CW00551535

SHANNON DEPARTURES
A STUDY IN REGIONAL INITIATIVES

Shannon Departures

A study in regional initiatives

BERNARD SHARE

GILL AND MACMILLAN

Published in Ireland by
Gill and Macmillan Ltd
Goldenbridge
Dublin 8
with associated companies in
Auckland, Budapest, Gaborone, Harare, Hong Kong,
Kampala, Kuala Lumpur, Lagos, London, Madras,
Manzini, Melbourne, Mexico City, Nairobi,
New York, Singapore, Sydney, Tokyo, Windhoek
© Bernard Share 1992
0 7171 1830 4
Index compiled by Helen Litton
Print origination by
Seton Music Graphics Ltd, Bantry, Co. Cork
Printed by Colour Books Ltd, Dublin

All rights reserved. No part of this publication may
be copied, reproduced or transmitted in any form or by
any means, without permission of the publishers.

A catalogue record is available for this book from the
British Library.

Contents

Acknowledgments   vii

Introduction   1

1   One Way to Run a Railway   5

2   A Laundry Basket from the Old Ground   26

3   A Genus of Small Rodent   55

4   A Shop on Drumgeely Hill   80

5   The Captives and the Kings   105

6   On the Way to the Technopolis   133

7   A Long Way from Tullyvarraga   165

8   The Matter of the Route   186

Select Bibliography   212

Index   215

Acknowledgments

I owe a deep debt of gratitude to the many people who consented to be interviewed on their involvement with or interest in the subject-matter of this book. Quotations within double inverted commas represent the material deriving directly from such interviews, and I trust that those involved will accept this as due acknowledgment of their assistance and co-operation. In the case of those associated with Shannon Development it must be pointed out, of course, that some responsibilities have changed since this book was first researched, and that their comments must be seen in this context. The company undertook a major reorganisation and restructuring in mid–1992.

Many others assisted me with advice and information: Gus Barrett of De Beers; Dermot Hurley, Jane Massy and Eileen Quin of Shannon Development; Dr Tony Ryan of GPA; Margaret O'Shaughnessy of the GPA Flying-Boat Museum; Desmond O'Grady (permission to reproduce part of his then unpublished poem 'Tipperary'); Marcus McInerney, Seamus Kearns and Michael Keating. My greatest single debt, however, is to Colman Garrihy of Shannon Development, without whose patience, efficiency, encouragement and unfailing good humour my task would have been immeasurably more difficult.

The illustrations were supplied by Dermot Hurley of the Shannon Development photographic archive with the following exceptions: Nos 5, 6, 10, 11, 12, 14, 16, 17, 18, 67, GPA Flying-Boat Museum; Nos 3, 4, 48, Seamus Kearns; Nos 13, 37, Michael Keating.

Publishers' Note

Grateful acknowledgment is made by the publishers to De Beers Industrial Diamond Division (Ireland) and Shannon Development for their support towards the publication of this book.

Introduction

Shannon: principal river of Ireland. Shannon: airport, Co. Clare, formerly Rineanna. Shannon, otherwise *Sionna, Sionnan*: town, Co. Clare. Shannon: rugby football club, Limerick city.... The list, eclectic and by no means exhaustive, serves to adumbrate the evasive sense of place which colours much of what is to follow. River, airport, town, all figure in this narrative (the football club is a regrettable omission) but this book is about something which makes a claim to comprehend them all: an entity known alternatively as the Shannon Region or the Mid-West. Even that claim to comprehension must, however, be confusingly qualified: for the Shannon river—which, after all, lends its name to this diversity—figures in the picture only in the lower part of its length. The Shannon Pot, Carrick on Shannon, Athlone or Portumna play no admitted role in this story.

To this already confusing picture there must be added the name of Shannon Development. To compound the confusion this title more usually appears with the geographical denominator in large capitals—SHANNON—followed by a discreetly smaller 'Development'. Shannon Development is the marketing name, adopted for convenience and euphony in the late 1970s, for the Shannon Free Airport Development.Company Limited, usually attenuated into the uncomfortable acronym SFADCo. SFADCo (the two designations will be used impartially in what follows, as much to avoid tedious repetition as anything else) is a state-sponsored body charged with a range of developmental activities in the aforesaid Shannon Region or Mid–West—an area which currently takes in Counties Clare and Limerick, north Tipperary, north Kerry and south-west Offaly, but whose writ runs no further north on the river itself than Shannonbridge: and that on the left bank only. In these circumstances it is not surprising that any sense of a Shannon regional identity should prove difficult to isolate and, once isolated, even harder to evaluate.

This said, there is no question but that the situation that has been evolving in the area over the past half century or so constitutes an attempt, part deliberate, part instinctive, to create some kind of regional identity and to explore just what that identity entails. It grew at first quite haphazardly from the siting of Shannon Airport and the perceived need, when its future was under threat for the first of many times by the eclipse of the piston-engined aircraft and the overflying jets, to discover some way of preserving jobs and sustaining local growth. Thus the Industrial Estate, or Free Zone, with its tax incentives; the new town that grew up to house its employees; the tourist business to lure transit passengers that developed a wider social dimension; and an increasing involvement on the part of the Development Company in virtually everything that moved, or hoped to move, between Loop Head and Ferbane, Fanore and Kilbehenny. Both the area and the emphasis were to change at the behest of successive governments which, having created and fostered the Shannon enterprise, seemed uncertain what should ultimately be done about it. Sometimes, when the Free Zone was returning a quarter of the new jobs created nationally, it was the white-headed boy; at others, when the activities of SFADCo seemed to threaten those of other state interests, it was rapped over the knuckles by the withdrawal of areas of responsibility or, even, by threats of extinction. Underlying all this was the knowledge, whether admitted or no, that what was involved was a real challenge to the growing centralisation of government, to the patently anachronistic local administrative system and—perhaps most potent of all— to the growing dominance of Dublin in the country's affairs.

Though the Development Company of necessity figures very largely in this study it is not a history of SFADCo, and in no way do the views it expresses or the conclusions it draws reflect SFADCo policy or thinking. It is important to clarify this in the introduction to a book of which Shannon Development is, for commercial reasons, a co-sponsor; equally important to emphasise that though I was given free access to both company records and personnel, no attempt whatsoever was made to 'guide' me in my thinking or direct my researches. I remain, however, deeply grateful to those many SFADCo people, both past and present, who enlightened me on many issues which would otherwise have remained obscure. "Recently a few of us have been saying," Tom Callanan observed to me in the course of one such conversation, "that the actual extent of the development and its contribution to the national economic and social revolution that took place in the post 1950s has never been properly tabulated, classified, examined, and the entrails picked over." This book is an attempt at some part of that task against the background of its historical origins and of a growing concern at the inadequacy of existing local government structures and the conviction on the part of many that if there is ever to be any meaningful regional democracy in Ireland, what has been happening in Shannon could profitably serve as an exemplar.

The undertaking arose initially from a chance meeting, after many years, with Brendan O'Regan and his diffident suggestion that the Shannon story might be worth the telling. It is, in my view, an experiment which has suffered from marked and frequently inexplicable neglect: no reference to Shannon appears, for example, in the index of either J. J. Lee's exhaustive study of contemporary Ireland or that of Tim Pat Coogan's *Disillusioned Decades—Ireland 1966-87*. In endeavouring to redress the balance I shall almost certainly stand accused of a debilitating want of the kind of civilised begrudgery intermittently exhibited in both these excellent volumes: that is as may be. Confronted with the dedication and achievement of those actually involved in the Shannon enterprise—and I speak not only of those within SFADCo but of a great number of people in the region in many walks of life—it would, in my view, be a gross distortion to withhold a positive response from what amounts to the only example of sustained and effective regional endeavour in the country in modern times.

In September 1990 a university academic, who had spent some time teaching in Cork but was then based in Britain, suggested in a radio interview that a new capital city should be built in the vicinity of Sixmilebridge in Co. Clare. Citing Canberra—unfortunately one of the less charismatic capitals in the world—and Brasilia as examples he even gave it a name: *Saibhreas*, the Irish for 'prosperity'. In choosing Sixmilebridge he paid tribute not only, as he acknowledged, to the importance of Shannon but (though he possibly did not know this) to the home town of the single individual most instrumental in its creation, Brendan O'Regan. If it is difficult to imagine the Dáil in session at Hurler's Cross with a newly-disadvantaged Dublin Region left languishing in provincial neglect, there is enough of the unconventional O'Regan vision in the proposal to see in it, perhaps, some kind of acknowledgment of what Shannon has achieved . . . and what yet remains to be accomplished.

Author's Note: I have employed the device of double inverted commas (" . . . ") to indicate direct quotations from personal interviews which otherwise appear without acknowledgment as to the source.

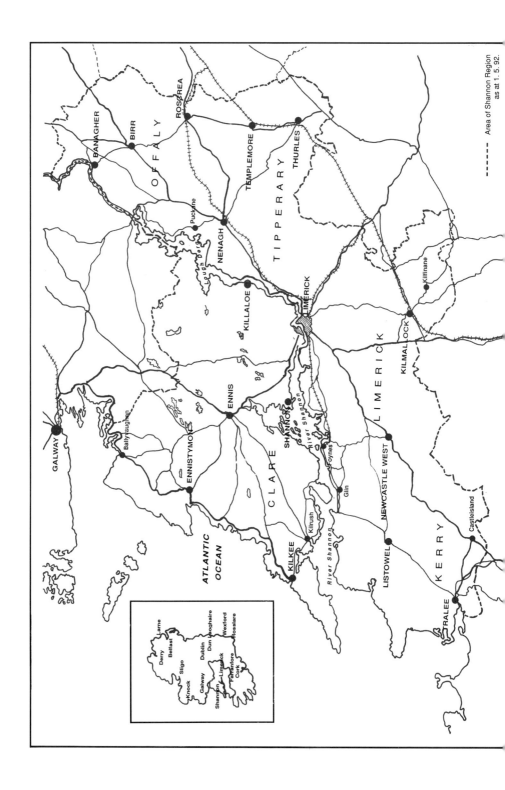

Area of Shannon Region
as at 1. 5. 92.

ATLANTIC OCEAN

GALWAY

BANAGHER
BIRR
OFFALY
ROSCREA
TEMPLEMORE
THURLES
TIPPERARY

Puckane
NENAGH

Lough Derg

KILLALOE

LIMERICK

Killfinane

KILMALLOCK

LIMERICK

ENNIS

Ballyvaughan

ENNISTYMON

CLARE

SHANNON

River Shannon

Foynes

NEWCASTLE WEST

Glin

Castleisland

LISTOWEL

KERRY

Kilrush

KILKEE

River Shannon

TRALEE

Derry
Larne
Belfast
Sligo
Knock
Galway
Dublin
Dun Laoghaire
Wexford
Rosslare
Shannon
Limerick
Fishmore
Cork

[4]

One Way to Run a Railway

The Clonmacnoise and West Offaly Railway is not, as its name might suggest, some fossilised relic of the Victorian era. It begins—and ends—at *Uisce Dubh*, a bogland some five kilometres from the river at Shannonbridge. *Uisce Dubh* is not even a name on a map. It is the local headquarters of Bord na Móna, the state-sponsored body responsible for the exploitation of the peat bogs; and the C & WOR is the recent brainchild of two Bord na Móna employees—Pat Dooley and Paddy Byrne—who saw in the vast network of narrow gauge tracks used to haul the milled peat to the power station at Shannonbridge the possibility of tourist development. With the encouragement of their superiors and the active co-operation of the Birr office of Shannon Development they refurbished a Wagonmaster diesel locomotive and commissioned a custom-built passenger coach from a firm in Edenderry which had built rolling-stock for the defunct West Clare Railway. The coach has a chemical toilet, wash-hand basin and public address system which carries a commentary on line-side items of interest as the little train trundles through a russet-brown desert at 20 kmph. The horizons are limitless, the power station, five kilometres distant, suggesting no more than a ten-minute stroll: a temperate mirage.

The C & WOR runs in a circle; and nowhere on its commodious route, in spite of the evocative nomenclature, does it touch upon the ancient monastic settlement of Clonmacnoise. In this it is at one with the territory of the Shannon Region, which stops a few kilometres upriver from Shannonbridge. The interests of Clonmacnoise tourism are the responsibility of an office in Mullingar, Co. Westmeath. That of the Industrial Development Authority (IDA), with a role in the development of major industry in South Offaly, is in Athlone. 'South Offaly' itself is a recent (1980s) invention, its boundary following no discernible precedent. "Some civil servant just sat down one day in Dublin and took out his map and did this," says Joe Price, Shannon Development's manager in Birr. Desmond O'Malley, as Minister for Industry, Commerce and

Energy its legal parent, later attributed its genesis to the necessity to placate a succession of deputies and deputations representing their disadvantages when compared with the prospering Mid-West Region. Thus with the stroke—or a few strokes—of a civil service pen (it is a convoluted boundary for all its arbitrariness) South Offaly sprang into existence as the north-eastern extension of the Shannon or Mid-Western Region: an area coterminous with the enlarged territorial responsibilities of the Shannon Free Airport Development Company.

On 4 August 1986 locomotive No. 5T of the Tralee and Dingle Light Railway was unloaded at Tralee, Co. Kerry, after its return from the USA, where it had been a museum exhibit since 1959. The Tralee and Dingle was a genuine Victorian creation, operating an unpredictable and infrequent service over a spectacular route from 1891 until the last cattle special ran in 1953. The repatriation of No. 5T was the first step in the contemplated reinstatement of part of the original line as an operating tourist railway. The re-opening of the section from Tralee to Blennerville is in the hands of a local group with the active participation of Shannon Development.

This involvement by the company in railway enterprises at the extremities of its territory is, to the outside observer, neither more nor less fortuitous than the extent of those territories themselves. North Kerry can claim a somewhat more respectable pedigree than South Offaly ("I don't know that it was a great success," Desmond O'Malley admitted of the latter: "it was something of an afterthought") since it coincides with a parliamentary constituency. It was included within the ambit of SFADCo responsibilities as recently as 1989. 'We see this development completing the full integration of the Shannon Estuary,' wrote the company's chairman, John A. Daly, in that year's annual report: 'Not only is the River Shannon the common bond of all the counties within our regional mandate, but the inclusion of the remainder of the southern bank of the estuary in our remit will strengthen the support we can provide for its development.'

Look at the map. Ballyvaghan, in north Clare, faces out across Galway Bay to Connemara. Thurles, Co. Tipperary, sits a short distance from a slightly older artificial border, instituted in 1838: that between Tipperary North and South Ridings. If 'Ridings' is a linguistic nonsense in this context (from Old English *thriding*, a third part) the responsibility of Shannon Development for one half of the county and not the other would appear scarcely more apposite. The map again: a 'monstrous cantle' of the sundered county divides SFADCo territory at Holycross Abbey from Galbally, Co. Limerick, gateway for the Glen of Aherlow, which, however, may not legitimately be featured in Shannon promotional tourist literature since it is administratively out of bounds. But start at Shannonbridge and travel south-westward on the river, 'common

[6]

bond of all the counties . . . '. Yes, but as far as a point a little north of White-gate on Lough Derg the starboard, or west bank is the territory of unincorporated Galway. At the southern frontier Tralee is within the pale, its airport at Farranfore within another jurisdiction. What is this thing called Shannon?

Offaly was for a period of some 400 years known as King's County, dubbed as such by the English queen, Mary, in the context of a plantation scheme in 1556. Before that it was O'Connor territory, before that again, in 1300, the sphere of influence of the MacCochlans and the O Melaghlins amongst, undoubtedly, others. It is necessary to retreat so far the better to come forward to face the complexity of present-day regional divisions. Since the shiring of the country on the English model by the invading Normans and their successors, local territorial boundaries have remained largely immutable, if not always the subject of such passionate adherence as at present. A mediaeval Kerryman might have asked, amending Shakespeare's Irishman in *Henry V*, 'What is my county?' but the decision of the newly-formed Gaelic Athletic Association in 1886 to set up county boards and organise games within these territorial limits secured the development of an allegiance verging occasionally on the fanatical. In the words of Desmond O'Malley, who, as iterative Minister for Industry in several administrations has been largely responsible for much of the legislation governing the development of the Shannon Region: 'Our counties are only historical accidents; they're simply an amalgamation of old English baronies, and the baronies themselves didn't really make sense.' Or, as Barry Brunt expressed it more formally: 'With an extremely strong tradition of local and county identities set against a background of growing centralisation at the national level, regional considerations remain under-emphasised within Ireland.'[1] 'Under-emphasised' is perhaps in itself an inadequate description of a condition which in many respects would seem to border upon the chaotic; and one for which the most recent reform of the local government system, preserving as in amber the strategies of a long-defunct colonial administration, presages no radical solution.

Consider an example from another part of the country relative to Water-ford's desire to expand across its river into Kilkenny: ' The sensitivities,' wrote Dick Hogan[2] 'take in provincial differences (Waterford is in Munster, Kilkenny in Leinster); diocesan differences (both banks of the river are in separate dioceses); political differences (if land were transferred, Kilkenny Euro-politicians could find themselves fighting the next direct elections to the European Parliament in a new and strange constituency); and even sporting differences (it has been argued that if the boundary is altered, Kilkenny hurlers

[7]

from the part of the county closest to Waterford would wind up wearing the blue and white of the neighbouring county rather than the famous black and amber of their own.' In a constructive attempt to neutralise such conflicting loyalties Tom Callanan, chief executive of the Plassey National Technological Park, proposed, together with a colleague,[3] a regional alignment based on the four European parliamentary constituencies: divisions, it must be said, that currently enjoy a very low level of public recognition.

Such considerations of demographic reform would remain largely theoretical and, except among administrators themselves, low in urgency were it not for the fact that the Shannon phenomenon exists. And phenomenon it is, by any standards: a region including the country's rapidly growing third city; its established transatlantic airport and focus of its growing aerospace industry; its greatest estuarine waterway, already the site for the country's largest heavy industry. It is a region which is differentiated from any other in that its commercial, industrial, social, educational, tourism and urban development has been or is currently the responsiblity of a state-sponsored body. The Shannon Airport Development Authority—its immediate predecessor—was originally charged with the creation of an industrial estate at Shannon Airport designed to counter the threat of redundancy posed by the introduction, in the late 1950s, of jet aircraft on transatlantic services.

In spite of this substantial assignment of responsiblity, modified over the years in the light of prevailing political perceptions, concomitant administrative power has not been forthcoming, so that SFADCo exerts tremendous regional influence without, except in the case of its own legislatively defined responsiblities, any mandated authority. Nor has its example been replicated anywhere else in the country. In the wake of the 1963 Local Government (Planning and Development) Act, nine planning regions were established; but, in the words of T. J. Barrington, one of the most vocal and authoritative advocates of regional development, 'In a somewhat disconcerting way, each government department has been defining its own regions . . . .'[4] Thus regions as defined by Bord Fáilte, (the tourism body), the Health Board and other state agencies established frequently incompatible sets of boundaries and within this cat's cradle of lines on the map some 200 public organisations involved in varying aspects of regional devlopment (as identified by the National Economic and Social Council in 1976) have been pursuing their diverse and often contradictory interests.

'It is really urgent,' wrote Barrington[5] 'that somebody get around to the task of defining regional boundaries for all purposes.' That was more than twenty years ago. The task remains to be completed, though in early 1991 the report on the structure of local government, drawn up by a committee of experts under the chairmanship of Dr Tom Barrington, recommended a three-tier system with regional, county and district councils. The existing regional authorities, according to a leaked version of the report[6] (which was not published) 'would rationalise the regional structures for planning, economic development, tourism, health, fisheries and the structural funds so that all would operate in the same areas of jurisdiction'.

'Dr Barrington has been an eloquent proponent of decentralisation,' *The Irish Times* commented editorially on the same day: and, indeed, at best, local democracy has been a vigorous force for regional development and diversity. 'In this State, SfadCO [sic] has been a notable success.' The Local Government Bill, introduced on 3 May 1991 took a few tentative steps down the road. 'As regards form or structures of local government,' wrote Richard Haslam, a former county manager of Limerick,[7] 'as it had been decided that the county was to remain the basic unit, appropriate bodies "above and below" needed consideration by the advisory committee [of which he was a member]. Regions were an obvious choice and it is satisfactory that the present Bill, so provides ... especially since the curious and unfortunate abolition of regional development organisations here in 1987.' The Bill provided for the establishment of eight new regional authorities to co-ordinate public services and the programmes of local authorities and other public agencies—but with no provisions for financing their activities. 'There is little use in designing elaborate structures and endowing authorities with impressive powers,' wrote Haslam, 'unless the wherewithal to implement them exists.'

In the late 1950s there was an active movement within New South Wales to set up a new Australian state of New England on the tablelands around the town of Armidale some 350 km north of Sydney. As you climb up the Liverpool Ranges from the coastal lowlands the countryside changes dramatically: oaks replace gum trees, the paddocks are almost an Irish green and there are functioning fireplaces in the substantial farmhouses. Armidale is a university town and centre of a prosperous rural area. But it was not so much this sense of difference that prompted the 'independence' movement as the conviction that everything in the State gravitated centripetally towards Sydney which was—and is—totally dominant in terms of population and influence. Given adjustments of scale, the perceived Irish problem is very similar. As Tom Callanan, with a background of long experience in SFADCo put it: "We have only one region and that's a place called Dublin."

In 1926, at the birth of the State, Dublin city and county represented seventeen per cent of the population; by 1985 this had risen to more than thirty per cent—'a centralisation of intellectual resources', in the words of J. J. Lee,[8] 'unique in northern Europe'. He attributed the failure to achieve the desired national economic goals to 'excessive centralisation' and stigmatised 'the internal colonialism of the centralised state' as inhibiting the development of

[9]

the true potential of the people.[9] The argument has been both universal and long-running. The Irish economist, painter and mystic George Russell (Æ) wrote in 1916: ' . . . in almost every country, politics, economics and social reform are urban products and the countryman gets only the crumbs which fall from the political table.' Advocates of regional devolution would argue that in this sense countrymen begin at the outskirts of Dublin and in the absence of any move to establish *metropoles d'équilibre*, as the French have done to counteract the predominance of Paris, Dublin is destined to grow at the expense of all other population centres.

Such counterbalancing 'growth poles' were, in fact, recommended in the 1968 Buchanan Report[10] which proposed three major national growth centres: Dublin, Cork and the Limerick-Shannon axis. Before that, however, the Lichfield Report, commissioned by the Minister for Local Governnment in December 1964 and published in July 1966,[11] listed in part XVI three main areas for action: regional planning, regional development and regional promotion 'to keep to the fore the concept of the region, to encourage people to think in terms of being part of a region, to have a sense of loyalty, to make the region a better place in which to live and work'.

Lichfield, which concerned itself solely with the Limerick-Shannon region, then defined as Counties Clare and Limerick and the misnamed Tipperary North Riding, was seen by some interested parties as an attempt by the minister to pre-empt the development of SFADCo. ("Lichfield was initially commissioned by Neil Blaney", said Paul Quigley, successor to Brendan O'Regan as the company's first general manager, "essentially to put us down. It didn't".) Be that as it may, it was the first serious attempt to address the issues of regionalism which had been raised, however tenuously, by the Underdeveloped Areas Act 1952 which introduced the first post-war regionally-differentiated grants and incentives. With the inauguration in 1956 of higher grants for underdeveloped areas and the establishment in the following year of Gaeltarra Éireann, a state-sponsored body with overall responsibility for the Gaeltachtaí or Irish-speaking areas, it was clear that the wider issue would have to be addressed.

Limerick and Clare County Councils and Limerick Corporation had been aware of some of the implications of the existence of SFADCo in advance of the publication of the Lichfield report. 'In that company,' said T. Brophy[12] 'they found a dynamic and progressive management, fully aware of the fact that consultation with the surrounding local authorities was not only desirable but essential because the company's functions impinged on a whole range of services previously exercised by local authorities or other agencies in the public service.'

[10]

'We recognised the need for a holistic approach' said Paul Quigley. 'We had to look at the whole life of the region from waste disposal to higher education. The latter we saw from the beginning as one of the key elements.' There were, of course, obvious sensitivities: local groups jealous of their powers had to be convinced that SFADCo was not a cuckoo in the nest aiming to abrogate all authority to itself. Lichfield indicated the path to be followed by recommending the establishment of a Regional Development Organisation. Quigley and his colleagues conceived a high respect for Nathaniel Lichfield and his team.

"I suppose the honest thing to say," admitted Tom Callanan, "is that we seduced Lichfield and his friend John Stephenson, who did most of the work, into the notion that really you couldn't conceive of Shannon developing in isolation but rather as part of a much wider issue." It fell largely to Brendan O'Regan to initiate the delicate process of meeting local representatives to discuss a constitution for the projected regional body. Under his guidance SFADCo adopted from the start a support role, carefully avoiding taking credit for actions which others might wish to claim for themselves.

The company, for similar reasons, never sought the chairmanship of the Regional Development Organisation (RDO), which quickly established itself as an effective, if circumscribed, forum for regional discussion. Its first director, Joe McHugh, was succeeded by Patrick Barry, 'a soft spoken, unpretentious man who was seconded from the Tipperary North County Council . . . to oversee the major task of weaning the people and organisations of the three counties away from traditional parochialism towards a regional view of life. His success is everywhere acknowleged', wrote Howard Kinlay.[13] Though lacking the power to implement decisions the RDO 'contributed significantly', in the view of T. Brophy, chairman of the organisation's technical committee, 'to a regional awareness and towards regional thinking in planning and development'.

'This group has, in my view, the best possible credentials as a regional body,' suggested Donough O'Malley, Minister for Education, at the inaugural meeting of the RDO on 23 February 1968. 'It began on local initiative in the region and was in no sense created or imposed from outside.' The main areas of discussion involved higher education, industrial promotion, communications, housing, tourism and amenities. In addition to the existing local authorities other interested parties such as the state-sponsored transport, electricity, postal and public works authorities became directly involved. The European Committee of the Conference of Peripheral Maritime Regions also participated, adding a wider dimension and a name to conjure with.

The great argument for a geographical area authority, in Barrington's view, is that it provides the opportunity for co-ordinating related services.[14] He added that experience elsewhere suggested that such an authority must be in a position of some power. In this latter respect the new RDO was conspicuously deficient. 'We have no voting process,' said Brophy: 'either a matter is agreed by all, or not agreed at all.' From the outset the new body suffered from a lack of executive power, inadequate financing and a relatively low status within the administrative hierarchy. "They tried to co-ordinate things by getting those who did have the executive powers to exercise them in a co-ordinated way," said Desmond O'Malley. "But when push came to shove the Clare County Manager did his own thing if he wanted to . . . you need statutory powers and the place where you need them particularly is in planning."

The RDO, with its thirty-two members and a technical committee of seventeen, was by its very nature a trammelled and cumbersome body, though it did go some way towards the co-ordination of public services at local level. For all its limitations it became the model for similar, if less successful, organisations in other regions. All of them were summarily abolished in 1987, indicating to many an unwelcome return to the centralisation of the development process and one which Desmond O'Malley regretted. He believed that the concept could have been the skeleton on which a real regional organisation could have been built.

In terms of creating an overall regional awareness, however, the RDO achieved little more than establishing a forum for debate. Overriding any tentative larger grouping, the county system remained—and remains—the prime focus of local loyalties in virtually every sphere. Desmond O'Malley pointed to the continuing habit of thinking in purely county terms in "the most regionalised of Irish regions" as evidence of the difficulty in establishing a regional concept. This is particularly true of the relatively recent accretions, south Offaly and north Kerry, which have little reason to look towards Shannon other than as a source of financial assistance. In both these areas, however, there was positive local pressure in favour of forming the association. Joe Price, who set up the SFADCo office in Birr in 1980, concluded that people felt that, geographically, they were not part of the midlands, though the relative success of the Mid-Western region obviously played a part in forming public attitudes favourable to seeking association with Shannon. In north Kerry there was, perhaps, a greater degree of ambivalence. A county which rejoices in its identification as the 'Kingdom'—even within inverted commas—must view any move towards partition with reservation. The impetus towards change came most strongly from tourist interests—the southern part of the county holding the advantage of incorporating the lakes of Killarney and the Ring—and from those anxious to see some progress made towards the exploitation of the Ballylongford 'land bank' which had been assembled by the IDA and earmarked for heavy industry but for which no occupant had been secured.[15]

1. *Specially-built passenger coach and refurbished Bord na Móna Wagonmaster locomotive on the Clonmacnoise & West Offaly Railway at Uisce Dubh, 8 February 1991.*

2. *The Plassey campus of the University of Limerick, formerly the National Institute for Higher Education. The River Shannon is in the foreground.*

Even within the company itself attitudes vary widely as to its relevance to any progress towards national regional development. Whilst Michael Tunney in Tralee believed that the re-creation elsewhere in the country of the Shannon Development model was long overdue, Paul Quigley, after a long career at Shannon, takes a more cautious view: "Some people look on Shannon Development as a model of a regional development organisation that could, if successful, be applied elsewhere. I don't think that is a fair way to look at it. It's a state agency that happens to be located here. There's no regional representation as such on the board, there's no local democracy. I don't think there should be. If I were arguing for the existence of a thing like Shannon Development in the country I wouldn't see the main benefit as arising from its regionalisation."

At another extremity of this uneasy aggregation there persists also a climate of disbelief. Tomás O'Domhnaill, in charge of the Nenagh office of Shannon Development, refuses to admit the concept of a regional culture. "We don't feel we are part of a region. I'm absolutely convinced that the only unit that people have feelings about is the county unit." He points, as a Tipperary man himself, to the lack of a following for the GAA Inter-Provincial Railway Cup matches: "people don't go to Munster against Connacht." Provincial identities, much older than those imposed by the Anglo-Norman shiring, now count for very little, particularly in the context of a sundered Ulster. Cultivated by politicians acutely conscious of their power-base, the county rules all. O'Domhnaill quotes potent local examples. The villages of Ballina in Tipperary and Killaloe in Clare sit at opposite ends of a bridge across the Shannon. There is 'murder' when there is a decision to locate in Killaloe and not in Ballina. Tipperary people, who will travel to Britain and the USA in search of employment, do not see the new aerospace developments in the Shannon Industrial Zone as a source of jobs. And again: "By any measurement Nenagh is a university town—about twenty miles away from Ireland's premier third level institution ... there's not a traffic light between here and Castletroy. But that's *Limerick* University...!" Though O'Domhnaill admits that the attitudes of the younger generation may be broadening, there is clearly ample mileage yet in the involuted flight of the *Skibbereen Eagle*.

☆ ☆ ☆ ☆ ☆ ☆

The village of Pocán in Co. Tipperary has, like many others in the region, its SFADCo presence: in this case a group of thatched cottages, in 1990 rather the worse for wear, built under the Rent-an-Irish-Cottage scheme (an ungainly name for a brilliant conception) which was inaugurated in 1969. Many of the occupants return year after year; and many are French and Germans who keep their own counsel, so that an hour before closing time on a fine spring evening Paddy Kennedy's pub is almost empty. But down on Lough Derg the mayfly are rising. At close on 11.30 the place comes to life with the arrival of two fishermen with a bag which they proceed to empty onto the floor in front of the bar. The two fine 4½ lb trout are evaluated and discussed to the accompaniment of several rounds of drinks which take those present well past the permitted hours. In one corner Patrick Walsh describes how he smokes his own pike, not a fish for which there is much local demand, and runs a successful craft business. "We should be looking towards Europe, not the USA," he says of the national tourism orientation—a running debate which invites wider participation. But, at this season of the year at least, there isn't an American in sight, and the few Germans in the bar have long since retired to their slumbrous cottages.

North Tipperary is bounded on the north by the Little Brosna river and on the west by the Shannon. For the rest, the dotted line on the map pursues an errant course, capturing the reconstructed abbey of Holycross but stopping a good deal short of Cashel which, according to a 1939 tourist brochure on Ireland's 'Premier County', 'because of its great antiquity, romantic history, and magnificent assemblage of ecclesiastical ruins, possesses a spell that few other towns can wield'. Wielding spells is an accomplishment that few, even the locally committed, would attribute to the principal towns within that section of the county which falls within the Mid-West region: Nenagh ('some buildings of historical note'—from the same brochure); Roscrea ('The Round Tower is in good preservation, its conical cap alone being missing') and Thurles ('pleasantly situated upon the upper reaches of the River Suir'). Apart from Nenagh, which is close enough to derive some tourist benefit, none of these centres is directly concerned with what happens on the Shannon, and the county (or half county) as a whole regards itself in many respects as the poor relation of the region. All the jobs, it is believed, are going to Clare: and, in spite of clear changes of policy in recent years people still see Shannon Development as the creator of jobs rather than, as current thinking would have it, the supporter of local initiative. And not just jobs for Tipperary North Riding: "Unless I can go down to Thurles," says Tomás O'Domhnaill " . . . and be able to demonstrate to them in a very tangible way how we have performed in their general area, we have been a failure."

He must make similar pilgrimages to Roscrea and Nenagh and to many smaller centres in between. The problem is to be able to transmute this strong, and understandable sense of local loyalty into something that will act for the Tipperary community as a whole, let alone for the wider interests of the region. O'Domhnaill likes to think that part of his strength is being well-placed to effect such a synthesis, and quotes the practical example of the Nenagh river, which rises near Borrisoleigh and flows north-west for some forty-five kilometres before entering Lough Derg at Dromineer. The fish in the river are owned by the ESB (because the Nenagh is a tributary of the Shannon) which leased the fishing rights to the Nenagh Anglers' Assocation; the riparian rights are owned by the local farmers; the Office of Public Works has a statutory obligation to keep the river dredged; the Central Fisheries Board is responsible for discouraging poaching; the County Council has the responsibility for access roads and bridges; the Irish Wildlife Conservancy has an interest in the local fauna. . . . When the river was identified as having tourist potential O'Domhnaill succeeded in bringing together these disparate bodies and instituted a pilot survey. One of the most important things this inquiry revealed was that the River Nenagh, for long thought of as a source of coarse fishing, was the fourth best trout river in Ireland.

Further investigation and co-operation followed, with the farmers, not amongst those most forthcoming with their initial support, being persuaded to become involved after a series of meetings and a personal visit to every landowner on both sides of the river—about 140 individuals in all. "That," in the view of Tomás O'Domhnaill, "is what development is about."

'Fatigued by the long walk of the day before,' wrote Le Chevalier de la Tocnaye in 1797, ' . . . I thought it well to stop in the village of Glin, which gives the title of Knight to its proprietor. There are but four places in the whole of Ireland which have this privilege, and all are in this part of the country.' The present Knight of Glin, Desmond FitzGerald, was expecting visitors at Glin castle—paying guests whose fairly substantial outlay on bed and breakfast contributes to the maintenance of the house ('castle', as the Knight explains, is a somewhat fanciful appellation) and its many treasures. These guests are an American couple, the husband with a background in the theatre, who seems a little bemused not only by the magnificence of Glin but by Ireland as a whole. Around the fire after dinner they are not without difficulty dissuaded from moving on to their next booked accommodation— a bed-and-breakfast in a sleazy area of Dublin's northside. Next morning we visit the tiny estate church, deconsecrated, but with the tombs of earlier Knights still flanking it in the family graveyard. Desmond FitzGerald is planning to recreate it as a heritage centre illustrating the relationship between the village of Glin and its 'proprietor' over the centuries. In the living room of the local pub, Maureen Barrett, County Councillor, imparts the welcome news that some financial assistance will be forthcoming. Desmond FitzGerald is addressed, formally but quite unselfconciously, as 'Knight'.

Shannon Airport—and the regional concept that grew from it—has its origins eighteen kilometres upriver from Glin at Foynes, where the transatlantic flying-boat base was established in 1939. With the shifting of the focus across the river to Co. Clare in the early 1940s, however, the western part of Co. Limerick found itself on the margin: the Newcastle West office of Shannon Development, responsible for activity west of a line roughly from Kildimo southwards through Croom, was opened in 1989, but its responsibilities were transferred back to Limerick two years later. During this brief period there was some local misapprehension as to its role and little real sense of regional solidarity. 'Are ye the same as the IDA?' was a question frequently addressed to Finbar Brougham, who was in charge of the office: "Very definitely," he said, "to some people in Newcastle West, Shannon Development is only an organisation to get in industry and that's it. Anything else is peripheral." He himself, a Limerickman, welcomed Shannon, in employment terms, as an oasis in the desert and worked on the industrial estate with a company which closed in 1976, after which he joined SFADCo. In his Newcastle West responsibility he was engaged with community groups, "trying to get them to take ownership of their own ideas". The initial expectancy was for funding, often without any developed ideas as to how and on what the money might be spent. The first step, Finbar Brougham suggested, is to relate the expectancy to the possibilities, to shift the initiative for development to the community and to establish the principle that any funds allocated will be largely to prime the pump.

With little in the way of small, indigenous industrial enterprises coming through, the concentration in west Limerick is heavily on community tourist projects, attempting to develop them to the point where they would possess something other than a purely local appeal. Like north Tipperary, it is not conspicuously a tourist area: passing traffic heading for the Tarbert-Killimer Shannon ferry has to be diverted, in both senses of the word. Thackeray, the English novelist, was, in 1822, moderately taken by Tarbert, which, he found, 'in the guide books and topographical dictionaries, flourishes considerably. You read of its port, its corn and provision stores, etc., and of certain good hotels, for which, as travellers, we were looking with a laudable anxiety. The town, in fact, contains about a dozen of houses, some hundreds of cabins, and two hotels ...' in one of which he was offered 'a good, large, comfortable bed.... The only objection to the bed, however, was that it contained a sick lady....'

The relatively cosmopolitan condition of Tarbert at the time was accounted for by the fact that it was a port of call for steamers plying regularly between Kilrush and Limerick. Though passenger traffic, apart from the cross-river ferry, is no longer a feature of the Shannon estuary, its development, an enduring source of controversy and conflict, remains crucial to the west Limerick and north Kerry sectors of the region. "If you want to look at the negative aspects of the regional concept," said Desmond O'Malley, "you have only to look at the estuarial side of it."

In 1983 a Welsh diver disappeared into a water-filled hole in the ground near Castleisland, Co. Kerry, to emerge a few anxious minutes later into a dark, dripping limestone cavern which had been closed to visitors since the last Ice Age. It was not entirely an accidental discovery—the Geological Survey of 1859 had acknowledged the existence of 'caves worn by water, some of which can be traversed for some distance' but it opened up for the owners of the land, Dr and Mrs Geaney, a whole new world, or underworld. Once a traversible passage was cut through the rock barrier Margaret Geaney "fairly bounded through it", as she put it, in the wake of her son David. Exploration revealed nearly four kilometres of caves and passages, striking rock formations and rivers—far too much for the Geaney family to keep to themselves. After a good deal of thought they took the decision to develop some 300 metres of the system, to be known as Crag Cave, for public access. Margaret Geaney now manages a busy souvenir shop and café at the cave entrance and the enterprise has become one of north Kerry's major tourist attractions. The project is one of those falling within the ambit of the Shannon Development office in Tralee.

Michael Tunney, who joined SFADCo here when the local office was opened in 1989, was previously a planner with Kerry County Council; in the light of this experience he feels that the proliferation of agencies now operating in the divided county might prove to be counter-productive. Shannon Development has responsibility for tourism in the north, Bord Fáilte in the south; the IDA functions in both sub-cantons; Údarás na Gaeltachta concerns itself with the Irish-speaking areas in the south; there is a County Development team in addition to Tralee Borough Council, the County Council and the County Manager. Yet there is no formal mechanism permitting all these people to meet and exchange ideas, let alone initiate cohesive action. Shannon Development has been generally well received in north Kerry; though *The Kerryman*, in a special supplement (21 July 1989) to mark the 'new era in tourism and industry', was moderate in its enthusiasm: 'We do not see north Kerry as a king or Cinderella within the new region. We join the partnership aware of the assets that we have to offer. . . . All the benefits of the marriage will not be exclusively to Kerry's advantage.' Many local people remained confused as to Shannon Development's role—it was seen as the IDA under another name or Bord Fáilte with a difference. There was a general perception, however, that it had the reputation for getting things done; but no awareness that any shift in fundamental loyalties might be expected on the part of those benefiting from its activities. It is difficult, for example, to envisage *The Kerryman* restyling itself *The Shannonman* or *The Mid-West Champion*.

☆ ☆ ☆ ☆ ☆ ☆

"It's where it stemmed from that's important, I think," says John Young of the Southill Development Co-Op Society Ltd. Southill is one of the vast housing estates built by the local authority on the periphery of Limerick city in the mid-1960s and early 1970s. Badly-planned, it lacks any degree of social mix and has been a centre of large-scale unemployment since its inception: those men who had jobs lost them when traditional industries closed down, some of them to be replaced by high-tech enterprises employing largely female labour. The case seemed hopeless: but the people of Southill took the matter into their own hands and approached Shannon Development for help. That was in 1978–79, and it coincided with a new brief which had been given to SFADCo by the minister, Desmond O'Malley, to become involved in the re-development of Limerick city in the absence of any firm initiative on the part of the City Council.

O'Malley, who himself sat on the Council for three years from 1974, is bitter about places like Southill. The then City Manager, he said, insisted that it was cheaper to put up huge, 1,000-house estates rather than tackle urban renewal in a city that was almost literally falling apart. The social cost, in terms of creating suburban ghettos where almost nobody had a job, was simply not taken into account. Families moved out from city tenements, many of them chronically unemployed, joining those in Southill who had lost their jobs due to redundancies and closures.

The involvement of Shannon Development in Southill is seen by O'Malley as valuable work appropriate to a regional authority: "You can't just concentrate on positives alone." The company worked with the Co-Operative in the task of creating local job opportunities by supplying a site and a 5,500 sq. ft building in three units and by providing financial support to get small enterprises off the ground. There was existing expertise in manufacturing, but virtually none in the necessary adjuncts of administration and, particularly, marketing. "We have learned a lot," says John Hanafin, Community Development Officer, "in terms of recognising that the expertise and skills we require are not all available in Southill. It's not the people: it's the way it was

[19]

designed and built." Shannon Development set about restituting some of the deficiency by forming partnerships or actually running businesses until they could stand on their own feet. A European Social Fund pilot scheme that ran from 1984–86 and involved the Southill Development Co-Operative, the Department of Labour and Shannon, produced thirty-two jobs in eight small manufacturing and service enterprises, all based in the locality.

The enterprises themselves reflect the traditional Limerick involvement in textiles: knitwear, leisurewear, casual jackets and a machine embroidery operation, originally designed to supply the needs of the centre but which has acquired customers throughout the city. The service sector embraces horticulture—plant supply, grass-cutting and garden maintenance—and a nursery and day-care centre with an important social dimension. The Co-Operative is restoring Southill House, built by Sir Peter Tait in the 1820s, as a centre for adult education and further enterprise development. John Young, who joined the organisation in mid-1990 to promote sales and marketing and to identify further opportunities for development, believes that the future success of the venture will depend upon co-operation and teamwork: "the hidden assets of the people involved are fantastic, but it hasn't so far been possible to extract the best out of everybody." A former motor mechanic, industrial employee and entrepreneur in his own right, he believes his varied background allows him to assess the current challenge in a clinical manner . . . to an extent: "I think this is a crazy job. But it's very satisfying."

Kilkee, Co. Clare: mid-October 1990. The only apparent movement is that of the incoming tide, flowing over the reef, replenishing the four natural bathing pools which the unseasonable sunshine would almost tempt you to investigate. The summer occupants of the elegant seafront houses have long departed for Limerick, Dublin or Germany. But the bar in the Strand Hotel now serves customers three nights a week in the winter, thanks to a population increase consequent upon the construction of Moneypoint Power Station on the other side of Loop Head; and, says Manuel Di Lucia, auctioneer, estate agent, restaurateur and diver, the demand for property is unprecedented. The resort now opens earlier and stays open later, and with the season expanding, local people are putting money back into the tourist industry. The town gleams with new paint, new building. A championship eighteen-hole golf course would be an asset, but the geology is against it. Kilkee tourism, however, is not over-commercialised: "We don't want that here," says Di Lucia.

Born in Belfast, he came to Kilkee in 1942, but is still often called a blow-in. "It's the stigma attached to the name: if I was Manuel O'Reilly or Manuel McNamara. . . ." But it is hard to pick up a copy of the *Clare Champion* without seeing the name Di Lucia. "I am a great believer in keeping in the forefront of things. A lot of people see this as a personal thing—that I'm pushing myself. But I believe that the more publicity an area can get the better. I'm the one personally responsible for pushing Kilkee as a diving resort." Chairman of the local development association, former chairman of the town commissioners, member of the festival committee, the Lions' Club . . . "as far as I'm concerned it's the best place in the world". One of the few places in the country that permits nude bathing. Men only.

Shannonside, the regional tourism organisation, the functions of which were taken over by SFADCo in 1988, helped Kilkee to build a children's playground and community hall; but since then, in Manuel Di Lucia's view, it has been downhill all the way in terms of securing financial support for local development. No Lottery money, nothing from the European Social Fund and no response from either Bord Fáilte or Shannon Development—though the latter did make some funds available for the reconstruction of the harbour wall destroyed during a storm. More damaging, perhaps, is the charge that SFADCo's executive, responsible for tourist development in Co. Clare, was invited three times to attend a meeting and three times failed to appear. "He never came near us. If he only came down and said 'Look lads, I can't do anything for you at the moment'. But all you get is promises, promises. There's no action."

In Di Lucia's estimation, Kilkee will never be anything other than a tourist resort. Industries—set up with the assistance of Shannon Development—did not last. A jeans factory, employing thirty-six people out of a total population of 1,500, was closed by, it is said, bad debts; another, producing gold plating for dentistry, only employed a maximum of two people and moved out to the Shannon Industrial Estate. Tourist-based craftworkers, on the other hand, are active. One of them, sculptor Jim Connolly, has initiated a novel programme of reverse emigration, persuading families from disadvantaged Dublin suburbs to resettle in West Clare. The requirements are a high degree of self-sufficiency (not necessarily money, but the ability to generate it) and, presumably, an enduring conviction that 'it's the best place in the world'.

The conviction, right or wrong, that local interests are being ignored in favour of somewhere else is endemic to an operation as geographically and politically complex as that of Shannon Development. Fergus Pyle was told in Co. Clare that 'They must get "Shannon" into all they do, instead of the names of local towns and villages. Rightly or wrongly', he concluded, 'a point is made that raises the argument above mere begrudgery. The Shannon Development Company is a functioning example of an unelected top-tier administrative entity, and as such is bolted onto the psychological landscape instead of growing from it.'[16] Such convictions are particularly acute in parts of Co. Clare, which saw the Shannon Free Zone growing up in its midst and apparently attracting industries to which other less advantaged areas might have made a prior claim. Kevin Vaughan worked for Clare County Council before becoming County Development Officer in 1966. At the time the only grants available were to the so-called Underdeveloped Areas.

Sean Lemass, who as Minister for Industry and Commerce had been responsible for the recruitment of Brendan O'Regan and for the genesis of SFADCo, had let it be understood that if there was a proposal for an industry for Ennis he would include the town within that designation. The Underdeveloped Areas were based on the concept of the old Congested Districts, and the whole county was so classified with the exception of a portion roughly corresponding to the Inchiquin estates; Lord Inchiquin apparently being of the opinion that the inclusion of his property would devalue the title. When Ennis was ultimately incorporated Kevin Vaughan was secretary of its Chamber of Commerce: "a fellow from the Department rang up and said, 'How will I describe Ennis? Wouldn't it be right to say Ennis Urban District?' 'Oh no', says I, 'there's factories outside the Ennis Urban District'. So he put in Ennis Urban and Rural District; and of course he didn't realise that the Rural District covered a huge area down to Newmarket and Shannon and Kilbaha. . . . "

Ennis was not slow to recognise the importance of Shannon to its own prospects for growth. On 14 March 1958 Kevin Vaughan wrote in his capacity as honorary secretary of the Chamber of Commerce to the Taoiseach, Éamon de Valera: 'As you are aware from long experience as Senior Deputy for Clare, Ennis is vitally interested in the fortunes of Shannon Airport. . . . We cannot but view with satisfaction the setting up of its Development Authority.' He went on to suggest that insufficient inducements were being offered to overseas industrialists by way of fiscal concessions to set up in Shannon and proposed tax relief in perpetuity for such enterprises. (The Finance [Miscellaneous Provisions] Act of 1958 set a limit of twenty-five years). Subsequent industrial development in Ennis was largely a spin-off from Shannon, and the town used its proximity to the airport as a selling point. In May 1966 the Clare Development Team invited SFADCo to a meeting to consider the promotion of an industrial estate in Ennis, and there were regular contacts thereafter until, in 1988, the County Development teams in both Clare and Limerick were abolished and their functions transferred, together with some personnel including Kevin Vaughan, to Shannon Development.

☆ ☆ ☆ ☆ ☆ ☆

[22]

There is a measure of reassurance—if allied to temporary inconvenience—in the discovery that the expense account restaurant on the Rue Archimède, a stone's throw from the centre of Europe of the twelve, accepts only one kind of credit card: Brussels has its provincialities. "There is no consensus," says Philip Lowe, former *chef de cabinet* to Commissioner Bruce Millan and now half way into his second day as Director of DG6 responsible for agriculture and rural development, "on precisely the way Europe's structures of government—national, regional and local—will go. There are several distinct attributes about the present community of member states which pull in the opposite direction to the Europe of the economic regions." The centralisation versus regionalisation issue of the Irish experience writ large.

Europe of the economic regions, he claims, is nevertheless a very real concept: "At the local authority and regional authority level people are coming together and saying 'well, how can we make sure that in our region, our area, we can attract investment and get our small businesses on a good footing? How can we get our research institutes, our academic institutes (like the University of Limerick now) as a central pole of attraction for people coming to our area?'" In the absence of political consensus, or perhaps as a prelude to it, the Commission operates a strong regional policy with the emphasis on local economic development in relatively disadvantaged areas, which means for the most part the rural community.

Philip Lowe was the architect of a pilot programme known as IRD (Integrated Rural Development) which financed twelve small schemes in Ireland, providing, through central government, funds to appoint a 'regional animator' whose task was to lead the individual project. It was, said Lowe, "an experiment in showing that there are people locally in every region who are willing actually to put their own money and time and machinery into doing jobs on a voluntary basis ...". The pilot scheme was the genesis of the 'Leader' programme for rural development announced subsequently by Commissioner MacSharry. "It is impossible to deal with rural development on a national basis," said Lowe, "even with three and a half million people. Rural development is about small communities and you need to be able to get down to that level to stimulate and encourage people, to give them the support they need without imposing schemes on them. In that sense Shannon is an important example. Both in the industrial area and, to a lesser extent, in the rural area they have been able to galvanise local support and interest in a way that is absolutely essential to regional development."

This principle of local self-help in a regional context is seriously complicated by the fact that, in the Community as a whole, there is no agreed definition of a region as such or commonality in respect of the degree of independence such

[23]

a phenomenon should possess. Some areas described as 'regions', such as Bavaria, Scotland or Sicily, have in the recent or distant past been politically autonomous in their own right; at the other extreme Shannon is the palest shadow of a constituted entity. "Ireland is all one region in the context of structural policies," said Tom O'Dwyer, Director General for the Co-Ordination of Structural Policies and formerly *chef de cabinet* to Ray MacSharry: "We negotiate with the Irish authorities on how these funds are to be used. It is only right and proper that funds are passed through this system."

"In Ireland there are specific economic reasons as well for arguing that you should deal with certain problems of regional development on a national basis," said Philip Lowe. "First of all, regional development is about people— and three and a half million people isn't very much. . . . The kinds of solutions you need for the problems of infrastructure in Ireland are probably best dealt with on a national level. Particularly, given the degree of financial resources available, you have to decide on priorities and those priorities have to be decided by democratic process . . . have to be decided in the capital."

All of which is cold comfort to an embryonic region such as Shannon seeking recognition not only by Brussels but by Dublin. Some member states, such as Germany, are quite happy to see requests made to Brussels by different *Länder*, a process not possible in, for example the French, British—or Irish—context; in a country such as Greece, said Tom O'Dwyer, whilst a major percentage of structural funds might be devoted to national programmes, a sizeable proportion would be channelled to regional programmes established within those regions themselves. Theoretically, he added, you should get an optimum distribution by allocating the funds nationally, but social and emotional considerations come into play. In the case of a small country like Ireland, however, there is a serious dilemma: "If you say that you are going to establish your priorities on the basis of regions you are sacrificing something in terms of economic efficiency." On the other hand, said Lowe, "Economic development would dictate more regional authority, because frankly speaking all our best experiences in regional development around the Community have been with the autonomous regions which have the power to do things on the ground, who are committed to it and are real partners. That's the lesson of everything we've done. . . . "

Brussels deals with governments. "Everything that comes in and out of our building," said Philip Lowe, "ultimately speaking has to be a piece of paper with the stamp of a central government. That is the law. In practice every country of the Community has a different constitutional structure and it can devolve its powers to whomever it pleases." The lesson for Shannon is that the path towards recognition and a greater measure of regional autonomy starts at the south Offaly border and leads through Dublin before it turns in the direction of Brussels. And that road has proved long and arduous.

Edward Walsh, president of the University of Limerick, was very encouraged by the establishment of the original Regional Development Organisation (RDO): "At that time it seemed to me that the whole regional thing would move and that the Shannon model would be adopted throughout the country and that's the great disapppointment. Coming back from the States I couldn't understand why we needed local authorities every few miles. I still don't understand.... The county towns were so geared that in a day's journey by horse you could be to the county town and back home before it got dark. You could do it now on the basis of a reasonable drive in a car. It seems to me that ultimately we will abandon the small local authority in favour of four or five regional structures."

Four or five, eight or nine? This year, next year? It is time to go back to the beginning.

References

1. *The Republic of Ireland* (Western Europe: economic and social studies), London 1988
2. *The Irish Times*, 17 April 1991
3. Tom and Brian Callanan: *Local Government in Ireland—the Regional Dimension* (unpublished)
4. 'Some problems of regional development', in *Administration*, 1970, p. 253
5. Ibid.
6. *The Irish Times*, 2 February 1991
7. *The Irish Times*, 13 May 1991
8. 'Centralisation and community', in *Ireland: towards a sense of place*, Cork 1985, p. 85
9. Ibid. pp. 95–96
10. C. Buchanan and partners: *Regional studies in Ireland*, Dublin 1968
11. N. Lichfield and associates: *Report and advisory outline plan for the Limerick Region*, Dublin 1967
12. *Administration*, 1970, p. 226
13. 'Developments in the Mid-West', in *Management*, November 1975, p. 16
14. *Administration*, 1970, p. 250
15. See p.153
16. *The Irish Times*, 27 June 1991

CHAPTER 2

A Laundry Basket from the Old Ground

In 1957 the New Zealand Airline TEAL—Tasman Empire Airways Ltd— was operating a regular flying-boat service from Auckland through Fiji, Western Samoa and the Cook Islands to Papeete, Tahiti. Flying-boats by that time were already an exotic survival, and the TEAL aircraft, a Short Solent, evocative of what even then seemed a more leisurely age. There was, for a start, an upstairs and a downstairs, connected by a spiral stairway that looked as if it had been salvaged from a Dublin tram. On reaching Apia, Samoa, nearly a day before starting from Fiji, courtesy of the International Date Line, the passengers were dispatched to a hotel to spend the rest of the day and the following night in whatever manner took their fancy. 'There is ... in favour of flying-boats,' an Irish Department of Industry and Commerce memo had suggested in November 1937, 'the psychological factor that passengers will consider they are safer in travelling over the ocean in these machines than in land-planes.' But as the Solent prepared to 'land' in a lagoon in the Cook Islands there was the strong impression that it was about to rip out its keel on the coral formations clearly visible below the surface— visible, that is, until the bow wave generated on impact substituted the conviction that the aircraft was about to plunge beneath the waters.

If, by 1957, flying-boats were an attractive novelty they had been taken much more seriously two decades earlier, when the debate as to their superiority or otherwise over land-planes for crossing the Atlantic was at its height. At a meeting between Irish and British officials on the desirability of establishing a transatlantic airport at Kilconry, Co. Clare, held in Dublin in July 1936, J. P. Candy, the chief engineer of the Office of Public Works, noted that a discussion took place as to 'whether passage would ultimately be made by land-plane or seaplane. The whole position appears to be still in a state of flux and it is for consideration whether it is wise to design the airport

3. Postcard view of the pier at Foynes early in the century.

4. Foynes in the flying-boat era: Pan-Am Clipper III, *moored offshore, July 1937.*

Come to Foynes
by
Sea or by Air

Luncheon

in honour of

Sean Lemass, Esq., T.D.

Minister for Industry and Commerce

on the Occasion of the Opening
by him of the New Pier at
Foynes Harbour

March 23rd, 1936

5. Menu of the luncheon in honour of Sean Lemass, Minister for Industry and Commerce, on the occasion of his opening the new pier at Foynes, 23 March 1936.

6. Special delivery: fuel en route to Foynes before the provision of more sophisticated services.

at the outset to accommodate both land-planes and seaplanes.'[1] In a letter dated 13 July 1937 from Charles Lindbergh, the aviation pioneer then technical adviser to Pan American Airways, to Juan T. Trippe, the latter's president, Lindbergh wrote that the Irish 'are constantly asking me about the future of flying-boats. I have told them frankly that my personal opinion is that the land-plane will be used for transatlantic flying in the future, especially on the Ireland-Newfoundland route. I told them there is no way of being certain how long the flying-boats would be used and that there was a great division of opinion in regard to the relative advantages of land-planes and flying-boats.'[2]

The Irish interest was something other than academic. In November 1935, at a conference in Ottawa, agreement had been reached between the governments of Canada, Britain, Newfoundland—then a self-governing British dominion—and the Irish Free State for the formation of a joint company to operate passenger and mail services across the Atlantic. Pan American had already indicated its intention to initiate such services, and would, under agreement, operate reciprocally with the British-based Imperial Airways, the chosen instrument of the joint company. Both companies would use flying-boats, since there were neither land-planes of sufficient range available nor airports to handle them. It fell to the Irish government to provide facilities for the proposed services, and on 16 December 1935 *The Irish Times* announced that Foynes, Co. Limerick, had been selected as the European terminal. The choice, which was not immediately confirmed, was regarded as a temporary expedient, investigations continuing as to the siting of an airport that would combine both flying-boat and land-plane facilities. J. P. Candy's report in the following July sounded a note of caution: 'It is a question for decision whether Foynes should not continue to be ... used for a time until the whole position as to the type of plane ultimately to be employed is clarified, bearing in mind that, by separating the land-plane and seaplane airports, the advantage of a central administration would be lost.'

When Sean Lemass, Minister for Industry and Commerce, opened a new pier at Foynes on 23 March 1936 he committed the government to providing the necessary facilities for the proposed transatlantic service. Lemass, already closely involved with the setting up of Aer Lingus, the national airline, realised that such an initiative was of very great importance to Ireland, a view shared by the Department of External Affairs which responded to a British offer to contribute a sum of £50,000 to the development of an airport with the comment that 'We cannot allow them to acquire a permanent or semi-permanent interest in this state enterprise, which has political and international implications of supreme importance to this country. We must

7. *The terrace of the restaurant at Foynes, formerly the Monteagle Hotel.*

8. **Yankee Clipper** *crew and aviation officials, Foynes, April 1939, on the occasion of its first visit. Foreground (left) in civilian dress: T. J. O'Driscoll, head of the Marine and Civil Aviation section of the Department of Industry and Commerce. On his left, also in civilian dress, is John Leydon, the Department Secretary.*

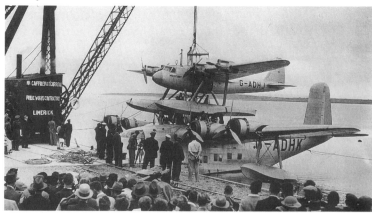

9. *Mayo Composite at Foynes. A heavily-loaded seaplane mounted on top of a flying-boat and launched in mid-air, this experimental British aircraft made its first revenue flight from Foynes to New York on 20 July 1938.*

keep a free hand for the future at all costs.' Brendan O'Regan, who was to open a restaurant at the Foynes terminal in 1943, said of this period: "I and the others who were with me regarded ourselves as the first generation of free Irishmen who were able to show in their own country the abilities that they had." When he got off the train at Limerick on the way to Foynes he overheard two officials of Imperial Airways telling a flying-boat crew that now that the Irish were taking over they were going to get bad bacon and eggs.

☆ ☆ ☆ ☆ ☆ ☆

May 1990, Killaloe, Co. Clare. Brendan O'Regan greets the interviewer in a large, empty room . . . . 'There was a table and two chairs' . . . the totally inappropriate lines from Louis MacNeice come to mind: 'Time was away and somewhere else.' For most people moving house is a painful actuality, not to be muddied over by remembrance of things past, but O'Regan sits and talks in that emptying house of events of fifty years previously as if they had happened the day before. He will, inevitably, figure largely in this narrative, since both ability and circumstance placed him in a central role in the events that were to flow from his employment at Foynes. In 1939, with the first commercial transatlantic service a reality after a series of proving flights, he was already making an impression: ' The Falls Hotel, Ennistymon,' said *The Irish Hotel and Caterer* for August 1939, 'is under the able and efficient management of Mr Brendan O'Regan, one of the youngest hoteliers in Ireland. Although but a youth at the helm, he steers a course that would reflect credit on older and more experienced pilots. . . . ' Here, amongst the patrons, he met some members of Dublin's venerable Stephen's Green Club who persuaded him to become its manager. He took up this position in the winter of 1942 and 'his success was so apparent to all that he was requested by the Irish Ministry of Industry to build up the catering at Shannon Airport'.[3]

"I certainly did switch the whole thing around including the profitability," O'Regan said of his time at the Stephen's Green Club. He attributed the offer of the job in Foynes to the fact that Éamon de Valera had been entertained to a meal in the Imperial Airways restaurant already operating there and concluded that such an undertaking should be run by Irish people. Interviewed by T. J. O'Driscoll, head of the Marine and Aviation section of the Department of Industry and Commerce, he received a contract from Sean Lemass, the minister, and the Department's secretary, John Leydon, (whose role in the early history of Irish aviation can scarcely be over-emphasised)— a contract which his father, a former chairman of Clare County Council and owner of the Old Ground hotel in Ennis, helped him negotiate. Thus Brendan O'Regan, at the age of twenty-six, became 'Catering Comptroller' at Foynes.

10. *Foynes, May 1943: An Taoiseach, Éamon de Valera (third from left) on tour of inspection.*

11. Opening of the restaurant at Foynes, 1943.

"It was a strange kind of thing—an agreement that I would do everything in my power to run a good catering service for the air crews, passengers and public, and that the capital would be put up by them but I would have to make it a profitable operation. I got £1,000 of a salary, £200 of the first profit and twenty-five per cent of any profits after that."

The arrangement was seen by some people, then and thereafter, as a licence to print money, and questions were reguarly asked in the Dáil as to the remuneration of the Catering Comptroller and equally regularly stone-walled. "No one knows what he was paid but it was supposed to be a big amount of money," said Kevin Vaughan: "You'd be happy getting two or three thousand pounds and he'd be getting £24,000." O'Regan himself acknowledged that he would have been a multi-millionaire had he stuck to the agreement, "but it became apparent very quickly that I would have been in trouble with the public . . . so I agreed over a number of years to have it reduced". A memorandum to government from the Department of Industry and Commerce dated 11 June 1955 explained that the Catering Comptroller 'is employed by the Minister . . . on a salary and commission basis' and that he was 'charged rent for the premises used and interest on the capital cost of the furniture and equipment supplied for the Catering Services together with depreciation charges on these assets. The net profits on the service accrue to the Exchequer'. It was a unique arrangement in civil service terms: but it was both an office and an undertaking for which there was no precedent.

When W. T. D. Harvey, a BOAC engineer, arrived at Foynes in 1940 to service the B 314 flying-boats recently acquired by the British airline from Pan American, he was 'surprised to see a small, one-street village: but it was an important one—flying-boats arrived there from the USA, England and many parts of Africa'.[4] The outbreak of war in 1939 had transformed the transatlantic operation into a vital strategic link. Passenger figures grew from 238 in 1939 to 9,599 in 1942, made up almost exclusively of VIPs and others having high priority to travel. Foynes itself, however, continued to function at the level of its minimal 1936 development. Maxwell Sweeney, who worked there in the early years, recalled the day in May 1937, just prior to the inaugural flights, when the railway station waiting room became the airport radio station.[5] The Monteagle Hotel, acquired by the government in 1936, had become the nerve centre of the operation, housing the airport management, the offices of the three operating companies, the meteorological services and the customs. Imperial Airways—subsequently BOAC—provided restaurant facilities in what became known as the Airport Office Building. A control tower was added in 1944. A terminal building, now the GPA Foynes Flying-Boat Museum, was situated close to the quayside.

12. *Shorts C Class flying-boat* **Caribou** *at Foynes, 1945.*

13. *The control tower, Foynes, 1944.*

14. *Mr Grogan in the modest power station at Foynes in the flying-boat era.*

As traffic grew the facilities both in the village and the surrounding area were stretched to capacity, both airline employees and passengers transiting having to endure primitive conditions as regards accommodation and sustenance. By 1943 the Airport Office itself was causing official concern: a memorandum from the Department of Defence described it as 'very open to attack' (it housed, amongst other things, secret radio codes) and requested an Army presence. The government refused this on the grounds that the character of the airport would be altered from civilian to military, with consequences for the country's policy of neutrality. (Even though it had agreed, in July 1942, to the stationing at the base of a British secret service officer.) Sean Lemass saw Foynes in another light, urging the Minister for Finance, Sean T. O'Kelly, to agree to the provision of uniforms for the airport staff: 'I think it is important from the point of view of national prestige that the appearance of personnel who come into contact with passengers using the Air Services to the Port should be beyond criticism.'[6] Finance agreed, subject to conditions, and the following year a blue, double-breasted uniform with lavender stripes on the sleeve, indicating rank, made its appearance.

Owing to shortage of local accommodation most people working at Foynes had to live in Limerick, some thirty-five kilometres away. A special bus service was provided, but the arrangement was far from satisfactory and in June 1943 Industry and Commerce announced plans for a 'staff inn' to accommodate fifty single men together with a restaurant project. 'No provision of married quarters,' however, 'is considered feasible.' Policy with regard to Foynes had been to provide the maximum operational facilities but to avoid capital expenditure on the basis of the planned transfer across the river to Rineanna. The UK authorities had, however, declined to make available dredging equipment necessary to complete the flying-boat base there. In the circumstances a survey had been carried out at Foynes and the construction of three jetties and a terminal recommended. Industry and Commerce were of the opinion that this should be proceeded with, suggesting that 'while the speculative nature of the Shannon project has always been recognised, it is a fair assumption that, if Shannon establishes its place in air transport, demands on its facilities will justify both Rineanna and Foynes.'[7] Approval for such development to proceed 'with all possible expedition' was given by the government on 9 September 1943. The Shannon Airport Restaurant was officially opened on 20 April 1944 under the management of Brendan O'Regan. Its first customers were passengers from Pan Am trip number 13067.

'You Irish are great for putting on a show, but you can't keep it up,' the second-in-command of BOAC said to O'Regan, adding, 'have you seen the awful chairs the Department have sent you down? We were satisfied with green but you have scarlet and red.'

'It is a spacious room,' a contemporary British newspaper reported: 'indirect lighting diffusing a cosy warmth over a moss-green carpet on which the cerise-upholstered Irish oak furniture makes a vivid splash. Most of the tables are arranged with wall settees in the corners, and the off-white buttoned cerise of chairs and curtains in dyed bawneen material.... From the windows, with their dainty geranium boxes, one looks at Foynes, its skyline dominated by a row of silver petrol tanks. Signposts in canary green, quite the neatest I have seen in design and lettering anywhere, indicate the many important airport offices. Dinner was a masterpiece of which Cesar Ritz could have been proud, yet its cook was an Irish chef, full and round-faced giant Joseph Sheridan, who hails from Tyrone...' Joseph Sheridan had already established a more lasting claim to fame. In 1938, according to *Time* magazine of 4 July 1955, he included whipped cream in his recipe for Irish Coffee. 'The passengers would come in off the launch shivering with cold,' he was reported as saying, 'so I thought up this stirrup-cup.' The claim has been contested, but, according to Brendan O'Regan, "he was certainly the man who gave it eye-appeal". The reputation of the Foynes restaurant grew rapidly, to the extent that the British newspaper *The People* characterised it as 'the most cosmopolitan publicity yet devised for modern Ireland'. In it lay the germ of much of what was to follow.

On the evening of 21 November 1935 a party of six Irish and British aviation officials set off from Dublin 'with the object', in the words of the government mandate, 'of finding bases in the Saorstát suitable for the operation of land-planes and seaplanes on a transatlantic service'. In one of the two cars heading west was R. W. O'Sullivan, newly-appointed Assistant Aeronautical Engineer to the Air Corps. Foynes had already recommended itself through a map survey as a possible location, but an examination of a suggested land site in the nearby Askeaton area revealed grave deficiencies—a road and railway would have to be re-routed at considerable expense. Athlone, Loughs Corrib, Ree and Derg and several other locations had already been eliminated. 'There was one more site remaining on the map survey,' O'Sullivan recalled,[8] 'which the senior members of the party deemed scarcely worth visiting since it was on the north bank of the Shannon. It was decided to let the two juniors, Hancock [F. G. Hancock, a junior official at the British Air Ministry] and myself have a look at it. It was at Kilconry or Rineanna at the mouth of the Fergus river....' The two men left the car at the nearest access point and set off across 'some pretty rough going over the kind of terrain that sportsmen and wildfowlers call "very close country"'. They disturbed a large flock of geese, which, according to local shooting men, read the signs aright and never returned; but decided, as they tramped along, that the location for a possible land site looked 'fairly promising, even in its flooded state. We climbed up on the slightly elevated ground at Knockbeg Point and it seemed to us that the area to the west of the point could be dredged out to provide a seaplane anchorage. If not as big as the area at Foynes, it might well prove adequate. It was, therefore, with feelings of high optimism but externally with deadpan caution that we reported to the rest of the party at Athlone, now well into their evening libations'.

Further investigations confirmed the judgment of the two juniors, who must take the credit for the 'discovery' of Shannon even if in the popular mind it was to become associated with Juan Trippe, the head of Pan American—who visited the site the year after the initial exploration—and Charles Lindbergh. Sean Lemass was not anxious to expose himself to the criticism that he was dependent solely on the British Air Ministry for advice in connection with the proposed airport, and sought the assistance of an expert from Pan American. Lindbergh surveyed Rineanna both from the air and on the ground and reported favourably. On 14 August 1936 the Executive Council (the equivalent of the Cabinet prior to the enacting of the 1937 Constitution) decided that the proposed airport would be built by the Office of Public Works and that a special Inter-Departmental Committee, comprising representatives from Finance, Industry and Commerce, Posts and Telegraphs and Defence (and later External Affairs), would be established to assist.

Immediately this committee was obliged to confront the dilemma as to whether land-plane or flying-boat facilities should be given priority. In November it recommended that the advancement of the latter should be postponed until further information was available and 'until it is possible to foresee future developments with a greater degree of certainty than can now be attained'. Both intending operating companies—Pan American and Imperial Airways—had expressed their satisfaction with the Foynes site. Nonetheless Industry and Commerce believed that 'in the light of the information at present ... it may reasonably be assumed that for at least five, and probably for ten years and *possibly* for even a much longer period flying-boats will be an important factor in transatlantic flying'. Lemass urged the preparation of permanent flying-boat facilities at the Shannon site. On 30 November 1937 the Executive Council approved the proposal, together with the construction of the 'land aerodrome' for a sum of £535,000.

Charles Lindbergh was at Foynes for the inaugural Pan American proving flight, though he missed the actual arrival at 10.41 on the morning

15. *Surveying the site for a possible base in the Fergus estuary (left to right): R. H. A. Delap, Joe Lynch, D. Bain, Capt. D. Campbell, resident engineer, Gus Connaughton, Gerard Mc Coy.*

16. *Rineanna, 16 September 1945, on the occasion of the arrival of the first transatlantic survey land-plane, a Pan Am DC4 piloted by Capt. Harold Gray, veteran of the Foynes service. (Left to right): Lord Headfort, BOAC station manager, Lord Inchiquin, Capt. Hedges, BOAC catering manager, Bob Dowley and Jesse Boynton of Pan American Airways.*

of Tuesday, 6 July 1937, when Captain Harold Gray put the Sikorsky S-42B flying-boat *Clipper III* down on the water off Foynes Island. 'After the Clipper took off for Southampton,' Lindbergh wrote to Juan Trippe, 'I went by boat to the location on the north bank of the Shannon where the new landing field is now under construction, and which we walked over when you were in Ireland last year. A large amount of draining has been done, including an open ditch around the outside of the entire area. As you know, they had a strike for about two months which set the work back materially.... Several barracks buildings are being erected on the north bank of the Shannon. I was informed that additional labour would be imported as soon as these buildings are ready for occupancy.'

The project had commenced on 8 October 1936 when Paddy Kelly, the works foreman, and a gang of about a dozen men recruited from the Ennis Labour Exchange cut the first sod. John Quinlivan was one of the early office staff employed. 'Miles and miles of drains had to be excavated,' he remembered. 'Concrete pipes of varying sizes were laid and interconnected to drain the floods and the surface water from a boggy area of more than a square mile of country.... The area had to be levelled and the old existing drains had to be filled up so that all the land depressions disappeared.... Two huge breakwater banks were constructed to connect Dernish Island with the Mainland. This was preliminary to the construction of a seaplane harbour....'[9] Gerard T. McCoy joined the resident engineer's staff a few months later. 'Conditions were hard in the early days,' he wrote, 'pay was poor and getting to and from work was difficult. The lucky men had bicycles but most had to walk some several miles morning and evening. In bad weather much hardship was endured for there wasn't much in the way of protective clothing to be had and anyway few men could afford it.'[10] The men worked a five and a half day, forty-eight hour week, the norm at the time, but the poor pay and conditions led to a strike, lasting six weeks, in February 1938.

The old name for the Rineanna area was *Trá Dá Rí*—'the strand of the two kings'—and development was proceeding on the assumption of a division of power between the land-plane and the flying-boat. A common terminal would provide facilities for both modes of transport, and the flying-boat base was to consist of a mooring basin dredged from the foreshore mud between Knockbeg Point and Dernish island, protected by two specially-constructed embankments. But even as the work proceeded doubts remained as to its relevance to perceived developments in transatlantic travel. Lindbergh was convinced that the future lay with the land-plane, and went as far as to express doubts as to Shannon's role even in that envisaged development: 'It seems to me,' he wrote to Trippe, 'that there is little if any possibility of Ireland being the transatlantic terminal.

I believe it is more probable that most transatlantic planes will not land at all in the future. . . . I am inclined to believe that the next decade or two . . . will see at least some schedules taking off from New York and flying non-stop to England and the Continent.' The prophecy was to prove uncomfortably accurate.

Another cause for concern was the mounting cost of the airport project. Sean MacEntee, Minister for Finance, wrote to Lemass on 31 January 1939 suggesting the re-siting of the land base at Askeaton near Foynes and the abandonment of the Shannon location altogether. Lemass was not amused. The suggestion, he replied, 'cannot seriously be entertained. The site is not nearly so suitable as that at Kilconry. It is saucer-shaped and there is a railway line running through it. It is five miles from Foynes and this, in my opinion, is a fatal objection'. Over £200,000 had already been spent at 'Kilconry' (the name was to have only limited currency) and whilst Lemass recognised the problems of developing the site he was fully aware as to the dangers of delay or divagation: 'It is particularly important,' he wrote sharply to MacEntee, 'to get traffic settled down on the lines we want in the early years; otherwise we may have lost our opportunity for ever.'

Though one of the operators—Imperial Airways—continued to express satisfaction with Foynes, the government decided in March 1939 to proceed with the Shannon flying-boat base. In December, three months after the outbreak of war in Europe, it agreed to instal hard-surfaced runways, a terminal building and hangars at the land-plane base, the seaplane anchorage to be 'further examined'. Though the development of the latter was again confirmed in January 1940, by July of that year shortage of supplies due to war conditions had forced the suspension of the terminal and hangar construction. Work on the runways continued, though in July 1941 the Department of Defence saw them as 'a menace to the defence of the aerodrome and an inducement to an enemy to make use of it as a base for operations'. Lemass disagreed, pointing out that war conditions had accelerated civil transatlantic traffic flying proposals to a remarkable extent and that 'services by land-plane of a frequency and capacity which in peace time would not have been achieved in years must now be expected within the next year'.[11] Defence was mollified by a promise of the provision of protection for the completed runways, but informed the Cabinet in November that the necessary equipment—to include two squadrons of fighter aircraft—was not forthcoming from Britain. In the circumstances of Ireland's neutrality and the progress of the war this can scarcely have come as a surprise.

The first aircraft to land at Shannon, on 18 May 1939, was an Avro Anson of the Air Corps, which was to occupy the airport for the duration of the Emergency. As wartime transatlantic traffic increased BOAC opened a shuttle service between Shannon and Britain to cater for passengers off the flying-boats. Though the latter continued to terminate at Foynes the issue of the Shannon base was still alive—and acquiring new political overtones. One of the motivations behind the proposed Joint Operating Company on the Atlantic had been the desire of the British, and to a lesser extent the Americans, to exclude mainland European airlines from the Shannon facility. 'Rynanna [sic] is the main gateway to the Atlantic', wrote Rupert Strong in the London *Daily Telegraph*, (as condensed in *The Irish Digest*).[12] 'There is, therefore, no country interested in the establishment of transatlantic air services that would not welcome an opportunity to make use of this focal point. It is known on good authority that Eire was prepared to invite Air France, KLM and Deutsch Lufthansa to commence transatlantic flights from the base in the event of a British base being established in Northern Ireland. . . . As matters stand at present the British Commonwealth have the almost exclusive use of Shannon. . . . ' The growing importance of the latter under wartime conditions had, however, caused the British to think again.

In 1943, in the wake of adverse criticism on the part of BOAC of the decision to develop the flying-boat base at Shannon, the Department of Industry and Commerce sought the advice of Commander C. H. Schildhauer, who had been manager of the Atlantic Division of Pan American up to 1940. He was currently a member of the US Naval Air Transport Services, which had a direct input into the operations of both PAA and American Export Airlines, which also served Foynes. Arriving in Ireland on Easter Sunday, 25 April 1943 from Lisbon, he was met by T. J. O'Driscoll. As a committed flying-boat man Schildhauer's endorsement of the plans for Rineanna came as no surprise; but his views on the attitude of BOAC, on his return from a visit to Britain, were perhaps more interesting. He reported that Campbell Orde of BOAC 'went so far as to say that with the immediate task in front of him of operating at Foynes, he felt it necessary to eliminate Rineanna from the minds of the Irish authorities so that they would be prepared to put far more into Foynes'. The Industry and Commerce memorandum[13] continues: 'Commander Schildhauer did, in fact, surmise that underlying this statement was the real objection, viz: the British opposition to the development at Shannon of fully-fledged operational joint flying-boat and land-plane facilities which would hold a paramount position in the post-war transatlantic traffic.' He was in general very critical of the British: 'to some extent probably he felt that we would be very receptive to such criticism.' The Department's response, however, was cautious: 'From this angle complete alignment with the Americans will require careful consideration.'

The flying-boat issue was, nevertheless, close to resolving itself. Though bigger machines were on the drawing-board both in the United States and Britain, it was learned that Pan Am had taken the decision to concentrate on the land-plane. In January 1944 General Critchley, BOAC's director-general, made it clear that he expected most of the post-war traffic to favour this mode, and predicted remarkable growth at Shannon. In the same month the government approved the extension of the existing runways as a matter of urgency. But the flying-boat concept was slow to die. As late as January 1945 the Department was noting that though the current trend was towards land-planes, 'increase in size may result in a swing back to flying-boats. A study of the topic was still inconclusive'. Plans for the Rineanna terminal still aimed to cater for both traffics, with an estimated nine arrivals and departures each day, of which six would be by flying-boat, each flight carrying fifty passengers and a crew of ten. Meanwhile, at Foynes, work was proceeding on the construction of three mooring jetties and ancillary facilities, though only one was eventually completed. A test docking was successfully carried out by American Export Lines on 28 May 1945, the month that the war in Europe came to an end. In September, Sean Lemass, on a visit to both Foynes and Shannon, said that it was proposed to proceed with the flying-boat base at Rineanna, but that work would take at least two years. It was never commenced, and the two retaining embankments at Knockbeg Point constitute the surviving monument to a brief but colourful era. On 28 September Lemass recommended to the government that the flying-boat base at Rineanna 'be postponed indefinitely'. On 28 October the first Pan Am passenger service, operated by a Douglas DC 4, landed at Rineanna. The battle of the two kings was, to all intents and purposes, at an end.

"... and on the day we put up the first meal at Rineanna they were expecting again that we couldn't do it. It was a super meal, and Lord Headfort said to me: 'That's quite extraordinary, we didn't expect anything like that. Could I congratulate your chef?' I said, 'But he's not on duty today'. And he said, 'My God, you can do it like that when the chef is off, what will it be like afterwards?' There was no chef, of course: the stuff was coming in a laundry basket from the Old Ground."

Brendan O'Regan moved across the estuary with the changing traffic, though for a time he ran the restaurants at both Foynes and Rineanna until scheduled services at the former ceased early in 1946. The Rineanna restaurant was housed in a temporary terminal which over the years acquired

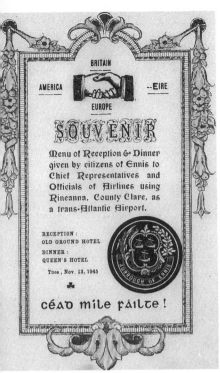

17. *Souvenir menu, Tuesday 13 November 1945.*

18. *Helen (left) and Lal Kirwan, first BOAC ground hostesses at Rineanna, 1945.*

19. October 1946 at Rineanna (left to right): Jesse Boynton, PAA, Bob Haight, Bob Dowley, PAA and Brendan O'Regan.

20. Shannon/Rineanna in the pre-jet era, Summer 1946: Pan American and TWA DC4s. The original terminal building is in the foreground. From a postcard published by Shannon Airport.

both the patina and the authority of permanence; though in 1952 Baron Inchiquin of Dromoland Castle—another local and vocal aristocrat—was to complain at the annual dinner of the Limerick Wine and Food Society that 'Shannon is the only airport in the world where passengers must enter and leave by a side door'. The *Irish Independent* of 17 September 1946 had been more favourably impressed: ' . . . the dining room is tastefully decorated, the best of any airport in the world I've ever seen, and the restaurant has 220 employees which gives some idea of the twenty-four-hour service maintained. Some 1,700 meals are served per day for international airline passengers, plus 600 on-board lunches.' O'Regan, 'a young man with imagination, ability, tenacity, patience and sparks in his eyes', according to the sister-paper the *Irish Press*[14] had had the room upholstered 'in báinín dyed red; the grill room in báinín dyed turquoise blue. The waiters are upholstered in white báinín jackets, grey bow-ties, grey trousers with white stripe'. The waitresses wore grey with white collars, cuffs and belts and all the uniforms were made by the Limerick Clothing Company: an early example of what Desmond O'Malley was later to term the 'genesis of regionalism'. Passenger courier Lal Kirwan wore a powder-blue uniform when stewarding the Pam Am courtesy flights introduced in January 1946. Shannon had become what one journalist described as 'the glamour spot of Ireland'. 'There is a really Irish invitation when one arrives at Rineanna,' commented *The Leader*, 'and when one descends from the air to Irish soil there is a warmth about the place, and this is largely due to the comfort awaiting the travellers.'

That comfort was not altogether the lot of those who worked at the airport. Most of them were obliged to travel daily from either Limerick or Ennis and the Department of Industry and Commerce proposed to the government in January 1945 the acquisition of a site 'of about 180 acres situated at the junction of the main Limerick–Ennis road and the airport road for the purposes of establishing a village settlement (self-supporting, but not profit-earning) for the staff employed at the airport'. The plan, the work of Desmond Fitzgerald of the Office of Public Works, who had been responsible for the design of the much-acclaimed terminal at Dublin Airport, showed a neat and self-contained layout incorporating a community hall, shops, a school, tennis courts, a sports club—occupying the existing Firgrove House—and a hostel for single male workers. Houses for married men were to be constructed by speculative builders, or by the State if such did not come forward. The village was never built, but the project can be seen as prefiguring the development of what was to grow into Shannon town.

Of equal urgency was the need to extend the airport itself to provide for the new generation of aircraft in prospect. The government agreed in

February 1945 to the addition of a further 800 acres in addition to the 850 already in use, and proposed to acquire this under the Emergency Powers (no 315) Order of 1944. Expectations in the area were high ('Prices are being demanded greatly in excess of the normal value of the land,' Industry and Commerce complained the following May) and on the 21st of the same month Fr M. Hamilton, parish priest of Newmarket-on-Fergus, wrote to the Taoiseach, Éamon de Valera, requesting a meeting on behalf of 'a reasonable, respectable body of men' whom, he suggested, were at the mercy of the Department. A document dated 27 May detailed the case *in extenso*: 'As a result of this compulsory acquisition quite a number of people are being deprived of their lands and houses, others are losing the major portion of their farms, others still a lesser but a substantial portion; some cottiers are being deprived of their homesteads and there are a few people such as herds and employed people who will also lose their livelihood . . . we look forward with confidence to our native Irish government to make adequate compensation for each individual loss, and to such an extent that there will be no undue subordination of the rights and liberties of any Irish farmer or labourer to the interests and convenience of trans-Atlantic Clippers and trippers.'

Claims were submitted to arbitration and the matter dragged on, but it was symptomatic of the manner in which Shannon was altering the expectations of its hinterland. Lemass had no doubts—at least for public consumption. In January 1946 he told the first annual dinner of the Limerick Chamber of Commerce that 'the Shannon airport [the definite article was still in general use] will serve as one of the symbols that all the qualities that mark a progressive people are coming alive amongst us'. He had few illusions, however, as to the fact that the airport, for all its growing international reputation, was living on borrowed time. Experts from Lindbergh onwards had been predicting that its role as a major transatlantic gateway would be limited, and in April 1946 the minister informed the government that 'two of the three US air companies operating services to and through this country have recently urged that Dublin Airport should be developed as our main Transatlantic Airport instead of Shannon. Transcontinental & Western Air Inc. [TWA] have been most active in pressing for Dublin'.[15] Thus the first intimations of an enduring challenge to Shannon's viability which was to evoke an equally consistent response. "We should almost welcome the threat," Brendan O'Regan was to say of the renewed controversy over the Shannon compulsory stop in the early 1990s, "because a threat is a way of invigorating the whole system."

The winter of 1946-47 was a harsh one. Electricity was restricted for cooking purposes and TWA crews using the Old Ground Hotel in Ennis were appealed to by the management to adhere to specific meal hours: breakfast, 7.30–11 a.m.; morning coffee, 10.30–12 noon; lunch 1–3 p.m., afternoon tea 3–5 p.m., high tea, 5–9 p.m., dinner 7–9 p.m. and supper up to 1.30 a.m. Bill Dixon, a TWA pilot, expressed himself puzzled as to what hours the meal service might have encompassed before the restriction.[16] Uncertainty was in the air. The previous November, Industry and Commerce had admitted, in a statement on the development of civil aviation, that ' … in view of rapidly changing circumstances in the realm of air transport it is quite impossible to foresee developments even a year ahead with any measure of confidence'. Recognising the possiblity of overflying, it did, however, envisage a role for Shannon for second-class stopping traffic (it was presumed that first-class, non-stop services would carry a premium) and 'for traffic in the carriage of goods by air, which is only in its infancy'. The terminal building, which had been repeatedly extended to meet ever-increasing demands, had now reached the stage when further expansion would be unwieldy. Provision of a new terminal, however, was estimated to occupy five to seven years. The memorandum added, almost as an afterthought: 'The Minister for Industry and Commerce intends to introduce shortly a Bill to create at Shannon the first free airport in the world.' A small warehouse and a customs hut would be required.

Customs-free status, first announced at the Ottawa conference in 1945, came into effect on 21 April 1947. There were now seven scheduled airlines operating through Shannon: three American, one Canadian, one British, one Belgian and one French. (The Aer Lingus transatlantic service planned for 1948 and for which male stewards had been recruited from the airport staff, was to fall victim to a change in government.) Nine hostels, each with twenty-two bedrooms, had been built to accommodate overnighting passengers and the restaurant, lounge and kitchens had been extended: the following year 1,033,000 meals were served by an organisation operating round the clock. The 1948 Report on Civil Aviation prepared by Industry and Commerce stated that the number of terminal passengers at Shannon now equalled landings at Cobh, the calling-point for transatlantic liners, but the bulk of Shannon's business was in transit traffic: between 1947 and 1958 nearly fifty per cent of North Atlantic flights were routed through the airport. Against this background it is easy to understand Brendan O'Regan's retrospective judgment that the most valuable innovation in the Shannon context was the duty-free shop, the first of its kind in the world. The customs-free airport concept had been introduced principally with freight development in mind, but the expected entrepôt trade failed to develop. The shop, 'occupying but a tiny space in a corner of the passenger lounge', as the *Irish Press* saw it in August 1948, 'is one of the country's best and most industrious dollar-earners'. The same year, however, it came under criticism from one Colonel Pozzy, an American who, according to the 1949 Report on Civil Aviation, complained of bad quality goods, badly displayed and the poor position of the shop itself. He recommended that Irish whiskey should be on sale, advice which was promptly and advantageously acted upon.

The principal focus of the catering service, however, was still the restaurant. In 1949 O'Regan arranged interchanges between Shannon staff and the KLM restaurant at Schipol, Amsterdam and the TWA flight kitchens in Paris. Two years later, in co-operation with Clare County Council, he introduced the Shannon Airport Catering Service Staff Training and Advancement Scheme—hastily abbreviated to SACTAS—which provided daily classes and an exchange programme with Swiss hotels. Less than a month after the scheme opened on 16 July it had enrolled 100 pupils, and Professor Wickenhagen of the Lausanne hotel school had been engaged to advise on the curriculum. This initiative developed into the Shannon Hotel Management School, the first of its kind in the country. Pupils, who were taught foreign languages as well as catering and management skills, gained practical experience with the catering service and subsequently in the Shannon International Hotel which was opened at the airport in 1964. A steady stream of graduates secured employment both at home and overseas.

At a time when there were few restaurants of quality outside Dublin and Irish cuisine had little relevance beyond the circumambience of the frying-pan, Shannon shone like a good deed in a naughty world. 'The Rineanna terminal is a revelation' said the *New York Herald Tribune* in 1945. 'The airport restaurant, where all arriving passengers are immediately taken for a complimentary meal, is something that every US airport should see and make an attempt to copy.'

'His aim is to combine good Continental cooking with traditional recipes, using materials fresh from the garden, farm and fishing attached to the hotel,' *The Irish Hotel & Caterer* had said of Brendan O'Regan in 1939; a typical Shannon menu of the post-1945 period indicated that these predelictions had not altered. 'Traditional Irish Specialities' included 'Baked Stuffed Duckling Cathal. (Tender Labasheeda [Co. Clare] Duck cooked with Apple and Bread Stuffing and Whiskey Sauce)'; 'Killybegs Potted Herrings' and 'Coddled Bacon Dublin Style'. If in some cases the tradition might, on investigation, have proved to be of recent provenance, such a menu was, in the context of the period, a major innovation (though the term 'natural cheese' concealed the still ubiquitous 'mousetrap'). It made its impression equally

21. *The Old Ground Hotel, Ennis in 1963. It was formerly owned by Brendan O'Regan's family.*

PRONNLANN SAORPHORT
NA SIONNA,
ÉIRE

SHANNON
FREE AIRPORT RESTAURANT,
IRELAND

22. *Airport menu, 27 October 1960. The occasion was a luncheon in honour of H. Thomas Hallowell, President of SPS (Standard Pressed Steel), one of the first companies to establish on the Industrial Estate.*

23. *The world's first duty-free facility, Rineanna.*

24. *The singer Bing Crosby admires Waterford glass in the Shannon duty-free shop, October 1965.*

on transit passengers and a substantial earthbound passing trade, for which the novelty of being able to dine at any hour of the day or night in an atmosphere of sophistication *va et vient* with the added opportunity of observing at close quarters the passage of the rich and famous proved, in those less sophisticated days, a powerful social attraction well worth the 2s 6d (12½p) parking fee and 6d airport admission.

"The one thing about Brendan O'Regan which his detractors have never given him any credit for is that the man is one of the original macro thinkers," Tom Callanan, a colleague from 1959 onwards, was to say of him; but he was somewhat less complimentary on his grasp of detail. One of the details with which O'Regan, on his own admission, failed to come to terms was the nature of labour relations. At the end of February 1952 there was a lightning strike of waiters and lounge porters at the airport—the complete night staff walked out. The action arose from the fact that four waiters had been given a month's leave without pay as an alternative to a winter lay off. At noon on the 23rd a Labour Court representative opened a hearing involving the Catering Comptroller, strikers' representatives, and an official of the Limerick branch of the Irish Transport and General Workers' Union. The strike, O'Regan was to admit, 'was mainly my fault: I didn't understand the unionisation problem. But once we solved that and once we set about making the traditional union force within the organisation work we never looked back'.[17] He was referring in this comment to the Sales and Catering Service and its immediate successors. The industrial relations situation in the context of the wider development at Shannon was to prove somewhat less amenable to instant solutions.

In 1954 the success of the duty-free operation led to the establishment of a mail order service: one of the first requests, according to the *Sunday Independent*,[18] was from San Francisco for 'two Kerry Blue dogs and a bottle of St Colman's water'. The initial catalogue ran to eight pages and featured Irish goods only, albeit of a more predictable nature; by 1969 it contained sixty pages listing a range of international items from Swiss army knives to Scottish sweaters. With this development O'Regan's organisation changed its name formally to Sales and Catering: profits of £7,574 in 1951 rose to £75,298 in 1955. Underlying this positive trend, however, was the abiding threat to the airport's international status, which, according to the 1948 Report on Civil Aviation, 'has brought prosperity to Limerick, Ennis and a large hinterland at a time when the concentration of industry and commerce in the metropolis is one of our most serious economic and social problems'.

In the general election of 4 February of that year Éamon de Valera's Fianna Fáil government was replaced by a coalition of Fine Gael, Labour and smaller parties including Clann na Poblachta, founded by Sean MacBride who became Minister for External Affairs. On 13 January 1950 MacBride wrote to George A. Garrett, US Minister in Dublin: '. . . the Government must set its face against giving its approval to any proposal which is likely to have adverse effect on the financial position of Shannon or the employment it provides.' The letter went on to suggest that in return for a waiver on the compulsory stop, as established in the 1945 bilateral agreement between Ireland and the United States, carriers might agree to pay a fee whether they landed or not and, further, that Shannon would be used as a dispersal centre for all transatlantic air freight destined for Europe.

The first part of the proposal did not appeal to the US Minister or his advisers, but, replying from Washington, he offered a crumb of comfort. 'The feeling here is that the development of the air freight potential is indeed a promising element in the future of Shannon and one which warrants careful exploration. If you can make Shannon the most efficient and economic dispersal center for such operations we are confident that traffic will come and your financial load will be eased.'

The portents were not good. Ireland became an independent republic on 18 April 1949, severing the last link with Britain, but as the decade progressed large numbers of its citizens were obliged to seek employment in the latter country and elsewhere abroad as the economic climate worsened. In 1951 Fianna Fáil returned to power following the collapse of the inter-party government on the socio-religious issue of free medical care ('The Mother and Child Scheme'). The septuagenarian de Valera was again Taoiseach, Lemass his Minister for Industry and Commerce. One of the coalition's innovations in the latter area of responsibility had been the establishment, in 1950, of the Industrial Development Authority: an organisation, according to one view, which 'was expected to perform many of the functions of a government department without having access to the requisite resources or authority to achieve its objectives'.[19] Lemass, on returning to office, was proposing to dismantle it, but was persuaded by its chief executive, Dr Beddy, to reform it as an organisation which would in future concern itself exclusively with the promotion of new industry in areas where none had hitherto existed. The establishment of An Foras Tionscal in 1952 was instrumental in facilitating, for the first time, the attraction of new companies to specific locations. The groundwork for state-assisted industrial development had been laid.

Lemass, a pragmatist with a commitment to socio-economic change at a time when national political attitudes were still dominated by the legacy of the 1920s civil war, recognised that in the Irish context the small, inefficient and non-innovative private industrial sector, largely the product of the 1930s protectionist policy, could not undertake the major developments required if the economy was to expand. The position was not doctrinaire: in 1961 he paid tribute to 'the vast dynamic of growth which is inherent in free private enterprise', but added that 'it cannot be fully availed of without government drive and leadership'. In the terms of the mid-1950s that largely meant himself. De Valera's comment to T. K. Whitaker on the subject of economic planning—'Tá rudaí eile níos tábhachta'—[20] was a fair indication of the commitment of the Fianna Fáil leadership to revolutionary economic ideas.

Lemass had the ability not only to make plans but to identify the people to carry them out. He owed much to his departmental secretary, John Leydon. "The fact that he coincided with a good civil servant," said O'Regan, "was tremendously important. This duality was able to perceive that we needed mechanisms that could compete, almost, with private enterprise. . . . " The mechanisms were put in place, together with the men who were to control them: J. F. Dempsey in Aer Lingus; M. J. Costello in Comhlucht Siúcre Éireann (the state sugar production company) and O'Regan himself in Shannon. These and other state-sponsored undertakings were considered to be the only practical method of pursuing major economic goals, and current con-demnation of the state sector on ideological grounds obscures and distorts both their origins and their functions. In many cases ad hoc solutions to specific problems, some failed fully to come to grips with their brief whilst others grew into formidable organisations, becoming major instruments of state policies whilst at the same time preserving a high degree of independence of action. They can be criticised on several grounds, but not convincingly as representing a committed ideology, unless it was one of sinn féin. In O'Regan's words, in respect of his own involvement: "a marvellous opportunity to show what Irish men and women could do in an international setting."

In 1957 the economy was in the depths of its worst depression since the foundation of the State. The view of the Department of Industry and Commerce that 'judged by any standards, the [Shannon] airport must be regarded as a major industry situated in a part of the country where such an industry is badly needed'[21] was challenged by the Department of Finance, which estimated the capital cost of providing each of 1,600 jobs at £1,720. 'This is a high price for the taxpayers at large to pay for the employment provided, particularly in view of the fact that if Shannon were closed down some at least of the redundant staff could be absorbed at Dublin to meet the increase in traffic there.' Industry and Commerce was asking the government to approve the construction of new runways to cater for the jet aircraft which were anticipated to come on stream in 1959–60, whilst recognising that these 'may eventually result in the general by-passing of Shannon'. The Department also recommended the deletion of the clause in the bilateral agreement with the United States whereby every translatlantic service entering Irish air space was obliged to stop at Shannon—a provision increasingly evaded by flying a more southerly route. On 20 April the government agreed to both proposals, and to the associated request that the two decisions should be announced together to avoid any implication of a diminution of Shannon's role. On 16 October 1957 a further memorandum from Lemass's Department proposed the establishment of a Shannon Airport Development Company.

References

1. National Archives, Roinn an Taoisigh, S 8814 A
2. Charles A. Lindbergh papers, Box 104, file 282
3. *The Leader*, Dublin, 6 April 1946
4. 'A BOAC engineer at Foynes', in *GPA Flying-Boat Museum* brochure, (N.D.)
5. *Travel Express*, Dublin, January 1975, p. 13
6. National Archives, S 8814 A, 15 March 1943
7. National Archives, S 8814 A CA 800, 9 June 1943
8. 'An Irishman's aviation sketchbook', in *Irish Aviator*, Dublin, 1988, p. 78
9. 'Shannon Airport: the beginning', in *Shannon Airport: 50 years of engineering*, Shannon 1987
10. Ibid.
11. S 8814 A, Industry & Commerce memorandum CA 1285, 17 July 1941
12. October 1938, p. 30
13. S 8814A, CA 800, 9 June 1943
14. 28 January 1946
15. S 8814 B2, CA 29/11/1
16. *TWA Magazine*, 3 April 1947
17. Interview with Padraig O Raighillaigh, RTE Radio, 4 June 1990
18. 20 March 1955
19. Brian Girvin: *Between Two Worlds*, p. 177
20. 'There are other things more important', quoted in John F. McCarthy (Ed.), in *Planning Ireland's future: the legacy of T. K. Whitaker* p. 51
21. S 8814C, CA 2838/12, 25 February 1957

CHAPTER 3

A Genus of Small Rodent

A soft autumn morning in 1990, damp in the air and the suggestion of mist haloing the modest summit of Tullyvarraga hill. To the incurious eye the Shannon Industrial Estate, with its well-kept roadways fringed with tidy grass, resembles nothing so much as a sleepy garden suburb. At ten o' clock on a working day the atmosphere is more evocative of Sunday—no suggestion of movement from the now-superseded customs post, a few stray figures waiting for the bank to open, the Garda barracks a hive of masterly inactivity. The impression, if deceptive, is at least partly attributable to the fact that, since the Free Zone attracted its first industries in the late 1950s, the nature of its enterprises has undergone a change: from small, labour-intensive manufacturing projects to high-tech operations and service industries, the principal tools of which are the facsimile, the computer and the international jet.

The manufacturers, however, are still here—several of them successful survivors of the pioneering days. Behind the discreet walls and strict security checks of De Beers, massive hydraulic presses crush raw graphite in the manufacture of synthetic diamond. The graphite is imported, from Australia and elsewhere: virtually 100 per cent of the product is exported. At SPS, tools are fabricated from imported steel from Germany, Austria, the UK: close to 100 per cent of the output is for export. For both organisations the beginnings at Shannon were small and, to a degree, tentative. Today the De Beers plant is the largest diamond processing factory in the world. And SPS has become a factory of another kind. "I suppose," says Joe Walsh, managing director of its Hi-Life division, "you could easily count fifty people in the country who are ex-SPS and who now have successful businesses in their own right or are MDs or senior executives with other companies." He has a photograph—of a reunion group at a degree-conferring ceremony in the University of

Limerick—to prove it. 'I was the first person employed by SPS International,' Noel Mulcahy told the Seanad on 1 March 1978: 'It was there that I got a grounding in industrial management. Sometimes that aspect of the contribution that has been made is forgotten. There are other people like me working in firms and state bodies throughout the country who acquired their skills in the industrial estate in Shannon.'

The Shannon Free Zone and all that was to flow from it was the product of a complexity of initiatives, some national, some personal. At the national level the economic situation was undergoing, through the disastrous 1950s, a major reappraisal. Foreign intervention had been anathema to orthodox Fianna Fáil thinking as expressed in the protectionist policies of the 1930s and after; and if it was the foundation, under the aegis of the inter-party government of 1948–51, of the IDA and Córas Tráchtála (CTT), the export board, that acted as a signpost to the way ahead, it was the re-orientation of Sean Lemass and the publication of Whitaker's *Economic Development* that cleared the path. The results were remarkable. In 1958, as Basil Chubb put it, 'with dramatic suddenness the State lurched into the middle of the twentieth century'.[1] That is probably a fair description of the change in the intellectual climate. The practical implementation of Whitaker's conclusion that the attraction of skills and techniques of foreign industrialists was the only remedy for the disastrous economic situation was to be something less than sudden in its fulfilment.

Whitaker had conceived of such industrialisation as being located in or near large urban centres, for obvious reasons relating to the supply of labour and services. Shannon was a special case to be argued, as O'Regan realised when, in 1957, with the threat of overflying a reality, he persuaded the Department of Industry and Commerce to call in J. Buist MacKenzie, Scottish director of the consultants Urwick, Orr and Partners (Ireland), to look at the situation. MacKenzie recommended that there should be an organisation 'specifically charged with seeking ways and means of developing activity at or in the neighbourhood of the airport', which could become ' . . . an important trans-shipment centre for freight. There is good reason to believe that the very satisfactory activities of the Catering Comptroller have resulted in stimulating a passenger demand for a stop at Shannon'.[2] O'Regan, already made a director of Bord Fáilte by the coalition government, was appointed its chairman in 1957. With that body's recognition that, in the Shannon context, the task was to convert the transit passenger into the disembarking passenger, the ground rules were established for a blueprint for the airport's future based on the development of both industry and tourism.

25. *Erskine Childers in Factory No. 1 on the Industrial Estate, then occupied by International Dynamics Industries. The company ceased production in 1960.*

26. *Pigs have wings: an unusual freight problem, Shannon Airport, February 1976.*

Lemass was thinking in terms of a new state-sponsored body to engage in these enterprises, but the Cabinet was not immediately receptive, and on 25 October 1957 he gained approval only for an extension of the functions of the Comptroller of Sales and Catering to embrace the development of transit traffic, of tourist facilities at or near the airport and the active promotion of freight traffic including, if necessary, a direct handling unit. Independent industries were as yet not envisaged. 'Lemass had authorised me to spend £50,000 of the profitability of Sales and Catering in the first year on finding ways to stop the overfly,' said O'Regan.[3] 'None of us knew how it could be done. . . . ' In lieu of a fully-fledged state-sponsored body a committee was formed chaired by O'Regan and with his key Sales and Catering personnel as members: J. C. Lynch, with responsibility for freight development; J. G. Ryan, industrial development; J. McElgunn, tourist development; and P. R. Donnelly, development promotion. There was also a consultative committee consisting of R. C. O'Connor, principal officer, Civil Aviation division, Department of Industry and Commerce; Col P. Maher, the airport manager, and J. Buist MacKenzie.

From the regular brain-storming sessions of this group there emerged the idea of industrialisation, at first on a limited scale. "I looked at the Hamburg Free Zone where they did processing," said O'Regan, "and the idea began as a processing zone." Following a press release in November 1957 the first enquiries began trickling in. In February and March 1958 two meetings of prominent Irish businessmen and industrialists were held to canvass support for the scheme; but private-sector thinking was not ready for such a revolutionary departure and the results were somewhat less than encouraging. Later in March, O'Regan visited New York to launch a promotional brochure 'Your Base in Europe' and went on to inspect the free trade zone at Colón, in Panama, and similar facilities in Puerto Rico. The idea was taking shape. Lemass, approached personally and persuasively by O'Regan, agreed to make land available for industrialisation at the airport for a shilling (5p) an acre. The legislation to permit tax relief and custom-free facilities for companies establishing at Shannon was introduced under the Finance (Miscellaneous Provisions) Act, 1958, and the Customs Free Airport (Amendment) Act of the same year. The latter fundamentally altered the administrative system, with a Customs Surveyor based in Shannon with authority to pass goods destined for the Free Zone through any port of entry. By July negotiations for establishing Shannon-based industries were at an advanced stage with Jacob Feldman, diamond merchant, Antwerp; Hiller Helicopters, Palo Alto, California; Romac, London, manufacturers of rubber goods; and Edward F. Casey, Fleetwood Chinchilla Farms, Lancashire.

O'Regan had given the name Shannon Free Airport Development Authority to his ad hoc organisation. In December 1958 he proposed to the Department that formal legal status was necessary to the conduct of its business and the minister agreed, pointing out to the government that industrial development at the airport would 'present very special problems with which neither the IDA nor An Foras Tionscal is equipped to deal satisfactorily', though full co-ordination would be maintained with both these bodies. The embryo Authority became the Shannon Free Airport Development Company on 28 January 1959, with two new appointments: T. Callanan as developments officer and J. Dilger as commercial manager. "The whole development of the concept was revolutionary," said Tom Callanan. "A lot of the early thinking was revolving around a very simple concept—how do you change an expected pattern of development using the resources you have in such a way that they reinforce rather than detract from what's happening? The airport, clearly, was both under threat and equally provided an opportunity."

As a very junior civil servant Tom Dunne had involvement with the establishment of the company and the drafting of the 1959 Act. "I have great memories," he said, "of pasting pieces of a Bill on pieces of paper, helping the then principal of the Aviation Division over in the Dáil when Minister Childers was putting it through the House." Dunne, subsequently to become the company's chief executive, had attended several meetings at which Brendan O'Regan was present in the late 1950s and had come to know him slightly. "It was very interesting as a civil servant to see the extraordinary level of support that O'Regan was able to command in Government circles because effectively he had his mandate from Sean Lemass. He [O'Regan] and a wonderful character called R. C. O'Connor, in charge of the Civil Aviation Division, agreed that it would be helpful to the new Company to have a civil servant attached to it for liaison purposes. O'Connor got me to attend a meeting at which O'Regan was present. I was interviewed for the liaison job without realising it." Tom Dunne joined the company in this capacity in 1960 on a term of three years' secondment, after which he had the choice either of going back to Dublin as a civil servant or accepting a permanent appointment. He decided to stay, and became assistant secretary on 8 May 1963. "I very quickly became heavily imbued with the sense of mission and the sense of something important happening down here which was all around us in those days, and has never really disappeared."

One of Tom Callanan's first jobs, as a Spanish speaker, was to translate the laws of Panama in relation to the Colón Free Zone. O'Regan had this facility—a combined seaport and airport—in mind as a model, with the

Shannon Estuary serving in the future as the sea mode. The immediate task, however, was to establish the nucleus of the industrial estate, which, it was decided, would be built not, as was originally intended, at the rear of the existing hostels on account of possible interference with runway construction but on the east hangar site. T. Garland & Company were appointed site engineers, with Frank Gibney advising on aesthetic and architectural aspects of the project. Pending the completion of the first standard bays, temporary buildings were provided to house Co-Am-Co, manufacturers of electronically-controlled coin-operated amusement machines, and Chinchilla (Ireland) Ltd, importers of dressed pelts for manufacture of fur coats. The intention of the latter company to import live chinchillas for breeding purposes was for the time being blocked by the Department of Agriculture, which expressed concern as to the possible danger of foot and mouth disease from this unfamiliar genus of small South American rodent.

The success of the Free Zone was still seen in terms of the development of air freight. "The idea was," said Callanan, "that the way you pulled aircraft out of the sky was by providing them with cargo payload." But first you needed your aircraft. 'As head of the Development Company,' O'Regan testified in 1972 at a hearing marking a further stage in the continuing overflying argument, 'I had many discussions with the leaders of US and other national transatlantic air companies. This was necessary because any development inevitably needed appreciation of the situation as it was and forecast of growth targets. The picture which I ... got from such discussions was extremely gloomy because the airline estimates of the traffic to and from Ireland were low. One American airline assured me at that time that the traffic could be served by routing an average of one Boeing 707 flight daily through Shannon. My clear conviction was that if Shannon had to depend on foreign carriers alone, growth of business of the airport would stagnate in spite of even the most dramatic developments in the fields of tourism and industrial promotion which we were then planning as a means to foment the interest of the carriers and their customers. Fortunately the government took the decision to re-establish the national transatlantic airline. . . . '

Aerlínte, the long-haul subsidiary of Aer Lingus, opened its service from Dublin through Shannon to New York on 28 April 1958, and though O'Regan's close friendship with J. F. Dempsey, the airline's chief executive, ensured practical co-operation between the two state enterprises, their interests and priorities did not always coincide. SFADCo, for example, saw connecting services from Shannon to points in Europe, particularly London, as essential to the viability of the airport, services which Aer Lingus could not foresee operating economically. In 1965 the airline opposed the application of

Loftleidir, the Icelandic carrier, to route through Shannon, to the dissatisfaction of the SFADCo board, which expressed itself as 'at all times anxious to assist and co-operate with Irish International Airlines, but when the interests of the two companies clashed the Board must act firmly in the Development Company's interest'. Nor was the accession of the Irish airline to the transatlantic routes an unmixed blessing: at the first meeting of SFADCo on 4 February 1959, J. Dilger, the commercial manager (aviation) had reported that all the airlines he had contacted on a recent US visit stressed that the principal reason for cutting the Shannon service was that Aerlínte had captured the traffic which previously had made the Shannon landing attractive and worthwhile.

With the prospects for entrepôt trading based on high air freight volumes looking increasingly uncertain it was essential that the Free Zone acquire an 'anchor tenant' of high international reputation to give the undertaking credibility. Several of the initial enquiries had come to nothing, and of those firms which had established, not all were to sustain a lasting and effective presence. By June 1960, official objections having been overcome, there were 250 pairs of chinchillas domiciled in the country under the watchful eye of an active Chinchilla Breeders' Association, and though a continuing market was envisaged for their progeny, by September of the same year SFADCo had written to Mr Casey seeking the suspension of further sales until the question of a pelting station could be settled. A year later breeders who had purchased stock were complaining of being left with quantities of fecund rodents on their hands. The firm, with a staff of six, had restricted its activities to the making of chinchilla cages. Of other early starters, Rippen, a Dutch piano manufacturer, was to experience serious trading difficulties and another, W. B. Pink, laid off staff as early as 25 November 1960. SFADCo, concerned at the serious effect which it considered would attend the dismissals without payment, made loans to eight of Pink's employees equivalent to the wages due to them.

There was an air of mystery surrounding what was going on at the Industrial Estate, Bill Jones of Lep Transport remembered: "There was Chinchilla. And there was talk of SPS, De Beers . . . . " An accretion of legend in the intervening years now makes it difficult to be certain of the factors instrumental in securing the first major international tenant—Standard Pressed Steel of Jenkinstown, Pennsylvania—for Shannon. 'At a very early stage'—in Brendan O'Regan's recollection[4]—'we got an artist's impression of what it should be like, a model of an industrial zone and of a town. SPS's Tom Hallowell looked at it and said "are you going to do that?" I said that's what we were going to do. "All right," he said, "I'm in then". It was the

[61]

bigness of the idea that got him.' But Hallowell, according to Joe Walsh, who joined the firm at Shannon in 1961, subsequently had a change of mind and O'Regan had to convince him to go ahead. Be that as it may, the decision was taken and SPS began making threaded fasteners in a 50,000 sq. ft building on the estate, setting up a small ancillary tool facility. By 1965 they had run out of space and added another 50,000 sq. ft.

There was a deliberate policy, according to Tom Callanan, to go for high-skilled mechanical engineering for the estate; but there was no industrial tradition whatsoever in the area. SPS, Kevin Vaughan recalled, were the first people to look for a lot of labour in the community: "I was involved in Muintir na Tíre at the time. We'd hold a meeting in Quin and Newmarket and Sixmilebridge and they'd talk about working in industry. . . ." Local enterprises such as a woollen mills in Sixmilebridge which employed orphans from Dublin, had given industry a bad name and SPS employed an industrial psychologist to counteract this prevailing impression. Everyone who joined SPS "had to do six weeks on the floor no matter what—after that you'd be apportioned". The factory opened in 1960, with SPS importing its own training programmes from the parent company, staff in specialised areas such as quality control going to the US for training. By 1965 local expertise had established itself to the extent that Shannon was manufac-turing for some of the twenty-two other SPS locations worldwide, and when AnCO set up the first industrial training programme at Shannon they recruited six SPS technicians as instructors. The last American to head the Irish operation left in 1969.

Though the firm has expanded steadily in the course of its thirty-year presence in Shannon, there have been problems, retrenchments and wrong decisions. One of the latter was the setting up of a plant in Galway to manufacture nuts for the US automotive industry, to which SFADCo gave encouragement. The move was based on the planned refurbishment of the port of Galway; and when this failed to materialise, the nuts, produced entirely from imported material, had to be freighted very expensively across to Dublin for shipment. The original intention had been to export from Foynes or, ideally, from Killadysert on the Clare side of the estuary. This would have involved bridging the River Fergus, and SFADCo felt that this would have to be considered in the context of the whole future of the estuary, an area which then lay outside its remit. Even had it fallen within the organisation's terms of reference, however, the likelihood of a decision favourable to SPS would have been slight, given the dismal history of attempts to secure local agreement on estuarial development.[5]

If the Galway move was a failure, the SPS experience of Shannon itself has been generally positive. SFADCo, according to Joe Walsh, was always very

27. *H. F. Oppenheimer, chairman of De Beers Consolidated Mines (foot of steps) arriving at Shannon with E. T. S. Brown, chairman of the board of Shannon Diamond and Carbide, for the opening by Jack Lynch, Minister for Industry and Commerce, of Ultra High Pressure Units (Ireland), manufacturers of synthetic diamonds, May 1963.*

28. *The De Beers complex on the Shannon Industrial Estate, 1992.*

conscious of not just creating new industries but of retaining existing jobs and identifying potentials for growth. One of the two largest employers on the estate in 1990, with a payroll of some 550, SPS had also adhered to the model envisaged in the original planning in that all its tool production was airfreighted to export markets, principally the USA. And the undertaking in its turn made its contribution. 'I took a reading at the end of 1989,' said Walsh. 'The total cost of running the two buildings here was £18.4 million. Of that, £13.1 million was spent in Ireland—not counting spin-offs such as cleaning, security, etc.'

'It's not so much that workers here are cheaper,' says De Beers of South Africa, whose Shannon subsidiary produces industrial diamonds, 'it's just that they're very good and very available.'[6] De Beers, established on the estate since 1961 along with SPS, is one of the two survivors from that period. In the 1950s its then head of industrial diamonds interests in Johannesburg, E. T. S. Brown, took the decision to establish a base in Europe from which to service both its European and north American markets. Monaco was considered, but Shannon was selected because of the financial climate that was being created, because Ireland was predominantly English-speaking and on account of the perceived calibre of the people. Following the favourable report of a survey team, Ted Brown became chairman of the board of Shannon Diamond and Carbide, retiring on the company's reaching its tenth anniversary in Shannon in 1971.

Shannon Diamond and Carbide moved into Bay 24 on the Industrial Estate on 20 March 1961 and by the end of that year was employing fifty people. A synthetic diamond plant followed in 1963 and further expansion took place in 1964 and 1970, by which time employment had risen to 550. The workforce in the early days, Chris Taylor, De Beers' managing director recalled in 1990, had divided loyalties: many ran small farms in the area and would give that activity preference at harvest time and other crucial periods. In-house training was introduced from the beginning, and in addition to drawing on the local labour pool the firm began attracting emigrants returned from overseas, a pattern that, through the 1960s and into the following decade, was to become characteristic of the industrial development of the region. The big breakthrough, according to Taylor, came when the company decided to own rather than rent its premises and bought the existing buildings together with a further twenty-three acres from the Development Company. Shannon now handles all sales, marketing and distribution for De Beers industrial diamonds worldwide. Taylor, who joined De Beers in 1967 from a computer business in the City of London, at first thought that he had made a serious mistake. But after a year in Ireland he was told that he was going to be tranferred to Paris. "I suddenly knew

I liked Shannon. You could get to the office—you were in a damned vibrant community." After two years away he was delighted to return. 'Possibly the happiest feature of the project,' John Burls wrote in the parent company's magazine *Optima*[7] 'is the fierce and almost nationalistic interest which overseas staff of the foreign companies on the estate have in the success of Shannon, and which goes far beyond purely selfish considerations.'

The fact of De Beers' South African provenance did not escape notice. The company kept a low profile, contributing to the local environment, underwriting the loan for the first Shannon town church, giving money to Co-Operation North and to the restoration of Limerick cathedral, but not seeking national attention. Though the group chairman, H. F. Oppenheimer, was on record as an outspoken critic of apartheid and the company was one of the first in South Africa to allow black employees to become shareholders, there had been criticism from Dublin-based anti-apartheid groups and opposition to the cathedral authorities accepting money from South African sources. According to Taylor there had been little hostility on the part of the local press. De Beers, the largest employer in the Mid-West region in 1990, has a history of good industrial relations, with no major dispute and only one period when it found it necessary to create redundancies. It acquired fifteen acres on the outskirts of Shannon town which it developed as a staff recreation area.

☆ ☆ ☆ ☆ ☆ ☆

Hello. . . . Would you like to know how to get a job with one of Ireland's biggest companies? An interesting and exciting job which offers wonderful opportunities for advancement? A job which will involve you in the rush and bustle of life at Shannon, Ireland's International Airport? Interested? Well, just read on and learn how you can become a member of the EI Company team!

If SPS and De Beers remained visible success stories, others who have come and gone have served to emphasise the fact that the development of the Industrial Estate has not been without its problems. The persuasive invitation quoted above is to be seen in the context of a promotional brochure directed exclusively at women. As early as October 1961 SFADCo was expressing concern over the tendency of firms to employ a relatively high percentage of female labour, a practice which it saw as giving rise to serious problems in creating a new community at Shannon. It did not, however, feel that it could refuse facilities to companies on these grounds, though by December 1962 it foresaw a serious shortage of female workers on account of the rapid expansion of firms like Lana-Knit and EI and proposed

[65]

the building of a hostel for girls, additional bus services and a ferry across the Shannon. At this stage community development was lagging behind industrialisation to the point where SFADCo felt it must cease to accept proposals from firms which would employ mainly female labour and even considered ending all industrial promotion.

This draconian view, fortunately, did not prevail. In March 1963 it was concluded that the labour position would have to be explained early in negotiations with all applicants and that if it appeared that an industry required too many female workers the promoters would be encouraged to seek a location elsewhere in the county and the IDA so informed. By September 1964, 1,155 women and girls were employed at Shannon, some from as far away as Tipperary, Ballylanders, Askeaton and Kilmihil. They travelled to work by bus, leaving as early as 6.15 a.m. and not seeing home again until 7.15 p.m. These services were to become a permanent feature: the 1990-91 Bus Éireann timetable showed early morning departures from Kilfinane, Galbally, Cappamore, Tipperary, Labasheeda and Scarriff. The earliest bus—from Galbally—was still 6.15 a.m. and these commuters were also the last to reach home at 6.25 p.m. Little had changed in nearly three decades.

By the end of 1964 the pool of women workers in Co. Clare was close to exhaustion. A year later the SFADCo board were informed that EI 'had recruited female labour at a rate greatly in excess of that which the company had advised as feasible and were experiencing, partly in consequence of this, a high rate of labour turnover. In recruiting at this rate they had created a shortage of women workers which inhibited the establishment of new industries and had upset the desirable balance between male and female employment on the estate as a whole'.[8] EI were employing 336 men and 686 women, with a target of a total workforce of 2,500. It was debated whether a fixed limit should be set to the size of any single firm, but the idea was rejected on the grounds that it might prove inhibiting to future applicants. In 1963 exports from the estate represented twenty per cent of the national total. "It really did constitute a headline for the industrialisation of the whole country," said Tom Dunne. "There were a lot of genuine firsts."

The Development Company was thus not anxious to place any barrier in the way of attracting firms to the industrial estate. One of the advantages perceived by overseas enterprises, particularly those of United States origin, was that an area such as Shannon lacked an effective trade union presence or tradition, though one of the first appointments was that of an experienced trade union official, Tom Sheedy, as Labour Liaison Officer. Some firms, nevertheless, actively prohibited negotiation with unions, a situation which, following a complaint by the Clare Council of Trade Unions, led to a meeting between the Minister for Industry and Commerce, SFADCo and the

29. *Sean Lemass (left) and Erskine Childers (second from right) with Mr Barcs (in white coat) of Clare Chemicals, Shannon Industrial Estate, 10 July 1965.*

30. *Diploma day at the Shannon Hotel School, 19 May 1966. Erskine Childers, Minister for Transport and Power (centre, front row), with, on his left, the school director, Mr Jorgen Blum and Brendan O'Regan. On his right is Jean-Marc Heidseick of the champagne firm and a graduate of Trinity College, Dublin.*

IDA in 1967. The situation had been brought to a head by the rapid deterioration of industrial relations in EI. On 29 May 1966 buses carrying workers to the factory from Limerick had been stoned and a major and bitter strike saw the situation go from bad to worse. In 1973 the board of SFADCo recommended that the company should seek acceptance by incoming industrialists of the rights of Irish workers and trade unions in the terms formulated and applied by the IDA, which made grant aid conditional upon the recipient's recognising the right of union representation.

The history of SFADCo's relationship with the Industrial Development Authority is one of almost Byzantine complexity.[9] It was understandable that the latter should regard the new body as something of a cuckoo in the nest, whilst as early as June 1959 the former was expressing itself as not entirely happy with the *modus operandi* which had been established between the two state organisations. It was agreed that close co-operation was necessary; but SFADCo was concerned that potential industries might be lost 'through slavish adherence to agreed procedure'.[10] Later in the year the IDA chairman, Dr Beddy, accepted that a degree of flexibility was necessary and that good relations were being maintained. But there had been created a fundamental convergence of interests which destined to make life difficult for both parties and to lead to several government attempts, more or less successful, at re-definition. The situation was further confused by the fact that the personnel tended to overlap. In April 1965 J. J. Walsh, a member of the SFADCo board, was appointed chairman of the IDA; a situation later to be replicated by M. J. Killeen, who had a particularly close personal relationship with Brendan O'Regan and who became a SFADCo director in January 1970 whilst IDA chief executive.

In 1969 the Industrial Development Act had reconstituted the IDA as an autonomous state-sponsored body outside the civil service, combining it with An Foras Tionscal and empowering it, amongst other things, to set up a network of offices to promote regional development. In the Limerick/Clare/ north Tipperary region SFADCo was to assume responsibility for building industrial estates and promoting industry: this extension of the latter's remit beyond the confines of the Free Zone clearly created a potential for conflict. The processing of grants both at Shannon and within the region generally would be carried out by the IDA with recommendations from the Development Company. The latter, which had been reporting to the Department of Transport and Power in respect of its functions in aviation and tourism, would now also report to Industry and Commerce on industrial estates, advance factories and Shannon town.

The move, in Tom Callanan's view, was prompted by the Limerick TD Donough O'Malley who was alarmed at the collapse of traditional industry in the area. Limerick city in particular was seeing long-established firms in the areas of bacon, shoes, leather and clothing, closing one after another. Progress at Shannon had also given a firm pointer as to the direction in which the IDA should be moving, but the new overlapping of responsibilities—not only in respect of the IDA but also of County Development Officers—was to create many problems and to stress the fact that SFADCo had been given responsibility without the necessary autonomous powers fully to exercise it. It commented in June 1970 on a draft agreement between the two bodies: 'From SFADCo's point of view the arrangements proposed ... meant the abandonment of the authority intended to be given to the Company as the essential counterpart of its responsibility for industrial development in the Mid-West region. ... The Company had undertaken the task on the clear understanding that it would have such authority, and the legislation had been designed to facilitate this. ... To accept a situation in which the Company became advisers to the IDA without power of decision in certain key areas would reduce the Company's effectiveness and ability to succeed. ... '[11]

SFADCo wanted to reserve the option to carry out its own promotion for the region should it feel it to be necessary and to retain some control over the awarding of grants, as heretofore. The new situation, in its view, meant that either SFADCo executives would report to the IDA board, in which case the former would effectively have no function; or they would report to the SFADCo board which would then report to the IDA board—with the same result. The IDA view was that an arrangement by which SFADCo would have power of decision in respect of incentives was not only illogical in that the government had established the IDA as the national authority, but would remove from the IDA control funds allocated to it and for which it was accountable. It would further create difficulties and embarrassment in dealing with other regions. The crux of the matter was, of course, that in no other region was there an organisation such as SFADCo or any existing development on the scale of Shannon. Government legislation had failed to take account of this fact and the consequences of the likely conflict of interests in the Mid-West. The IDA suggested that industrial development in that region required not delegation of decision-making in respect of incentives but close, harmonious working by the two organisations—an aspiration that was to prove consistently difficult to transmute into reality.

Agreement, however, was reached for the time being, the understanding being that incentive recommendations would be submitted to the SFADCo board and that decisions would be underwritten by the IDA and incorporated in the formal agreement between the IDA and the client. A year later, in June 1971, the procedures were still a matter for discussion and some disquiet. SFADCo's understanding of the situation was that the IDA would subject proposals for the Mid-West region to the same examination as Shannon proposals and advise the company whether they were grant-worthy; the SFADCo board would then receive the proposal with the IDA clearance and decide what grants and other facilities to offer in the context of IDA guidelines ... not exactly a formula for prompt and efficient decision-making. As the company had put it in April 1969 in the introduction to its five-year programme, the first of its kind in the country, for the industrial development of the region: 'The Industrial Development Authority is responsible for the promotion of industrial development for the country as a whole, so that there is an interlocking joint responsibility ... success involves mutuality of effort.' The will was not lacking: the 1974 five-year programme was prepared in consultation with the IDA, with a view to harmonising it as much as possible with the plans for other regions originated by that body. The IDA was asked to include Shannon, now feeling the effects of world-wide recession, in its list of problem towns.

The second five-year programme itself exposed a major divergence in the thinking of the two bodies. Whereas SFADCo had broadly accepted the concept of core area development as expressed in the Buchanan report (following political pressure Ennis had been added to the original Limerick–Shannon axis) the IDA plans for other regions did not concur with this approach, employing town groupings only as a means of defining or setting out job targets. In its view the clear designation of a group area was likely to revive the controversy about growth points which had arisen from Buchanan. SFADCo's reaction was that the concept of the core area in the region was so well established that to abandon it would in its turn cause considerable controversy, and in this it was backed by the Regional Development Organisation (RDO). The matter of regional development was, in Paul Quigley's assessment, the major difference between the two bodies. The IDA, he suggested, was an excellent promotional organisation, but it spent half its budget promoting itself. "They believed that what was good for the IDA was good for Ireland." But, said Quigley, they always disliked the idea of Shannon growing industrially.

A partial view, perhaps, but it serves to underline the inevitable dichoto-my between centralised and regional control—or the aspiration towards it. In 1970 SFADCo had launched its own advertisement campaign in Britain, a move which the IDA objected to on the grounds that other regions would insist on having public funds made available to them for similar publicity and that it should carry out all such promotion overseas to generate sufficient enquiries for the whole country. SFADCo accepted this view on the assurance that such IDA promotions would be adequate to achieve this end, but the enlargement of the company's remit had increased its propensity to think regionally. When the government had announced in October 1967 that it was considering extending the facilities existing in the Industrial Estate to Limerick and Ennis, the SFADCo reaction had been that such development could not be carried out without regard to the requirements of the region as a whole and that the company must be ready to participate in any discussions or action which might be necessary to solve regional problems and co-ordinate regional development. 'Industrial development will affect everybody in the Region,' said the introduction to the first five-year programme, 'directly or indirectly. The degree to which it is successful (and success should be measured in social as well as economic terms) will depend very largely on the degree of support which the people of the Region give to the objectives, plans and policies adopted.' The use of the capital 'R' was in itself significant.

These were heady days. ' The widely-accepted goals of the community,' the programme announced, 'are: first, full employment, which can be equated to an end to involuntary emigration; second, and concurrently, an improvement in the overall standard of living for all of the people and particularly for those whose standard is now lowest; and third, an end to the depopulation of rural areas'. The fact that the document regarded the last-named as the region's most pressing problem served to emphasise the strong social element present in the company's thinking at the period—not only in the industrial context but also in the spheres of tourism, the development of Shannon town and the improvement of rural housing. 'Viewed from the standpoint of regional development,' Brendan O'Regan wrote in 1973,[12] 'our various activities tie logically together as part of a coherent whole. . . . A healthy prosperity can exist only if the decline of small communities is stemmed; where these are yet too small to attract major industry, tourism activity, small industry, or industry within easy commuting distance may offer the best prospects for growth.'

A SFADCo director, N. A. O'Brien, on making enquiries from 'an independent source' discovered that though there was some uncertainty within the Department and Bord Fáilte as to the organisation's role its performance was highly regarded and its staff praised for their professional ability and approach. It was suggested to him that this arose from the degree of local involvement which injected realism into the company's attitude. Criticisms concerned its alleged tendency to try to divert business to Shannon with too little regard for the national need. . . . [13] It is perhaps a salutary exercise in this regard to take a thirteen-year leap forward to the report of the Dáil Committee on Public Expenditure on the Shannon Free Airport Development Company Ltd (1986): 'Shannon is ideally poised to pilot new approaches to industrial promotion and development with a view to providing the model

[71]

for other Regional development agencies in time.' Holding this poise whilst time ticked by was to prove a performance demanding both patience and some degree of political agility.

The 1968 mandate to promote industrial development in the region did not include small industries, the responsibility for which was retained by the IDA. Medium and large-scale industries require dedicated accommodation in the matter of siting, and thus SFADCo quickly found itself enmeshed in property deals under pressure, involving in some cases very expensive acquisitions from existing owners. This was particularly true in the case of Limerick city, which, in spite of the genuine intention to diversify in the matter of location, was recognised as the key to any meaningful industrial development in the region. In 1970 the company was able to report standard units under construction at Galvone and Corcanree, with a large site acquired at Castletroy. Acquisition at Raheen had been costly and difficult, one house with an estimated value of £6,500–£7,000 being bought for £12,000 on account of the need to proceed quickly. There was in general a lack of suitable serviced land, particularly in the city. Raheen, which was bought in May 1968, had to be rezoned for industrial use, a process which was not completed until January 1969, and there was no adequate water supply. The project was also delayed by a shortage of cement.

'Throughout the region we found that sites zoned for industrial development were generally the least attractive from the point of view of the prospective industrialist,' the 1970 supplement to the five-year programme noted. The prospective industrialist, in particular one envisaging establishing in Limerick, had also to surmount that city's appalling reputation in the matter of industrial relations. Cathal O'Shannon, in 1991 in charge of public affairs at the Aughinish Alumina plant on the estuary, recalled his father, a lifelong trade union official, telling him that 'the reason the Limerick workforce, especially those on the docks, were difficult and awkward was that the Limerick bosses were fucking lousers'. SFADCo put it perhaps more circumspectly in 1973: 'The reputation of Limerick as a place where labour relations were deplorable seriously hampered progress of industrialisation in the city and surrounding area.' Nor were the newly-establishing industries proving conspicuously successful in remedying the situation. Commenting on a widespread impression that there was a shortage of unskilled workers in the region, the SFADCo board suggested in May 1974 that 'this probably arose from the labour turnover problems of Ferenka which now employed 1,500 but in the last two years had recruited at least 3,000'.

The high turnover was due, not to shortage of men, but to Ferenka's unpopular four-shift system and the firm's poor industrial relations record. In early 1975 this steelcord manufacturer was the largest grant-aided employer in the State, occupying a forty-acre site at Annacotty on the outskirts of Limerick city. Its problems—and, indirectly, those of the region—were seriously compounded when on 3 October 1975, Tiede Herrema, the firm's Dutch managing director, was kidnapped by paramilitaries seeking the release of the imprisoned Dr Rose Dugdale. He was freed following an eighteen-day siege of a house in Monasterevin, Co. Kildare, which attracted world attention, but SFADCo's general manager, Paul Quigley, discounted any serious industrial repercussions in an interview shortly after the event.[14] 'I don't think the kidnapping hits the region particularly,' he said. '. . . it is quite clear now that it is an operation that extended over the whole country; it has got nothing to do with this region really. . . . At that level, I think, there will be some adverse effects on industrial promotion. I don't think it will be very grave because this kidnapping was an aberration, a peculiar thing that happened once, and, please God, is very unlikely to happen again.' Quigley was right in that the event produced no palpable effect on the level of industrial enquiries in the region; but two years later, following a protracted and bitter strike, Ferenka closed for good with the loss of 1,400 jobs.

This serious reverse took place against the background of a worsening recession and concomitant job losses. In January 1974 Lana-Knit, on the Shannon Industrial Estate, had made 110 redundant; their payment of three times the statutory amount plus a lump sum of £200 to each affected employee disturbed SFADCo, which felt that such generous terms might become the norm and create difficulties for other firms forced to take similar action. In the region as a whole 3,000 jobs were lost between January 1974 and September 1975; but the company was still trying to take the broader view. Whilst admitting the vital importance of job creation it did not feel that this should be achieved at any price. Jobs, it concluded, 'essentially were a means to improve the quality of life and the company must be aware that what was done now would affect the quality of life for generations to come and the selection . . . should be conditioned by this awareness'.

Whether this steadfast idealism would have registered with ex-employees signing on the dole is a matter for speculation. Out of a total of fifty-nine grant-aided industries established in the region between 1960 and 1973, fourteen had closed down by the latter date. 'We were involved in attracting new industry,' said Paul Quigley: 'and we knew we were taking a high risk with some of them.'[15] But by 1971 one of every four jobs was provided by an industry set up after 1961, the traditional sector having collapsed spectacularly. It is against this background, and in the broader social context, that the success of the industrialisation programme should be measured; though it is a matter for further speculation as to the number of major industries which might have located in the region had suitable sites been available. Ad hoc arrangements, such as those made for Burlington and Syntex, were successful but there is no meaningful measurement of the ones that got away.

On 9 December 1975, in the wake of the Herrema kidnapping, *The Irish Times* published a special report on the Mid-West Region. In recent years such supplements have largely degenerated into 'advertising features' of little informative value and questionable objectivity, but the contributions to this particular example ranged a good deal wider than those of the newspaper's own staff reporters and it offers an interesting and generally authoritative contemporary perspective of the Shannon phenomenon, if from a largely Dublin viewpoint. Liam de Paor on the Celtic tradition of the area, Ciarán MacMathuna on traditional music, Donal Foley on the Clare poet Brian Merriman, furnished the cultural underpinning for analyses of the industrial and economic situation, with Michael Dillon making the important point that agriculture was still the mainstay of the region and Fr Harry Bohan, founder of the Rural Housing Organisation, stressing that industrialisation alone would not stem the flight from the land. Henry Kelly, evaluating the role and influence of SFADCo, concluded that 'the Shannon publicity machine is so geared that it could probably run a mission in a brothel or sell Jack the Ripper to the public as a champion of moral rearmament. That it does not try to do so is either sheer honesty and integrity (which I think it is) or the subtlest piece of brassneckery this century'.

The general tone of Kelly's report evoked wonder at the acknowledged achievements of the region salted with a touch of incredulity that this could be happening in—to a Dubliner—a somewhat unlikely location. 'Essentially what has been proved in Shannon,' he concluded, 'is that a regional development body . . . can make itself a genuine presence if a few simple, but vital decisions are agreed at the outset: perhaps the greatest of these is that, without prejudice to an overall national economic plan, such an area must have a wide degree of local authority. In other words, one of the successes of Shannon is that so many decisions affecting the lives and future of its many dependent communities are taken within those communities themselves.'

Not all, however: the assumption by the IDA of regional planning subsequent to 1973 reduced SFADCo's high degree of autonomy. "We had to fall in line," said Quigley. "Our target was part of the national target from then on. Our plans wilted after that." On 1 January 1973 Ireland became a member of the EEC; the following month a general election installed a Fine Gael/Labour coalition government and attitudes to state bodies underwent a change. The new Minister for Industry and Commerce, Justin Keating, visited Shannon on 20 July 1973 and asked for the company's thoughts on regionalism and that it should consider participating in the equity of new

31. *Captain J. C. Kelly-Rogers, who piloted British flying-boats through Foynes before and during World War II, with Justin Keating (right), Minister for Industry and Commerce, at an aviation exhibition at Shannon, July 1973.*

32. *Paul Quigley, former managing director of SFADCo, with a bust of himself by Marjorie Fitzgibbon in the University of Limerick, which conferred an honorary doctorate on him in March 1992.*

industrial firms and try to encourage new projects which could be operated by a combination of public and private enterprise. There was, however, no evidence of real planning vis-à-vis the state sector and this was creating a vacuum where divergences of opinion within SFADCo were emerging as to the aims the organisation should pursue. It is fair to say that up to this point the philosophy of the endeavour had been very much the product of Brendan O'Regan's thinking; and this thinking was exhibiting a tendency to develop in directions which caused problems for those, such as Paul Quigley, who were responsible for implementing policy. "He became a little bit like he is today, a philanthropist," was the view of Arthur O'Keeffe, who had been interviewed by O'Regan in 1959 and worked for the company thereafter: "He began to look for challenges away from the main stream. He had given whatever he had to give."

Such challenges were discerned by O'Regan as lying more and more within the social framework. A note in the minutes dated 23 January 1976 is strongly evocative of this view. '. . . the essential character of the company's success was to be seen not in industrial development nor in tourist promotion alone. Rather was it in the stimulation of groups of local people in the countryside and villages to undertake or become involved in various kinds of development work in their own communities. It was this that marked the difference between progress in the Mid-West and other regions.' This minimalist view contrasted markedly, at first sight, with O'Regan's plans for involving the company in the Third World and in promoting an international trade centre at Shannon. For Paul Quigley, a former director of the Irish Management Institute and his obvious successor, this apparent dichotomy, which was in fact simply parallel manifestations of an innate idealism and social concern, was a source of some concern. He believed that in the light of the prevailing economic circumstances—the second SFADCo five-year plan had been put on ice and more immediate objectives assigned—the whole future of the company and its responsibilities needed serious rethinking, a view that was to be shared by Desmond O'Malley when he returned as Minister for Industry, Commerce and Energy following the general election of 1977.

☆ ☆ ☆ ☆ ☆ ☆

Do ghealadh mo chroí nuair chinn Loch Gréine,
An talamh, 's an tír, is íor na spéire;
Taithneamhach aoibhinn suiomh na sléibhte
Ag bagairt a gcinn thar dhroim a chéile.[16]

There was something singularly appropriate in the fact that SFADCo should choose the village of Feakle, Co. Clare, as the location for a meeting to debate the whole future of the company. Here Brian Merriman eked out a living as a schoolteacher in the late eighteenth century, and it is here that his deeply subversive poem, *The Midnight Court*, finds its setting. Merriman, representing both a concern for the decline of rural communities and a wide-ranging international interest (according to Frank O'Connor he was acquainted with the major European authors including Swift and 'most of all, Rousseau. How he managed it in an Irish-speaking community is a mystery') constitutes, in his own way, a simulacrum of the Shannon impulse. The meeting which convened at Feakle on 29 September 1977 cannot but have been aware of the long shadow of their visionary predecessor.

'It was important that the Company should do things which could be clearly seen to be related to it and which would be distinctive of it, things which could not be done by any other state organisation' the board minutes had asserted on Friday 13 February 1976. The voice is clearly O'Regan's, but the conditional mood suggests some uncertainty as to the way forward. The idea of a Shannon Trade Centre had come and gone;[17] an informal grouping of executives into an Enterprise Development Unit was being set up to bring to fruition opportunities for the exploitation of indigenous resources— people, materials, ideas—and had come up with plans for milking machines, vegetables and mead. At a meeting in March 1977 the minister, Justin Keating, had stressed the importance of developing non-economic activities by local communities and the need to counteract the growth of Dublin. The return to power in June of Fianna Fáil had, however, introduced a new note of urgency. O'Malley was impatient for change. There had been talk of abolishing SFADCo altogether and merging its activities with those of the IDA; but he took another view based on his concern that too much reliance was being placed on overseas firms in the drive for industrialisation.

' Those who control industry can exercise a considerable influence on the determination of national policy,' his predecessor, Sean Lemass, had concluded in the 1930s: 'If such persons are foreigners, to any large extent, their only interest in the country is the profit they can make out of it. . . . ' Whilst recognising that for the foreseeable future foreign firms would continue to play a major role O'Malley envisaged a much greater contribution from indigenous industry. The IDA had had nominal responsibility for this sector but, for one reason or another, little progress had been achieved. The situation suggested an urgent need for new thinking.

The conviction that change was in the air had played a significant part in the discussions at Feakle in September 1977, at which the SFADCo board took the decision that the company should seek to relinquish its role in industrial development. There was "a genuine clash between people who were attempting to find a new future for the company", Tom Dunne recalled, "and people who felt that the company was doing a damn fine job and needed to be supported in what it was doing and not undermined". Underlying the move to get out of industry was the expressed conviction that SFADCo's strengths lay more in the broader co-ordination of regional activity, with emphasis on its consultative function. Following the discussion O'Regan met the ministers for Industry, Commerce and Energy and the Environment and reported that he had received an encouraging reaction. A further meeting was arranged with Desmond O'Malley, one which Paul Quigley, whose views by this time were diverging sharply from those of Brendan O'Regan, looked forward to with considerable qualms. At its conclusion, however, his mind was considerably relieved: the minister had put forward his own proposals for the development of small indigenous industry and his decision that SFADCo should assume responsibility for a crash programme designed to provide a blueprint for similar development in the rest of the country. 'The task entrusted to the company', in the words of its 1978 annual report, 'was to be a pilot exercise, the results of which would be evaluated after about two years, when decisions would be taken about the extension of such an intensive drive to other regions.'

In February 1978 the report of an executive task force on the new role was put before the board, which now realised that, with the minister's announcement imminent, it was vital to move quickly, 'and to be seen to move quickly, towards the assumption of the new small indigenous industries role. This was known to be the wish of the minister who had also directed the IDA to move into Limerick quickly and to get on with the industrial functions which it was to resume'.

The decision, not for the first time, involved a rearrangement of the working relations with the IDA, represented on the SFADCo board by Michael Killeen. According to Tom Dunne he was "stronger than a minister in his day". The national authority resumed its responsibility for large and middle-sized industry in the region, delegating to SFADCo the grant-giving powers necessary to enable it to function in the indigenous sector, 'subject only to national sectoral considerations and to the reciprocal representation of each body on the other's small industries committee'. The two organisations were still committed to playing box and cox, and the IDA was not entirely happy with the arrangement.

For Brendan O'Regan, however, the new dispensation marked a redirection of policy so fundamental that it served to reinforce a growing conviction, born of the development of a range of new interests, that he could no longer remain as SFADCo chairman. On 16 December 1977 he attended his last board meeting in that capacity, though he remained a board member. The conferring on him of a doctorate by the National University of Ireland the following April was both a well-deserved recognition of his unique contribution to the Shannon enterprise and the marking of the end of an era.

'He did two things,' Justin Keating, former Minister for Industry and Commerce, told the Seanad on 1 March 1978: 'One was that he made things happen and the other was that he inspired other people to make things happen. He was the best sort of activist. I am very pleased that even though he does not remain as chairman, his enormous vision, wisdom, practical experience and drive will remain at the service of the board and of SFADCo. He has done great good for his country in his fruitful life.'

References

1. *The government and politics of Ireland*, 1970, p. 242
2. S 8814C, CA 5071, 16 October 1957
3. Interview on *Monday People*, Clare FM Radio, 7 May 1990
4. Interview with Padraig O Raighillaigh, RTE Radio, 4 September 1990
5. See pp. 129ff
6. James H. Winchester: 'Shannon: the airport that refused to die', in *Reader's Digest*, March 1970, p. 160
7. Anglo-American Corporation of South Africa, Johannesburg, September 1965
8. Board minutes, 1 September 1965
9. See 'Links with other State bodies', in *Report by the Dáil Committee on Public Expenditure: Review of Shannon Free Airport Development Company Limited*, Dublin 1986, p. 17ff
10. Board minutes, 3 June 1959
11. Board minutes, 24 June 1970
12. Chairman's introduction to SFADCo Annual Report for 1972–73
13. Board minutes, 2 May 1973
14. Howard Kinlay: 'Developments in the Mid-West', in *Management*, Dublin, November 1975
15. Kinlay, op. cit.
16. When I looked at Lough Graney my heart grew bright,/Ploughed lands and green in the morning light,/Mountains in ranks with crimson borders/Peering above their neighbours' shoulders. (Frank O'Connor's translation.)
17. See p. 170

CHAPTER 4

A Shop on Drumgeely Hill

From the direction of Ennis the junction at Hurler's Cross has all the appearance of a motorway flyover reduced to a single plane: to reach the N19 you must engage in a kind of reverse loop, then move smartly over to the left-hand lane to avoid an involuntary return to where you began. The N19 itself has little competition as the shortest National Primary Route in the country. 'When I first came here,' said a Shannon resident in 1968, 'I thought that the road that went up to the Airport continued on past, and the day I realised it didn't, that it was a dead end, I got an unpleasant sinking feeling . . . . '[1]

Even if the road had not been effectively neutralised by the main airport runway there would have been nowehere else for it to go. Beyond lies the featureless foreshore of the Shannon estuary—beyond and effectively on all sides, for the airport and its adjacent town occupy a broad peninsula surrounded by water. Poor land—barely supporting the occupants of half a dozen Land Commission houses before the builders moved on to Drumgeely Hill. 'The drumlins rise fairly sharply out of the alluvial flats and are the main structural feature of the new town site,' observed the Sheppard Fidler report in 1972. 'They provide some shelter to the northern and eastern slopes against the main prevailing wind from NW to SW. The slopes facing N and E are the coldest, and frost will tend to occur more frequently on these faces. The combination of the drumlins in the W part of the town provides some continuity of shelter but because of their rounded form the wind will follow the ground fairly closely.'

An unappealing enough location, on the face of it, for the country's first experiment in innovative urban development. Even thirty years on the initial impression is one of incongruity, of an *urbs in ruri* barely sustaining a civic identity in an inimical landscape. This initial reaction is at least partly due to the novelty of the phenomenon—an Irish town like no other, with no building or monument older than its oldest inhabitant, no tradition deeper than one generation, no agreement, even, as to what it is called. 'The name of the town at Shannon is "Shannon" simply, without addition of the word "town"', the SFADCo board enunciated in April 1967. But there was nowhere called Shannon in the 1990 telephone directory. In Irish it is, locally, *Sionna*; though the 1989 *Gasaitéar na hÉireann*, prepared by the Place Names Branch of the Ordnance Survey, lists it as *Sionainn*. The 1959 Post Office Guide had 'Shannon Airport, Limerick', or in Irish, *Aerphort na Sionnaine, Luimneach*, and a similar dislocation was visited upon the town. "You'd hear it from time to time as Shannon, Co. Limerick," recalled Michael McNamara, in 1990, property manager for Shannon Development, and letters addressed via Limerick would be delivered earlier than if endorsed for Co. Clare. Such problems of identity were to extend well beyond the limits of nomenclature and location.

There were those who believed that *Sionna*[2] should never have been built at all, or should have been sited at Sixmilebridge, or developed as a suburb of Ennis or Limerick. But the town was in fact far less formally conceived than, say, Westport or Birr. The perceived need in 1959[3] was to provide 'dwelling houses close to the Industrial Estate'. By the time the first meeting of the newly constituted Development Company was held on 2 February 1959, a plan already existed for an estate of sixty-seven houses, four shop dwellings, eight sites for hostels or flats and space for a small community building. The idea did not appeal to the Revenue Commissioners, who were concerned over possible unauthorised access to the duty-free zone. In September Brendan O'Regan proposed reducing the estate to thirty houses for key executives as a temporary measure, the Commissioners being asked to make clear how close to the airport they would agree to a larger housing concentration being sited. By October they had given their consent to development at Drumgeely and the architect Frank Gibney was asked to prepare plans for an estate of twenty-three houses, the Revenue insisting on a fence and the right to spot-check goods within the airport.

Sionna thus began in the manner of many Irish towns of an earlier era, as a settlement at a river mouth or, later a railway junction—except that in this case the intersection was between land-based activity and air transport. As Liam Ryan put it: 'Like many of its mediaeval counterparts, Shannon is a town built upon a bridge. It is a bridge between the new world and the old, between agricultural Ireland and industrial Ireland, between rural Ireland and urban Ireland.'[4] The decision to build on Drumgeely Hill arose from the expressed need of those working in the Free Zone for somewhere to live. It was not, initially, part of an overall plan for a self-sufficient new town. The likely scale of what it had undertaken was, however, not long in impressing itself upon the company. It quickly realised that neither had it the resources to provide the housing that would be required nor could the County Council be expected to undertake to build in advance of demand. The only recourse was to goverment to seek the same powers and financial assistance as granted to local authorities.

By January 1960 the concept of a new town had formally entered the company's thinking as 'the best practicable solution to the problem'. But what kind of new town? A town like Elizabeth, New South Wales, in the middle of nowhere? There was no Irish model and eyes turned predictably towards Britain and in particular to Lord Holford, who had pioneered planned employment location as a regional development tool in the 1930s, and to Ted Cage, sometime general manager of Crawley New Town and treasurer of the New Towns Commission. Cian O'Carroll, who was employed at Shannon at the time in the property management area, felt that, in hindsight, "we should have been drawing more on our own native inspiration rather than relying on formulas from elsewhere." But this was the era, not yet altogether superseded, of preferring the foreign expert in general and the British expert in particular. (Though in mid-1960 Frank Gibney and Paul Quigley, general services manager, went to Sweden to discuss plans for the new town and study Swedish co-operative house-building organisations.)

The xenophobic objection, is, nevertheless, not entirely facile. Events were to prove that what worked in English terms did not necessarily transfer effectively to Irish conditions, particularly as the composition and origins of the *Sionna* population was to prove to be markedly atypical in the context of the experience of either country. Some lessons, however, were learned: the nature of people's reactions to coming to live in a bleak, new place, reactions which were to be voiced with increasing clarity by the first citizens:

'Shannon is a town without history, without roots, without character. It is a collection of uprooted people in search of a job who will perhaps be on their way tomorrow if a better job beckons them elsewhere....'

'There are no local characters to have a yarn about, no town elders to give wisdom and stability, no mothers to offer advice nor mothers-in-law to fight with, no athletic or cultural achievements to enthuse over, and above all no real gossipers.'

'If I thought I was going to stay here for the rest of my life I would go mad. I couldn't bear the thought. I think that it is a place where one can get into a rut very quickly. I don't dislike life here. To start with I did. I loathed it. I thought that there could be no place as lousy as Shannon.'[5]

There were also political problems. The Minister for Local Government, Neil Blaney, wanted the housing to be the responsibility of the National Building Agency, which constructed the high-rise flats in Ballymun, Dublin, a landmark in several senses. His Department, was not, however, thinking in terms of a full-scale town for Shannon; but O'Regan fought the decision, relying on his 'direct line' to Sean Lemass, who had become Taoiseach in June 1959 in succession to Éamon de Valera. "Local Government didn't like it," recalled Tom Dunne. " [But] for as long as Lemass remained Taoiseach, O'Regan was on absolutely solid ground. That gave him the time he needed to get a head of steam and show it was working and was going to work. And once he had achieved that he was almost unstoppable." The proposal for a new housing company with directors representing Local Government, Transport and Power and Industry and Commerce (the same directors who sat as representatives of the latter two Departments on the SFADCo board) was, however, not acted upon and the company was given direct responsibility for building the houses and, *ipso facto*, the new town. An Outline Development Plan (ODP) was commissioned from Messrs Downes and Meehan and was ready for consideration by January 1962. Frank Gibney, who had been responsible for the development of the Industrial Estate, refused to collaborate with other town planners and stood down.

Many of those who were to become key figures in the subsequent development both of the town and the whole regional enterprise were recruited at this time. Cian O'Carroll, with a Dublin background in auctioneering and property management but with a strong interest in history and folklore inherited from Gaelic-speaking parents, found O'Regan "the kind of person whose enthusiasm could be very convincing". Paul Quigley, then in charge of the Irish Management Institute in Dublin but with an Army engineering background, was, in his own words, "mildly headhunted" by J. Buist MacKenzie, the management expert who had been a member of the consultative committee of the original Authority and was subsequently a member of the SFADCo board. Tom Callanan came from Dunlop in Cork as "the first employee, because I was the first person from outside the system". At the end of 1957 he had been offered a choice of jobs in Canada, Norway or Northern Rhodesia, as it then was, but was attracted by what he had read of O'Regan's efforts to introduce a new development concept. He became his personal assistant. It was a small, tightly-knit group with a formidable range of responsibilities. By March 1961 the total SFADCo staff numbered only twenty-three.

There were other people on the move in the direction of Shannon. Bill Jones, working in Dublin with the air cargo handlers Lep Transport after a period in London, was sent down to report on the feasibility of opening a branch office and in the meantime to cover the area as a representative. He reported favourably, and landed himself with the job, moving into Hostel 3

33. Shopping centre, Sionna (Shannon town), 18 April 1967.

34. The first Sionna generation, Drumgeely Hill, June 1965.

at the airport and conducting his business from a small hut. A few years later, in 1964, Chris Taylor, who was to join De Beers in 1967, passed through on his way from London to Killarney on holiday and also stayed in the hostels. Out of curiosity he went to look at the flats which had been built on Drumgeely Hill and remembered saying to himself 'God, I'd never live here!' From what he saw he doubted whether the whole concept could survive.

It was the obvious place to begin: a gentle eminence overlooking the customs post at the entrance to the Free Zone and an easy distance from the airport, upon which the first residents of the 157 flats and ten executive houses depended in more ways than one. "We used to go up to the flight kitchen and Chef Ryan used allow us buy fillet steak and butter and rashers," Bill Jones remembered. "You found you were really living on the fat of the land at £8 a week, which wasn't exactly good economics." Joe Walsh, who joined SPS on the Industrial Estate in 1961 as a toolmaker, was another airport customer. With no car, he walked up or took the bus for bread, steaks and roast beef. The bill came after six months. More extensive shopping had to be done in Limerick or Ennis. Not surprisingly many wives, reared in Dublin, Cork or Limerick suburbs, found their introduction to the embryonic *Sionna* more than a little disconcerting.

Jones and his wife Eileen—from Dublin's Griffith Avenue—were the first couple to occupy the new apartments. It was rough on her, he recollected, though they both found the accommodation agreeable and moved three times within the complex before buying one of the first speculative houses, built at Tullyglass in 1966. Joe Walsh and his wife were the first Irish couple to occupy the second block of flats. The first year was anxious and trouble-some. The women at first did not mix socially, and British wives of the returned emigrants who constituted a major sector of the early population found conditions particularly dismaying. But it was not long before a community spirit, born both of the straitened circumstances and of the unique population mix, began to emerge.

'It is not a proper home for human beings,' Fergal McGrath, S.J., had written three decades earlier.[6] 'In the history of the world has man ever, except under dire necessity, resorted to the strange device of building his home on top of another man's house? Should the threshold of the home be a concrete parapet heavily railed in? Can the most ingenious architect obviate the moral dangers of the common staircase?' It was a measure both of changed times and the uniqueness of the Shannon experiment in the Irish context that this traditional view found little support amongst the early flat-dwellers on Drumgeely Hill. Chris Taylor remembered the apartments as

[85]

"very livable-in", occupied by people of the same young age group united in a common concern as to whether their jobs on the estate would survive. 'They have a character of their own which you won't find elsewhere in Shannon,' said a respondent to the 1969 survey;[7] another recalled that the first Irish residents of Drumgeely Hill were regarded as a novelty: Bill Jones was convinced that he would come back to the flats one day and find IRISH GO HOME scrawled on the wall.

The international mix would account in some measure for the spirit which developed amongst the flat dwellers, who began visiting one another and holding welcoming parties, often at the airport, for each new arrival. The first block of flats was occupied very largely by personnel from the SPS parent company in the US, sent over to train the local workforce; and even by 1975, when many temporary foreign residents would have completed their assignment and returned home, a census of the town population[8] showed that virtually everyone came from somewhere else, either within Ireland or outside it. "The thing about Shannon," as Joe Walsh put it, "was that everybody was away from home. They were fabulous times . . . a great relationship between people."

Others saw it through spectacles of a slightly less rosy complexion. Drumgeely Town, as it became known in Limerick, was characterised as a glorified itinerant camp. The level of criticism directed at SFADCo, as town manager, was considerable and sustained. The company was, of course, a sitting target, though in the view of many residents it was not sitting quite close enough to its area of responsibility. The charge that many of its senior executives chose to live elsewhere than in the new town was sustained, with a large measure of justification, over the years. It was widely felt that to see the top men coming and putting down roots would be a guarantee that the whole experiment was going to last. Those directly concerned made the case that to live so close to the job would deny them any degree of privacy—a view which was supported by at least one resident in 1964. 'They have done far too much for people. Shannon people are utterly spoiled. They get everything for nothing, and if they want anything they go running to the Development Company for it and they get all hot and bothered if the company doesn't do it for them. No other community in the country could get away with this carry-on.'

No other Irish community, of course, was constituted in a manner similar to that attempting to secure its future at *Sionna*. The closest comparison— most apposite, perhaps, in these early days—was with a commercial company town where all aspects of a resident's life come within the ambit of offical policy. Thus SFADCo from the start concerned itself with qualifications for tenancy (only persons employed at Shannon, primarily on the Industrial Estate) as well as with housing design and layout itself; and, through force of circumstances, many of the pioneering commercial enterprises in the community in the early days enjoyed an effective monopoly. The fact that for many years there was only one licensed premises—a situation by Irish standards almost beyond credulity—induced in one resident a 'feeling of unreality' which was almost certainly widely replicated.

Though Dr Mill of Arthur Guinness, Son and Company of Dublin had visited Shannon as early as the autumn of 1960 with a proposal to finance and build a community centre, the effective presence of the brewery was not established until 1965 when 'The Crossroads' pub at Drumgeely shopping centre was opened, the attendance including Patrick Monahan, president of Shannon Community Association, established in 1964. Before that, however, what would generally be considered as more essential facilities had been put in place, if on a very limited scale. In 1961 a shop opened on Drumgeely Hill. It was housed in the new community hall which also did duty as primary school and social centre, and it was operated on a self-service basis by the Shannon Sales and Catering Organisation on behalf of SFADCo. A temporary measure, it was to be the sole recourse of the expanding community for three years; but at least it obviated the long trek to the airport, 'a welcome relief for the flat-footed and those like myself with fallen arches and corns', as one local historian put it.[9]

Meanwhile the political controversy over the further development of the town had not been entirely stilled. In March 1963 the report of an inter-departmental committee recommended that Local Government Commissioners with powers of a local authority be appointed responsible for community development. SFADCo's board reacted strongly, holding the view that such an approach was not in line with the directives previously given to the company and not designed to facilitate industrial development to its full potential. It believed that it should continue to hold direct responsibility, and was reinforced in this opinion by doubts being expressed by key industrial tenants such as SPS as to the future availability of housing and the absence of any long-term plan. The lack of executive-type housing, the board was told, was making it impossible for managements to attract suitable people. They feared that such a deficiency would induce incoming personnel to look for accommodation outside the airport area, a move which they foresaw as detrimental to the balanced development of the new community.

The company's view prevailed, and new legislation introduced in 1963[10] empowered the Minister for Finance to advance monies for financing house building. By March 1962 there were 300 people living on Drumgeely Hill, and a contract was signed two months later for major housing development at what was to become Drumgeely proper. By November 1963 all the 186 houses on the scheme had been allocated. The following year four shops— including a chemist and a newsagent—opened on the Drumgeely estate. Chris Taylor helped Bart and Jim Clancy stock up their premises the night before it opened. A temporary interdenominational church had been provided in 1962. With the inauguration of two primary schools—St John's and St Senan's—in 1964 and the pulling of the first pint in The Crossroads, the community could be said to have come of age. The shop on Drumgeely Hill closed its doors.

People missed it, Seán O Nuanáin remembered, because of the sense of community it represented. Joining SFADCo in 1964, he became a *Sionna* resident when the population stood at 600–700. As the town grew, the pioneer days quickly became only a memory, or in the words of one resident: 'just a dream, or at least dream-like; though some probably thought of it as a nightmare. We lived on a hill. There was a muddy track to get off it, so unless you went in a car nobody left the hill. We had no school, no shops, nowhere to go....'[11]

The Outline Development Plan prepared by Downes & Meehan was based on the prospective creation of 10,000 jobs in the Free Zone at a rate of 500 per annum with an annual average construction rate of 435 houses per year rising to 1,375. The related population estimates were 6,000 by 1967 (actual 1,717); 16,000 by 1970 (actual 3,153); 27,000 by 1972 (actual 5,091) rising to 35,000 in 1982+ (the 1981 figure was 9,900). The Sheppard Fidler reappraisal of the ODP in 1972 acknowledged even at that point that these projected figures were unlikely to be realised, but suggested that *Sionna* was capable of growing to 50,000 'by 2000 or earlier' and to 25,000 by 1986, below which figure the town, it argued, would not be viable. In spite of this, development had proceeded in close accord with the original ODP provisions in the matter of the dispositions of housing and industry and the overall layout.

'Ten years from now the air traveller who comes through Shannon to visit Ireland will find, as he leaves the airport, a well-planned and pleasantly landscaped town set on the banks of the broad river,' a booklet produced by SFADCo in 1970 predicted:[12] 'The highway which divides the town from the thriving industrial zone ... will be tree-lined and traffic will move freely past carefully-designed junctions. The town on the right of the highway will be comparable with any of the best planned towns of its size in Europe, with ample space for public entertainment. Wooded parks and playing fields will lie between it and the river, while the civic centre will nestle between two of the most prominent hills, Tullyglass and Tullyvarraga, where attractive dwellings command a view of the Shannon river beyond the town. . . . '

The vision, given the promotional prose, was not misplaced, inhibited only by the failure of *Sionna* to grow into the major urban centre that was envisaged for it. Today the roads skirting Finian Park at the eastern end dissipate themselves rather folornly into proximate nothingness. Seven years ago, said Michael McNamara, SFADCo's property manager in 1990, there were bigger gaps: "I would have completed the Drumgeely end of it before I went further." But the scaled-down community has a solidity and integration which, admittedly, on account of its planning and layout requires several visits fully to apprehend. The 1970 booklet quoted above accurately reflected the concept embodied in the ODP; 'the most remarkable feature of the town will be the care given to making it safe for pedestrians and children, while still ensuring ample parking facilities and complete freedom from congestion due to motor traffic. The majority of housing will be within three-quarters of a mile of the main centre; within one mile of the industrial zone; and immediately adjacent to the residential open space in which will be located primary schools, churches and other residential amenities. A system of pedestrian pathways will give access through to the main recreational parkland to the south of the town centre. . . . '

The ODP adopted a scheme which is known as the Radburn system of pedestrian/traffic segregation, a formula that had been implemented in several of the British new towns. It is a concept that looks very attractive on paper, the houses grouped 'in enclaves with landscaped corridors.'[13] It is based on the assumption that people of similar incomes would live in such enclaves with access to open spaces shared with other neighbouring housing groups. The emphasis on space as an integral element of the planning was no doubt influenced by the British experience of catering, in new towns, for emigrants from congested inner-city conditions; but it proved to have only limited appeal for the first *Sionna* residents, most of whom came from very different backgrounds. In this respect the Ryan survey of 1964 is particularly illuminating, derived as it was from 'a highly educated, highly skilled, highly articulate group enjoying a reasonably high standard of living',[14] many with overseas experience. One respondent characterised this element not as open space but as 'empty space' and suggested that most residents saw it more as a problem than as an amenity. Others suggested that there was too much space between the areas and not enough between the individual houses. 'Towns are for people and the goal must always be to build so as to allow a full and satisfying life,' the Sheppard Fidler 1972 revision asserted; but to a sizeable segment of the early townspeople this objective had been subsumed in a planners' dream. The sylvan pedestrian pathways of the ODP became exposed, muddy tracks in the Shannon winter. You either walked or you had a car—not by any means a universal possession in the early days. And if you had a car, you still had to walk a good distance to get into it. By 1964, when seventy-three per cent of the residents had cars, only thirty-three per cent had a garage. As one inhabitant put it: 'If it is presumed that people have cars, why didn't they build garages? If it is presumed that people walk, why didn't they build footpaths?'

It was a bit like a jigsaw, in the view of Cian O'Carroll, the town's first property manager for SFADCo, because the logic of the plan did not become overtly apparent until later and the first occupants of Drumgeely could not be expected to live in the future. Within the imposed boundaries of the site between the airport and the estuary there was only one direction in which to develop, and it was an extraordinarily difficult place to build. The poor quality of the land demanded piling for major constructions and from the beginning it was recognised that landscaping would have to play a major role in humanising the environment. Two playing-fields were provided in 1962 and four years later a programme of extensive tree-planting was undertaken, 48,000 being planted in 1966–67 on the three hills: Drumgeely, Tullyglass and Tullyvarraga. Quick-growing coniferous species were employed and were sufficiently mature for the first leisure area to be opened for public use in 1975. In pre-development days the land had been drained by open ditches, both natural and artificial, a system not suited to an urban environment. A major drainage and reclamation scheme was therefore undertaken in 1969 with considerable favourable impact on the settled areas.

Apart from small schemes at Tradaree in 1970 and later in the town centre, no more flats were built at *Sionna* after the initial development on Drumgeely Hill. 'Look at the little garden bright with flowers or stocked with useful vegetables and the patch of grass where the smallest children can play in safety,' wrote Fergal McGrath in the article quoted above. 'Notice the quietness of the house even when the hall door is open. When you look out of the window, you see, not empty space or the back wall of the opposite house, but the worker's little estate surrounding his little castle.' The planners of *Sionna* shrank from the desiderata of suburbia, however, believing that they knew what people wanted better than they knew themselves. They built to a density of fourteen to the acre—with all the space in the world at their disposal; and the house design itself, clearly a product of male rather than female thinking, evoked reactions in the early residents ranging from anger to derision. The development of the 'G area' was, in the words of one of them, like 'something you'd see out in Peru or somewhere: little humpybacked things with a bit of a garden, and railway sleepers outside the door . . . for a long time I didn't know which was the back or which was the front—nobody does'. The open-plan concept was, in the view of one mother, 'just a dead loss', the children walking in from the garden dragged the mud right through the house. The general layout put one male respondent to the 1964 questionnaire in mind 'of some fellow who must have got drunk one night and got a load of houses to deliver and he just dropped them off the truck as he went along and some day maybe when he sobers up he will come back and collect them'.

It may well be, of course, that such reactions were as much a comment on the aesthetic perceptions of the early residents as on the shortcomings of the planners; but when the first speculative McInerney-built semi-detached three bedroom houses were constructed they sold, in Cian O'Carroll's recollection, "by the new time". The company, with a continuing responsibility for housing development, duly took note and took note, also, of the natural landscape. The original plan had sought to impose an urban shape, removing natural features such as hedges and ditches. Subsequent thinking was to respect natural boundaries and build around and within them. After all, as Fr Liam Ryan put it, 'there are no broken-down buildings to explore, no trees to climb, nothing to discover, none of the things which children normally do and from which they derive initiative and originality'. In this context a robin's nest in a hedge could speak louder than volumes of planning theory.

By 1972 the Sheppard Fidler revision had taken some of this new thinking on board, to the extent of stressing the desirability of accepting any opportunity for creating character and individuality through an unusual building, 'especially one with an interesting silhouette'. Its continued adherence to planning imperatives, however, savoured of Big Brother. 'It is recommended that strict control should be exercised over the design, size and location of garden sheds . . . it will be important to avoid poorly-maintained unscreened gardens facing onto public places. . . . ' The justification for these authoritarian strictures was that 'standards of design . . . will have a palpable influence on the residents and give them a feeling of satisfaction and well-being'[15]—a feeling that might have been more appropriately created by the provision of adequate domestic amenities in the first place. For better or worse, however, the standards of suburbia were to replace the imaginative, if not always practical or acceptable strategies of the ODP. But in one respect at least *Sionna* had side-stepped what might be termed the Dublin Downs syndrome (Cowper Downs, Sandyford Downs, Roebuck Downs, Thormanby Downs, Rotunda Downs et al). After the initial adoption of English-language names, followed by a brief experiment with bilingual versions, the new

35. Work in progress on Croí na Sionna, the Shannon Town Centre, January 1972.

36. The Irish identity, Shannon Town Centre, June 1973.

developments—Cluain Airne, Ard na Mara, Rinn Eannaig, Dún an Óir, Ard na Gréine—were named in Irish only.

When Seán O Nuanáin became a *Sionna* resident in 1964 he started to work for SFADCo in the industrial sphere. In the beginning he was reluctant to push his identification with the Irish language, partly for personal reasons, and it was not until a small group attending German classes came together and discovered a mutual interest that *Club na Sionna* was founded, initially associated with the language and rural development organisations Conradh na Gaeilge and Muintir na Tíre. This first step was followed by the establishment of bilingual nursery schools and an all-Irish primary school, which in 1990 had an enrolment of 135 from many nationalities. When an Aeroflot crew member stationed at Shannon later sent his child to the school he progressed so well in the language that a prosperous future was predicted for him with the KGB. When the town centre was developed in 1972 it acquired the name *Croí na Sionna*[16] as part of an attempt to give a modern shopping complex an Irish character—though its usage is not strongly in evidence. On the other hand, during the protracted rent strikes of the early 1970s the office of property manager Cian O'Carroll was picketed by tenants carrying placards proclaiming *CIAN AGUS CÍOS*.[17]

In one respect the advocacy of and enthusiasm for Irish—notably among many families with an exclusively anglophone background—can be seen in the context of the broader need among the early residents to develop some sense of identity. With North Americans constituting a significant proportion of the initial population the embryo culture was perhaps best described as mid-Atlantic, with the Irish element clinging, perhaps protectively, to its roots elsewhere in the island. At weekends and at Christmas the emergent town was largely deserted as people returned to what they still regarded as their home place. Culturally, at this early stage, *Sionna* was an island: apparently unwanted by Co. Clare and resented by Limerick city itself. There were few contacts between the townspeople and the local population. Farmers coming to Mass often bypassed the new church in *Sionna* and continued on down the road to the one at the airport itself. Several respondents to the 1964 survey commented on a sense of isolation, with the bi-monthly trip to Limerick as much a psychological necessity as a shopping spree. 'It is so unusual here,' said one resident: 'you have no background to go on . . . and not knowing people's background you don't really know them at all.' Michael McNamara, who came from a small town some twelve kilometres away, noticed that here it was possible to be anonymous, that neighbours would not intrude unless you positively needed help. The big vacuum, in Cian O'Carroll's view, was the absence of kinship, the close network of extended family that exists in most Irish towns.

One of the overriding problems was the slow pace of growth, contributing to the sense of precariousness and impermanence. The population in 1965 was only 1,192 and the company agreed that in the interests of raising morale and of encouraging more people to take up residence it was desirable to give wide publicity to the plan for a community of 6,000—even though it was aware that such a plan would inevitably be delayed by problems over land acquisition. In November 1965 a development of 125 houses at Tully-glass was authorised, but in the following spring tenants had to move out of Drumgeely following the discovery of chimney defects. In March 1966 notice to quit was served on ten residents, and the newly-formed Shannon Community Association wrote to the minister asking him to consider changing the restrictive clause in the tenancy agreements which limited occupancy to those employed at Shannon. The company, consulted by the minister, expressed itself as reluctant to vary the conditions, but suggested that tenancies might be permitted to continue if the tenant had been in residence for a miminum qualifying period.

The ten executive houses on Drumgeely Hill were the forerunners of similar developments on the other two eminences as the town grew. As a resident of the flats Bill Jones used their front rooms as tennis pavilions. Class distinction, he believes, was not and has never been a part of the *Sionna* ethos. But there was a view that as each new housing sector developed it was a little better—and a little dearer—than what had gone before, and that 'upward mobility' was becoming a fact of life. For one resident the town recalled a Welsh mining village, with the 'folks who live on the hill' looking down on the grey-roofed workers' houses in terraced rows below. Michael McNamara maintained that people on Tullyglass Hill are not, metaphorically, looked up to "in any way I know", though a house there would command a greater price. Bill Jones decided early on that he could not afford to live there.

Many early residents, however, continue to stress the tangible sense of community that transcended (and, they claim, still largely transcends) any putative class boundaries: *ar scath a chéile a mhairimid*.[18] As a result of the significant role played by the clergy in the early years of the town a 'parish feeling' developed. With the initial international mix it was generally supposed that the community would be multi-religious, which in Irish terms means a mixture of Catholic and Protestant. Two denominational schools shared the facilities of Drumgeely Community Centre before permanent premises were built, but the Protestants never progressed beyond a temporary building. Many people regarded this as an opportunity missed to educate children of both faiths (or none at all) together, thus creating, again in Irish terms, a completely new community. But as late as 1980 the local Catholic bishop, Dr Harty of Killaloe, was of the opinion 'that there was no evidence of community demand in Shannon for non-denominational or inter-denominational primary education ... he and other members of the Catholic Hierarchy were totally committed to the preservation of the present arrangements'. The stance was endorsed by SFADCo, which felt that the promotion 'of this concept of primary education could be highly divisive at this stage and could encounter major opposition in the Town'.[19]

In the beginning, in the times of Fr Gaynor and his Church of Ireland opposite number, Rev. Baxter, there had been a real spirit of ecumenism, and this well before Vatican II: if the Catholic priest encountered difficulties with resident wives he referred them to the minister's lady. But *Sionna*, for all its pioneer origins, was to develop its religious and educational facilities largely on conventional lines, due at least in some measure to the fact that it became, in the course of time, overwhelmingly Catholic in its adherence. A clergy-man who served in the town in the early years suggested that this was due to the fact that immigrants from North America or Europe would have been given ground rules by their employers: do not become involved in either politics or religion. And since most of them would have seen Protestantism in terms of its Northern Ireland politico-social identity they were reluctant to declare themselves, even if of that persuasion—a simplistic argument, perhaps. A more plausible explanation may be sought in the findings of the 1975 census, which revealed that sixty-five per cent of the 3,000 adult population responding originated in other parts of Ireland. By this year, also, the community was itself generating over a quarter of its population increment— 227 births in 1974 out of an increase over the previous year of 849. *Sionna* was, in religious complexion at least, conforming to the national norm.

The broader social problems were, however, more specific to its status as a new town. Among the first employees of the Development Company was community officer, Josephine Glynn, who called on new residents a day or two after their arrival and encouraged the establishment of community organisations—sports clubs, social clubs, debating clubs, flower clubs .... 'The local pub,' complained one resident, 'is almost the only place where one can relax without helping some cause or other.' At one stage some thirty per cent of the population was involved with the Musical Society, whilst an Archaeological Society, another early foundation, provided, in its researches into the previous history of the area, some sense of local identity. Monks came across the islands on the Fergus river on their way from Kilrush to Rome. Hugh O'Neill camped at Smithstown, where an industrial estate was to be established, on his way to the battle of Kinsale in 1601 ... bridging a hiatus almost of the dimensions of that which lay between the Australian aborigines and the European colonists of 1788.

[95]

The first residents were, nevertheless, firm in the defence of their nascent identity and, though often complaining about the way SFADCo was running things, would unite against criticism from outside. Outside—in Limerick, Ennis, and particularly in Dublin—there was little understanding of what was afoot. In 1964 Bill Jones was involved in the arrangements for bringing down an Oireachtas delegation on a tour of inspection, but the parliamentarians were sparing with their enthusiasm, and Jones detected the beginnings of the long-running Dublin–Shannon begrudgery. "I thought," he admitted, "that it was going to do a lot more than it did."

As in most communities a handful of committed activists attempted without marked success to make waves on the large sea of passivity representing the majority of the population, but a sense of purpose, was, nevertheless, discernible—one with which the more socially-conscious residents could identify. "We always felt part of the growing up of Shannon," Joe Walsh recalled. "We were all party to making decisions with the local priest." The Americans in particular settled in well. The most uneasy were those who had moved in from Limerick and Ennis and who returned 'home' every weekend. Their sense of uncertainty was shared by the Development Company, which expressed doubts in 1967 as to whether it was the right instrument for building the town, and, if so, whether it would not be better to create an entirely new body on the lines of the New Town Corporations in Britain. It was felt that it might be more appropriate to seek responsibility for the three non-technical state services at the airport—airport development, airport management and sales and catering. This view did not, however, prevail, and a decision was taken to address the problems of the town within the existing format. One of the most urgent of these was the provision of a town centre.

In the meantime, however, the growth of the population, particularly of school-going age, was focusing urgent attention on educational requirements and on the provision of facilities for sport and leisure activities. A full-time youth officer was an early appointment, supported after 1972 by a Youth Advisory Council; and at an equally early stage the necessity of planning for second-level education was identified. This fortunately coincided with the introduction of comprehensive schools in several centres in the country with an approach to educational methods refreshingly different from the established pattern. The opening of the comprehensive school in *Sionna* in 1966 was, in the view of many of those involved, one of the major factors in the bonding of the community. The headmaster, Diarmuid Ó Donnabháin, established not only a local but an international reputation and has been equated in terms of vision and influence with O'Regan himself. The school was, and is, multi-denominational. Its influence both in setting and maintaining high educational standards within the community and in giving the rising generation a positive sense of belonging would be difficult to exaggerate.

Whilst those with roots elswhere remained to some extent ambivalent— 'If Wexford is playing Clare I'm a Wexfordman. If Clare is playing anybody else I'm a Clareman!'—their children found little difficulty in identifying themselves as 'Shannonites'. The term is not euphonious and is accepted, it would appear, for want of anything better; the Clare identity is easier to enunciate and, particularly in the sporting connotation, more immediately positive. The Wolfe Tones Gaelic football and hurling club provided the focus and its successes over the years undoubtedly contributed in no small measure to civic pride. The same might be said of the golf club, an early priority and the particular concern of Dr Bill Flynn, ex-RAF officer and first Shannon medical practitioner. Land close to the airport was leased by the Minister for Transport and Power to SFADCo who sub-leased it in 1966 to the Shannon Golf Club, which had a membership of 150 before a sod of the first green had been turned. Bill Jones, a founder member, claimed that from the beginning there was no social exclusivity.... Always provided, of course, you were of the male gender.

The first substantial group immigration to *Sionna* followed upon the destabilisation of the Allende government in Chile and the consequent flow of refugees. The local community was very sympathetic and many who were offered sanctuary subsequently intermarried locally. Kevin Thompstone recalled on first coming to Shannon in the 1970s hearing "a couple of Chilean kids speaking with Northern Ireland accents!" On 15 August 1969 British troops had moved into the Bogside in Derry and shot dead five civilians. One of the consequences of this and subsequent events in the North was an influx of refugees into the Republic, many of whom found their way to *Sionna*, since housing was readily available and they had, rightly or wrongly, the expectation of securing jobs. Their impact was considerable and the consequences far-reaching. Some established businesses in the town (today Northern accents are as common in the Town Centre as those of Dublin); some returned whence they came as the situation improved; others created serious problems and were a source of friction with the established residents. The majority of those who stayed went to Cronan estate which was opening up at the time, but they were not seriously ghettoised. Perhaps their most lasting contribution has been to the politicising of the community.

The Shannon Community Association, formed in 1964, elected annually an eleven-member council and often acted in a representative role in dealings with the Development Company. It was complemented subsequently by the Shannon Town Alliance, a forum composed of representatives nominated by individual groups and clubs; but this was stigmatised

37. *Michael Keating, who worked at Shannon in the 1950s, with his model of the expanding airport, 1956.*

38. *Fairway to runway: the original Shannon golf course was designed by John D. Harris for £2,500. He subsequently returned to design the second nine holes. At 6,890 yards the course was for many years the second longest in Ireland.*

as non-democratic and its validity seriously questioned. Attempts by the company to secure some form of legal status for *Sionna* were met with the response that local government was being reformed and that local authorities would be merged into regional structures. In the meantime widespread dissatisfaction over rents had led to the formation of the Shannon Tenants' Association and strike actions, involving the withholding of rents and the cause of great acrimony between the company and its tenants, took place in 1971–72. The system appeared to many patently inequitable: a man on Social Welfare was paying the same as a high earner. The company, its room for manoeuvre to some extent restricted by the legislation under which it was operating, found the strike extremely difficult to handle and a serious shock to the delicate structure of the community system. Negotiations with pressure groups were abandoned on the grounds that they were not representative and company staff embarked on an arduous house-to-house canvass over a period of four to five months to explain the situation as they saw it, whilst continuing to hold a harder line.

'Arrangements were being made to issue proceedings for recovery of arrears,' the board minutes recorded.[20] 'For practical reasons it appeared that proceedings could not be served on the whole [sic] tenants involved at the same time. Groups of 20–22 were being taken and the leaders of the STA [Shannon Tenants' Association] were included in the first group.' This policy of attrition culminated in September 1971 in the serving of civil bills on 250 tenants. The STA was receiving support from the militant National Association of Tenants' Organisations (NATO). Roads were blocked; tenancy agreements burned. The company recognised that if the legal process were pursued to finality it would end in evictions, and decided, before this stage was reached, to review the whole matter. A final settlement was achieved in June 1972, a five-year agreement between the STA and the company phasing rent increases to October 1976. An Estates Arbitration Committee was established and a tenants' purchase scheme introduced in October of the same year. Though inhibited initially by lack of mortgage facilities, it consolidated the trend towards home-ownership and the disposal of SFADCo-owned houses which resulted in a figure of eighty-two per cent owner-occupation in 1990, one of the highest rates in the country. In the long term the strike had the effect of stimulating the desire of *Sionna* residents for effective local representation—an ideal which was still eluding them in 1991.

In the 'Social Diary—Events of Interest to Shannon Folk' issued on 20 October 1970, it was announced that the exhibition 'Shannon Town—planning for the 1970s' would remain open in the Development Company's office block until 23 October. The presentation included a model of proposed future expansion in which the new Town Centre occupied a prominent position. The 'Diary', the responsibility of the Community Officer, Frances Condell—subsequently to become Limerick City's first woman Mayor—is an indication of the wide range of activities then flourishing in the town. Cratloe Rovers Football Club was holding its Carnival Dance in Tullyvarraga Hall (opened the previous year) on the 25th, admission 6s (30p). Other events scheduled for the week included: Tuesday, Shannon Country Market, badminton and bridge; Wednesday, bingo, badminton, bridge practice and a film *Till death us do part* in Drumgeely Hall (there was no cinema proper); Thursday, *claisceadal* (choral singing), a céilí, physical training and a parent/ teacher association meeting; Sunday, Oakfield Beagles meet at Croom; Monday, Shannon Community Association Open House, which all residents were invited to attend, a child welfare clinic in Drumgeely and fire brigade drill at the fire station . . . the 1st Clare Scout troop, Shannon, was collecting waste paper. Art classes commenced at the comprehensive school, where the ladies' choir also reassembled for the season on 21 October. Sister M. Sunniva of the Dominican convent, opened in 1966, was providing a nursing service for residents in the absence of Sister M. Josepha. All these activities, with the exception of the meeting of the beagles, took place in disparate locations in the individual housing estates. The need for a central focus for the town was becoming critical.

The Development Company had from the outset intended to retain ownership of the proposed centre rather than concede it to outside interests, but recognised in April 1967 that this would be feasible only if there was a long-term commitment from central government. In September the minister was asked to approve the development of a centre to cater for a population of 6,000 by March 1973. The company was also concerned at this time over the lack of amenity areas, which, they believed, would inhibit future development and decided that a suitable site would be drained and cleared. On 26 March 1969 the minister indicated in a letter that the Town Centre should be constructed through an arrangement with a commercial developer. The company was subsequently informed by the Department of Finance that since the minister's letter the forward financial situation had deteriorated and that it was even clearer that the government could not undertake to finance the work directly through the company. It would, however, allow SFADCo to borrow from the Shannon Diamond Group—formerly Shannon Diamond & Carbide, subsequently De Beers—with whom negotiations had already been opened.

In the event Finance came to accept that a town centre was mandatory and that SFADCo would be involved in expenditure for which state capital would be provided. In these new circumstances the company decided to issue an open invitation to developers and Cian O'Carroll was instructed to drop all other responsibilities and progress the proposal, with the result that an agreement with the developer John Sisk & Co. (Dublin) Ltd was announced to the residents in October 1970. The £1 million first phase of the project was opened by Brian Lenihan, Minister for Industry and Commerce, on 15 March 1972. It provided some 50,000 sq.ft of shopping space and included as anchor tenant a Quinnsworth supermarket.

The deal with Pat Quinn was concluded very quickly, O'Carroll recalled. One day there was hardly any shopping, the next *Sionna*, with a population of some 3,000, had better facilities than many towns three times its size. Concerned about creating an Irish character for the Centre, he was disappointed in only being able to influence Sisk's in this regard in a superficial manner relating largely to lettering and other small details. But he did persuade them, with the local bishop's agreement, to include a church, for which the developer made available a unit free of charge: a move which was criticised in some quarters as constituting a somewhat hypocritical attempt to reconcile God and Mammon. The Development Company ordered a reprint of a major coverage of the Centre in the *Irish Independent* and delivered a copy to every home in the town. After the initial euphoria, the shopping precinct experienced difficulties, with a high turnover of commercial tenants and the fear that Quinnsworth would withdraw completely; but Sisk's, and in particular one of its directors, Neil Connolly, maintained a strong interest which resulted in further development in the 1980s.

The area set aside for *Croí na Sionna*—the entire centre which embraces the shopping complex—is one of forty-eight acres lying between Tullyglass and Tullyvarraga Hills. Owing to the overall shape of the town site it can be a 'centre' only nominally, occupying as it does an area on what remains the eastern fringe; but with the accretion of the new SFADCo headquarters, government offices, a library, a filling-station, a Garda station, a health clinic and other amenities it steadily reinforced its role as the focus of town life. The latter still lacked, however, a discernible constitutional status. In May 1973 the Development Company expressed the belief that it was desirable to hand over as many of the town services as possible to Clare County Council, which remained reluctant to assume a wide responsiblity, claiming that it lacked the necessary resources. The townspeople, for their part, were concerned that if they were to be taken over, monies generated in *Sionna* would be dispersed throughout the county.

In February 1974 SFADCo submitted a proposal to the Minister for Local Government, in the context of a local government reorganisation discussion document, that the electoral boundaries for a putative Shannon Urban District Council should take in 'the areas scheduled for development by

SFADCo up to the 25,000 population stage, also surrounding areas in the immediate vicinity which form a natural extension to the town ...'. The general feeling has been, and remains, that an Urban District Council is the best option, but that solution, at the time of writing, lies in the future. In the meantime, following considerable debate, it was decided to seek the appointment of Town Commissioners under the 1854 Town Improvements Act.

Though there are some thirty towns in the country governed by Town Commissioners this antique piece of British legislation is a total anachronism, and recourse had to be had to the Stationery Office in London to secure a copy. The Act conveys the power to regulate the speed of carriages and to make rules for the storage of gunpowder. To hold an election under its provisions a notice must be nailed to the door of the Protestant church ... and of the Catholic chapel if there be one. Elections were, nevertheless, conducted in *Sionna* in March 1982 and the nine Commissioners, with Fianna Fáil representation generally predominating, have since then dutifully exercised their strictly limited powers. They are answerable to the County Manager. They can 'provide allotments, school meals and parks ... maintain a town hall, advertise the amenities of the town, provide and improve the markets. They also have powers to provide public lighting, insist on removal of obstructions and dangerous buildings, erect a public clock, license cinemas, and control offensive trades'.[21] The County Council remains responsible for roads, for the public library and other amenities, nor do the Commissioners have any formal arrangement with SFADCo, though there is regular contact on maintenance issues. The Commissioners can, and do, however, make their voice heard on wider political issues and in acting as hosts to visiting dignitaries and politicians assume at least the outward appearance of corporate authority. 'The transfer of the administration of Shannon Town from SFADCo to Clare County Council ought to be proceeded with forthwith,' the Oireachtas Joint Committee on Public Expenditure recommended in 1986—a recommendation which, in early 1992, had yet to be acted upon. SFADCo, for its part, would be comfortable with the handing over of its responsibility to a properly-constituted body.

☆ ☆ ☆ ☆ ☆ ☆

As late as 1975 there were still doubts. 'Since, on the face of it, the evidence seemed to suggest that many Shannon workers did not need the town, it was necessary to re-examine why the town was being built,' the SFADCo board concluded. 'Even if it proved that the original purpose was no longer valid, to build the town to regional rather than simply Shannon needs could still be worthwhile. . . it should be assessed not only by its current problems but also by its potential . . . .'[22] Today, in the neat housing developments flanked by maturing trees, in the public spaces and amenity areas, in the busy shopping centre—attracting visitors from a widening hinterland—it is clear that a great measure of that potential has been achieved. In the Knight's Inn, the pub provided as part of Sisk's development, though the voices at lunchtime denote the broad provenance of the town's population, the conversation is for the most part uncompromisingly local. The USSR airline, for some years highly prominent in Shannon, has just announced its sponsorship of the County hurling team. At the bar there is animated discussion of future nomenclature. "Clareoflot," suggests one pint-drinker. "Hammer and *Sliotar*"[23] counters another.

The roots are down.

References

1. Fr Liam Ryan: *Shannon—Ireland's New Town: A Social Survey*, Shannon 1969, p. 37
2. To avoid confusion the Irish form will be used throughout this chapter as denoting the new town.
3. Shannon Free Airport Development Authority: Report to the Minister, 1 August 1958–31 January 1959
4. Ryan, op. cit., p. 8
5. Ryan, op. cit., pp. 1, 34, 42
6. 'Homes for the People', in *Studies*, June 1932, p. 271
7. Ryan, op. cit., p. 52
8. *Social Trends in Shannon Town, Report of a Special Census*, Shannon 1975, p. 6
9. Desmond Donnelly: 'Shopping at Shannon—One Man's Views', in *5th Annual Shannon Recreation Week Souvenir Booklet*, 1982
10. Shannon Free Airport Development Company Amendment Act 1963
11. Ryan, op. cit., p. 31
12. *Shannon Town—Planning for the 1970s*, Shannon 1970
13. Sheppard Fidler, op. cit., p.27
14. Ryan, op. cit., p. 13
15. Fidler, op. cit., pp. 30, 33
16. 'Heart of Shannon'
17. 'Cian and Rent'
18. 'We live in the shadow of each other'
19. Board minutes, 18 January 1980
20. 2 June 1971
21. James O'Donnell: *How Ireland is Governed*, 2nd ed., Dublin 1970, p. 60
22. Board minutes, 25 March 1975
23. The ball used in the game of hurling

39. *Lord Gort, whose restoration of Bunratty provided the initial impetus for the tourist development in the Shannon Region, photographed in the castle in 1969.*

CHAPTER 5

The Captives and the Kings

I am going to give you the first two lines of a limerick and I want to see if you can finish it before the end of our trip this evening. You may be able to read it out at the Mediaeval Dinner tonight at Bunratty. If it is not a good one we throw you into the dungeons. Here are the first two lines:

> *'There was a young lady called Brewer*
> *Who booked on the Mediaeval Tour. . . .'*

☆ ☆ ☆ ☆ ☆ ☆

A damp May morning sometime in the 1960s. It is Sunday, and the Limerick–Ennis road is empty of all but a few early spectators taking up their positions for the passing of the Circuit of Ireland rally. As the castle comes into view, grey stone against a grey sky, the Australian historian is markedly unenthusiastic. Suspicious of Arnold Toynbee's dictum that history is both a science and an art, he is disinclined to accept that the physical re-creation of the past can add anything of significance to a contemporary perception of battles long ago. Bunratty stands, mute and apparently deserted, testifying apparently to nothing but its own enduring presence, now confirmed for the indefinite future by the work of restoration. Steps lead upwards to a door which, quite unexpectedly, lies open. Inside, the great hall is empty, but empty in a manner that eerily implies a recent and potent occupation. A scattering of fifteenth-century objects on a long table; a heavy chair set askew; the vibrant heraldry of an escutcheon: it is as if something has impelled the

[105]

40. *Every inch a king: Clement Freud filming for BBC television, Bunratty Castle, November 1971.*

41. *The widely-travelled Bunratty Entertainers, January 1986.*

inhabitants to depart with a suddenness that has left an overwhelming sense of their continuing presence. The Australian, on his own admission, senses the disconcerting dimension. It is only a mildly ironic coincidence that some years later a 'Bunratty Castle' could be discovered, offering its own accommodation with a doubly-distant past, in the unlikely environs of the city of Melbourne.

Bunratty is in many respects a metaphor for the whole Mid-Western endeavour. ' The essential element of tourism is the difference,' said Brendan O'Regan.[1] If Shannon did not invent the mediaeval banquet, it enlarged upon it to a degree which set a headline for any imitators, conceiving of it not just as an isolated initiative but as a nucleus around which to assemble an interlocking and durable complexity: the folk-park, the Bunratty Singers ... and the many private commercial enterprises which have also taken root. As for the banquet itself, the Herbelade Allowes and the Salomene Chekyns in Brownet have been laid before a succession of revellers in the course of a performance which has now been running longer than the London theatre's *Mousetrap*. There was even an early plan, to remain unfulfilled, to acquire Dirty Nelly's—the then aptly-nicknamed pub at the foot of the castle walls—to round out the integrity of the concept. But if this came to nothing the basic idea proved highly susceptible of outward expansion, leading to the acquisition of Dunguaire and Knappogue castles and their development on parallel lines. King John's castle in Limerick was identified for similar treatment as early as 1966, though in this case the realisation was to await the passage of some twenty-five years.

Kevin Vaughan, who attended the first Bunratty banquet, traced the origins of the concept to a request from George O'Malley of the Limerick Wine and Food Society to be allowed use the restored great hall for a function. Though the castle had been opened to visitors in 1960 by the Minister for Transport and Power, Erskine Childers, it had been under-utilised: there was no water and certainly no cooking facility. George O'Malley's request met with little enthusiasm but he enlisted the support of the minister, who was closely involved in the proposals for tourism development for Shannon. The celebration, based on an authentic menu from the period of Henry IV of France and irrigated by, amongst other things, a 400-year-old sherry that was so concentrated it had to be 'extended', was a marked success. O'Regan, who was present, discerned in it the seeds of what was to follow. "He had a tremendous facility for collecting people's ideas," said Vaughan, "and of putting them all together."

Bunratty had been restored by Lord Gort (who had bought it for £1,000) with the assistance of the Office of Public Works. The Vereker family, of which he was a member, had settled in Roxborough, Co. Limerick in the early seventeenth century and supplied the city with several Mayors. They later acquired Loch Cutra castle, Gort, Co. Galway, but sold the estates in 1840, donating the proceeds to the relief of famine in the neighbourhood and moving to England. Lord Gort, brother of Field-Marshal Viscount Gort, VC, from whom he inherited the title, made a fortune in coal-mining and hotels in Canada and when he returned to Ireland originally intended to buy the old family property of Loch Cutra. The castle, however, was in poor condition and he was persuaded by John Hunt to buy and restore Bunratty instead. A board of trustees was formed on which SFADCo was represented; and in January 1960 the minister approved the assumption by the company of the responsibility for its operation. The entertainment functions were to be exercised by the sister Sales and Catering Organisation, which following the establishment of SFADCo continued to work closely and harmoniously with the new body.

The happy circumstance which brought Lord Gort and John Hunt together was thus to lay the foundation, not only for the preservation of one of the country's most important mediaeval buildings and its furnishing with equally important contemporary artefacts, but for the development of a major commercial asset. Hunt himself, a Limerickman who had been consultant to Sotheby's of London on mediaeval and early Celtic art and who was an expert in the field, became honorary curator of Bunratty. In 1965 he bought Craggaunowen Castle, Co. Clare and established there a museum to display part of his own collection of some 2,000 artefacts collected by himself and his wife over a period of fifty years and conservatively valued in 1991 at £35 million. In 1976 part of the collection was put on display in the Hunt Museum in the University of Limerick and in the autumn of 1991 a committee was established under the chairmanship of Tony Ryan, chairman and chief executive of Guinness Peat Aviation, to co-ordinate the project to refurbish the Custom House in Limerick as a permanent home for the collection. According to Paul Williamson, curator of sculpture at the London Victoria and Albert museum, to which part of the collection was on loan, it was 'by far the strongest collection of mediaeval works in Ireland, if not in Europe'.[2]

At Craggaunowen Hunt was also responsible for the building of a replica of a Celtic lake-dwelling, or *crannóg*, which was to prove a lasting tourist attraction. He was further instrumental in securing the removal of the cottage on the site of the runway extension at the airport—an act which led to the establishment, also enthusiastically promoted by Erskine Childers, of the Bunratty folk village.

The first detailed proposal for this latter scheme—by Kevin Danaher of the Folklore Commission—was made in September 1959 and in April 1960 it was agreed that the project should proceed with the assistance of a grant and loan from Bord Fáilte. With the world-wide proliferation of folk parks and similar phenomena from Old Sydney Town to Williamsburg to the Fortresse de Louisburg in Nova Scotia and back to Ballarat, it is important to acknowledge the innovative role of the Shannon experiment. For experiment it was: there were no relevant models to follow in that a major tourist attraction was being created in almost complete dependence on whatever traffic could be captured from the movements at a neighbouring airport—movements the very uncertainty of which provided the compelling impetus for the endeavour.

Few women grace this narrative. For this the temper of the times, the ban on married women continuing to work in state enterprises, the traditional pattern of rural society, may be held responsible—though it is worth noting that in 1991 there was no woman holding a senior management position in SFADCo. In 1945, however, Maeve Fitzgibbon had been successful from among 300 applicants for a job with Pan American at Foynes. Transferring to Rineanna when flying-boat services ended, she worked subsequently in the PAA Dublin office and, again at Shannon, with KLM before two serious crashes involving KLM aircraft ("people ringing from all over Europe . . . a most heartbreaking experience. I was numb with grief myself") convinced her that her involvement with aviation was over. Her brief retirement was brought to an end by a friend's suggesting that Brendan O'Regan might have a job for her. The duty-free facility had just opened, but once transit passengers had made their purchases from the limited range of goods on offer there was little else to occupy them. O'Regan had observed Noel Coward on one occasion sitting on his own in the transit lounge for three hours awaiting a delayed flight. There was nobody, apparently, ready or willing to engage him in conversation. There should, thought O'Regan, be somebody here who could do that. Maeve Fitzgibbon, who was, of course, already well-known to him in the Rineanna context, seemed to him the right person for the task.

"The whole thing about it was excitement and fun," said Cathal O'Shannon. "That was the great bloody thing about Shannon, and I think it was engendered by Brendan. He could pick people." O'Shannon's experience went back "to the old days when I was in *The Irish Times*. They were a wonderful organisation then. For a journalist nothing was impossible—whether it was a trip to the US for some specific purpose, whether it was to meet somebody of importance or consequence who had to do with Shannon or the area or whether we were down there covering air crashes, as we quite often were, Brendan personally saw that everything was done. He had wonderful people working for him. The two I remember most vividly and with greatest warmth are John Dilger and Maeve Fitzgibbon, a wonderful woman. . . . "

Having made a decision regarding an individual O'Regan would then leave him to his own devices—a propensity that was, in this case, to transcend the sexual barrier. When he departed on his six-week promotional visit to the United States he left Maeve Fitzgibbon in charge of the embryonic tourist information bureau, designed by Louis Le Brocquy, but with minimal resources and, for its principal occupant, virtually nothing in the way of a job description. 'What will you call yourself?,' O'Regan had asked her before leaving. "I said what about Passenger Relations Officer? He said 'that sounds very good.' I said to Jack Ryan, his second in command: 'I need a uniform!'" Maeve Fitzgibbon took a room in one of the airport hostels, since the flight pattern involved working a sixteen-hour day and made commuting to and from her home in Limerick out of the question. From then until she was sent to New York in 1962 to open a SFADCo office she embodied the spirit, since much-devalued, of *Céad míle fáilte* in a manner which was both warmly authentic and firmly authoritative. Airline economics of the period meant that the transatlantic passenger profile was shaped largely by two extremes— the rich and famous and the refugees fleeing from continuing or intermittent oppressions towards the prospect of a better life. The former category was, in the nature of things, the larger concern of Maeve Fitzgibbon. "I had people like Paul Gallico. He was writing *The Steadfast Man* at the time and was staying at Ashford Castle. He kept coming up and down to Shannon because he was madly in love with an exquisite creature. . . . "

That from this markedly personalised beginning there was to grow the highly organised and commercially-aware Mid-West tourist industry was not untypical of the genesis of many Shannon initiatives, undertaken more from immediate conviction than on the basis of far-sighted schemata; deriving from an intuitive response rather than a formulated prognosis. From the need to keep a sedentary Noel Coward happy there sprang, for example, the idea of catering for transit passengers on a more general scale, an idea which evolved into the 'Free Day' promotion, the aim of which was to induce passengers bound for Europe to break their journey in Shannon with consequent benefit to the local economy.

A short distance from here we are going to turn off the track usually taken by tourists and travel through a part of the country that was old in story when Columbus set sail to discover the New World. As you know, you will be winding up this tour with a fifteenth century dinner at the ancient castle at Bunratty. The fifteenth and the twentieth centuries are never far apart in Ireland. Just a few minutes ago you were passing through a jet-age industrial estate and in another few minutes you will be riding through what would have been the domain of the Great Earl of Thomond who ruled from Bunratty Castle and at whose table you will dine this evening. We are going to travel through villages where life goes on in the same pleasant tempo as it did 500 years ago, when the Great Earl ruled all these lands. So as we go along I want you to relax for a little while and fall back into the easy and gentle way of life that belongs to the people you will see on this journey.

A special travel section, headed by Ray Joyce who had been recruited from American Express in Dublin, had been set up within the company in July 1962. Its principal task was initially the promotion of the Free Day Tour. By October it was realised that the scheme was not economically viable and it was replaced from April the following year by the One Day Tour for which a charge was made of $15 inclusive of a meal in Bunratty. The profit on each participant was calculated at $1. At the same time it was recognised that the future of tourism lay in the growth of terminal traffic, and it was with this in view that the New York office was opened—a move which caused some embarrassment since the IDA had not been officially informed. The office, managed by Maeve Fitzgibbon and initially staffed by members of the Sales and Catering publicity division (the two bodies were under O'Regan's chairmanship) was envisaged as largely a public relations operation. Industrial enquiries were passed to the New York office of the IDA for processing. A separate press and public relations section within SFADCo was formed in November 1963 and took over the running of the New York office; by this time the company had defined its tourism objectives as 'the encouragement of the improvement of tourist amenities ... by active participation with residents, voluntary groups and societies and Local Authorities; development of tourist "products" ... with a view to getting amenities within the region and particularly the immediate hinterland of the airport ... improved by such means as the clearance of derelict sites, painting of houses in villages, landscaping villages and cottages by planting trees and shrubs and the establishment of gardens. The company's activity in this would be mainly to act as leader and spur...'.

Among projects to be examined were farm and village holidays, holiday camps for children, a holiday village and the improvement of vacant labourers' cottages for holiday letting by the Rentavilla system. "Brendan got a yen at that time for what he called social tourism," Kevin Vaughan remembered; but underpinning this obvious element was the aim of making

Shannon the gateway to the West of Ireland by offering low-cost 'centred' holidays. In this the company found itself up against the continuing inadequacy of air links with mainland Europe: in October 1963 Mr de Graff, who owned a hotel in Kilkee, complained of the lack of charter services. The problem was to acquire, over the years, a quality of permanency.

And now you can see through the trees in front the battlements of Bunratty Castle. . . . We are going to stop now in the shadow of its walls at an Irish farm cottage where the woman of the house will serve you bread, tea and scones, which were cooked this morning over the open turf fire.

'How may worthy features of the old traditional way of rural life be preserved in the rapid advance of industrialisation and urbanisation of the modern world?' asked Kevin Danaher, effectively the originator of the Bunratty Folk Park.[3] ' . . . this is the question which confronted those responsible for the development of the Shannon Airport region in 1959 when an extension of the airport runways made necessary the demolition of a little old farmhouse. . . . Could a little house of this kind be preserved as it deserved to be? Ways and means were sought and found. The businessmen of Shannon were then practically interested in the restoration of the great mediaeval castle of Bunratty, and when they learned that, in the old days, there were numerous thatched dwellings of the lesser folk under the shadow of the lord's castle, they decided that the farmhouse from the airport should be erected there.'

The Folk Park became a functioning reality in July 1964 when Erskine Childers formally opened a pair of farm gates which had been brought to the site from Galbally, Co. Limerick. Inside were two small farmhouses, a fisherman's house and a forge, with other exhibits under construction. "It is an attempt to interpret Ireland as it was at the turn of the century," said Cian O'Carroll, managing director of Shannon Heritage, the SFADCo subsidiary responsible for the Park, more than quarter of a century later. "It may be somewhat selective—there are no warts—but you have to recognise that we are really in the area of theatre." Critics have described it as an architectural zoo, and the debate on the aesthetics of this and similar developments is likely to continue. 'At first some doubts were expressed at the historical propriety of having a series of small thatched dwellings in the immediate vicinity of a great Mediaeval Castle,' wrote Christopher Lynch, its first manager,[4] 'but little research was necessary to show this was normally the case in former times. When Rinuccini visited Bunratty in 1646 he wrote to

42. *Teacher Noel Murphy (extreme left) with Raisa Gorbachev, wife of the USSR President, at the school in the Bunratty Folk Park, April 1989. Also in the picture (left to right): Russian interpreter, Mrs Haughey (wife of the Taoiseach), John A. Daly, then chairman of Shannon Development and Cian O'Carroll, managing director of Shannon Heritage.*

43. *Irish night at Teach Ceoil, Murroe, 2 May 1978. The attendance included members of a visiting ODA (Overseas Development Aid) group.*

44. *Dunguaire Castle, Co. Galway: a 1970 publicity photograph.*

45. *Mark Edwin Andrews, owner of Knappogue Castle (left) with Erskine Childers at its opening for mediaeval banquets in 1967.*

Rome: "The great estate on which the castle stands is full of thatched wooden huts peopled by countless servants and a thousand soldiers...."

'From the beginning certain principles were adopted and rigidly adhered to throughout,' Lynch added. 'In the first place it was decided that the exhibits should be replicas of houses in the Shannon region; secondly, they should be entirely authentic in representing Irish country life in or about the first decade of the present century; and thirdly, the presentation should be warm and alive, avoiding as far as possible the static presentation popularly associated with a museum.' The warmth and vitality remains an essential element of the Folk Park ethos, fortified in recent times by the addition of a full-scale pub; and the authenticity received perhaps its most definitive endorsement when Raisa Gorbachev, wife of the Soviet President, was clearly uncertain as to whether the activities of the village school—which she inspected during the course of a visit on 2 April 1989—represented the Ireland of today or yesterday.

In August 1964, following on the success of Bunratty, the company agreed that other castles in the region should be surveyed with a view to preservation. Although transit traffic at the airport had fallen substantially since 1959, some 4,600 people took the One Day Tour in the course of the year and accepted the invitation of the Earl of Thomond to dine at his table and languish, if only temporarily, in his dungeon. The sixteenth Baron Inchiquin, however, was to object to SFADCo inviting and imprisoning guests in his name. 'The title ... has been with my family and although it is now extinct we hold title to it,' he protested.[5] 'The last person to hold the title was the Marquess of Thomond, who died in 1855....' After an exchange of views the clash between illusion and reality was amicably resolved. In October 1964 the company decided that Knappogue Castle should be bought for £1,800 'with a view to reconstructing parts of it for use as the focal point of a tour'. In 1966, however, before this decision could be implemented, it was acquired by a wealthy American, Mark Edwin Andrews, who subsequently agreed to participate in its restoration.

On 6 October 1965 an offer by Lady Ampthill to sell Dunguaire castle to SFADCo was accepted by the board. Dunguaire—physically in Co. Galway and therefore technically outside the Region proper—was, nevertheless, developed as a third banqueting centre and became the focus of one of the Mediaeval Tours. The entertainment in this case, with a script, *Saints and Singers*, by Carolyn Swift of the Dublin Pike Theatre—was of a markedly literary cast and perhaps, with its '... celebration in Song, Verse and Anecdote of the Saints and Sinners, Scholars and Songmakers, Kings and Queens, Poets and Patrons of South County Galway ...' a little recherché for some of the captive audience which had spent the day touring Connemara by bus. This further territorial extension, whilst in accord with the company's designation of Shannon as the 'gateway to the West', could be seen to be poaching on broader Bord Fáilte territory; though SFADCo conceived of Castle Tours as an operation complementary to, rather than in conflict with, national tourism policy.

Castle Tours, a major development in the company's tourist activities, was the direct result of the collapse in 1969 of Shannon Travel, a private handling company providing services to US tour operators. Its failure had posed a serious threat to tourist business in the area and the government agreed that SFADCo should make good the deficiency, arranging package tours which were subsequently marketed by its personnel in the United States. The arrangement was to fall foul of CIE, the national transport authority, in its marketing activities directed at overseas travel agents. After strong objections from that body, which had a well-developed organisation in the United States, agreement on a joint policy was reached in March 1971. Such differences—which occurred also with Aer Rianta, the airport management authority[6]—were in a sense landmarks in the expansion of SFADCo's tourism operations from a very modest beginning to a programme which inevitably cut across other established interests.

The situation had been further complicated by the setting up, in 1964, of regional tourism organisations. The new Limerick offices of Shannonside, otherwise the Mid-Western Regional Tourism Organisation Ltd, were opened on 14 April 1969 by T. J. O'Driscoll, director general of Bord Fáilte, who complimented the new body on its 'essential network of almost a dozen servicing points throughout the Mid-West which are contributing enormously to the enjoyment of visitors through the provision of advice and guidance'. There was an obvious danger of duplication of effort, (Shannonside's activities were, in fact, to be eventually taken over by SFADCo) and the company for its part was concerned that its own role would come to be seen as that of an administrative organisation operating an established system rather than as the source of new ideas. On a practical level, however, there was a high degree of co-operation among statutory bodies functioning in the region, specifically in one of its most original and far-reaching tourist developments. Writing in the first issue of *Shannonside Courier* in December 1968 the organisation's chairman, B. G. O'Malley (the 'onlie begetter' of the Bunratty banquets) referred to '. . . our lead story in this issue on the "Rentan-Irish-Cottage" project. This is one of the most exciting ideas in the last ten years. It is yet another "first" for this region, and we are pleased to be part of the regional team working on it'.

The Shannon enterprise, whatever about its successes on the ground, has been intermittently unhappy in its choice of names with which to crown them. The ungainly 'Rent-an-Irish-Cottage', an unimaginative derivation from the only marginally happier 'Rent-a-villa', was in a sense a by-product of a larger-scale scheme to construct 'Cottage Courts' (essentially hotels in a rural idiom) which had incurred the displeasure of the minister, Erskine Childers, who would not countenance SFADCo's engaging in the hotel business in competition with the private sector. In February 1966 a proposal from US interests for the construction of a Cottage Court hotel at Craggau-nowen seemed to point to a way out of this difficulty whereby the company would act for a period of years as agents for the owners, but the scheme came to nothing. Other locations were nevertheless considered, the shortage of accommodation for 'inclusive tourists' (the term was still sufficiently novel to merit inverted commas in the minutes) having become acute, and options were taken on sites at Quin and Miltown Malbay in Co. Clare and an architect, T. Sheahan, appointed. Again, no results were forthcoming and the idea, though remaining in theory at least a company objective, was effectively extinguished by the Rent-an-Irish-Cottage scheme (for both brevity and linguistic decorum hereinafter referred to as RIC).

'Yet another of history's wheels has turned full circle,' said *The Irish Times*[7] 'and the thatched cottage, new status symbol of our time, is more likely to have a Jag outside the door than most urban villas.' The idea was O'Regan's—though refined in the heat of energetic argument with associates such as Kevin Vaughan—and the schemes designed by SFADCo's architect W. T. Smyth. As the concrete blocks were put into place at the first site in Ballyvaghan, Co. Clare, there were those who expressed concern for the integrity of the village and the uneasy concordance with existing traditional buildings of the same type. Would prospective occupants bother with pothooks when they were supplied with electric cookers? Few, however, were prepared to fault the social thinking behind the scheme, which argued that the villages themselves would be enhanced by a development that in some cases would replace derelict buildings; that since the cottages were designed to integrate with the community the economic benefit would be substantial; and that local groups would participate directly in the ownership through holdings in a limited company. 'A new and readily marketable element will be added to the National Tourist Plant,' the introductory prospectus claimed; and such, indeed, proved to be the case.

In the summer of 1969 an agreement was reached between Bord Fáilte, Shannonside, the County Council and local committees on a programme to improve those villages in which RIC schemes were to be sited. For SFADCo, which was to provide executive and planning staff, the scheme was an ideal complement to its parallel aim of upgrading villages on the route of the Mediaeval Tours and served to underline its continuing commitment to the social content of its development strategy. In the same year, 1969, Fr Harry Bohan became the Muintir na Tíre community organisation officer for the region, and the company decided to contribute to his proposed scheme for rural development 'as [it] could be co-ordinated with work at present being done by SFADCo and Shannonside . . . '. Fr Bohan's concern was that small towns and villages in the proximity of major industrial development were not benefiting to any discernible degree. ' There is in the region a "hierarchy" of centres,' he wrote.[8] 'This hierarchy comprises a series of market towns distributed at points around the region. Within commuting distance of these towns, there are villages. In the main, these villages have not been touched by development. The reason for this must be stated clearly. Conventional industrial policies are derived from the First and Second Programmes of [sic] Economic Expansion and the Third Programme for Economic and Social Development. Through our work we have discovered that the social content of current development is virtually nil.'

By the time he wrote this Fr Bohan's Rural Housing Organisation, (RHO) established in 1972, had built 150 dwellings in ten centres, with construction in ten further locations at the planning stage. He quoted the case of the Co. Clare village of Kilkishen, population 100 and some twenty-five kilometres from the airport, which up to 1974 had exhibited all the hallmarks of stagnation: a decline in the primary school roll and only eight houses built in five years. With the completion by his organisation of a scheme of twenty-four houses the school enrolment increased by one-third virtually overnight and the population doubled. A new industry was established which, together with another 'in the pipeline', promised jobs for 100. 'A policy which helps people to live and work in their own communities,' he concluded, 'turning to their own natural resources (human and material) will in the long term bring about a more stable community. A properly defined social development policy supported by good organisation can achieve this. The demand for such a policy is pressing. This demand has been demonstrated in the Mid-West. Something is being done. . . . ' The communality of concern as between the RHO and SFADCo had led, in 1971, to Fr Bohan's being appointed as consultant to the company on community affairs.

Fr Bohan's achievement has been considerable: not only in material terms, but in raising the morale of small communities to enable them the better to confront the perennial problem of rural depopulation and disadvantage. Some have been more successful than others: whereas Sixmilebridge, Co.

Clare, has grown into a virtual dormitory town for Shannon, with new executive-style housing far removed from the Rural Housing Organisation's simple structures, Glenanaar, Co. Limerick, has virtually vanished from the map. Glenanaar? The novelist Canon Sheehan wrote of it, in the early years of the nineteenth century, as a thriving community. There is nothing there now. Ballyorgan, on the north-western rim of the Ballyhoura mountains, has recently lost its post office and single shop, and its school is under threat. Ballyorgan is about eight kilometres from Kilfinane, a village of some 700 people with a centre which exhibits all-too-visible signs of creeping dereliction. "Can you say," asks Carmel Fox, "that Kilfinane will exist in fifty years' time as a community?"

Behind the main street, on the left as you come in from Kilmallock, is the Kilfinane Education Centre, housed in the former vocational school. Carmel Fox is trying to explain the nature of her responsibilities as manager of Ballyhoura Fáilte Society Limited to two Poles who have come to Co. Limerick to learn something of the possibilities of agritourism, as the verbal shorthand has it. She cannot pronounce their names; and they, for their part, are experiencing obvious difficulties not only with the language—the medium is Hiberno-English—but with the whole concept of private enterprise as it is practised in Kilfinane and environs. They cannot understand, for example, how a farm that makes cheese in commercial quantities can also cater for paying guests; or how a state body such as Shannon Development can come to be involved with a man with ponies for hire or the tourist promotion of a steam-operated creamery in Drumcolliher.

One cannot blame the Poles, strangers in a strange land: until recently many in Kilfinane itself would have been hard put to it to make a connection between these and other similar, and dissimilar, activities which now fall within the ambit of Ballyhoura Fáilte. As to the part played by Shannon Development: 'Well,' said that body's Jim Beary,[9] 'I can best describe our role as a combination of a number of elements of planning, support, direction and funding. After recognising the opportunity presented by the resources of the area, [this includes] organising, motivating and developing linkage and co-operation, promoting the partnership approach with all the parties and players, setting goals; influencing the structuring of long-term and short-term plans; identifying funding sources for the various projects and development requirements, providing linkage through its network to all sources of assistance and expertise, tourist promotion, etc'.

'From Marsaaxlokk to Marsakala', according to Stuart Rossiter's *Blue Guide to Malta*, 'is a rural walk of 3¼ m . . . a track leads round St Thomas Bay to join the by-road from Zejtin. . . . " The Guide was published in 1968. By

1991 the rural element of the walk had been drastically diminished. The beginnings of the track now threaded its muddy, rubble-encumbered way through a gaggle of half-built 'villas', the nucleus of yet another holiday development. Marsaaxlokk is—or was—not very much bigger than Kilfinane; and the fate obviously in store for it must, or should, influence the thinking of all those who promote large-scale tourism in small-scale places. Fortunately, in this regard, Kilfinane cannot guarantee unclouded sunshine and the mindless inactivities that go with it. But there are other ways of ruining an environment, or simply of getting it all wrong. "We don't see the area moving into mass tourism," said Carmel Fox with some conviction. "We're starting from a very low base." It is against this background that one must read Jim Beary's management-speak: in this context 'influencing the structuring of long-term and short-term plans' means helping a farmer to decide whether to put a bit of money into converting a couple of spare rooms for visitors . . . this year or maybe next year. 'Recognising the opportunity presented by the resources of the area' means coming up with a little financial support to enable Ballyhoura Fáilte to map out a few walking trails through the mountains. It would help, of course, if somebody bothered to produce decent large-scale maps for tourists at a national level—it would help, but it is not a disaster. Ballyhoura is all about making something out of virtually nothing; and not falling over itself by trying to make too much too quickly. Ballyhoura, in Jim Beary's words 'has one of the key ingredients essential to the development and planning of Rural/Community tourism—it is an unspoilt area of outstanding natural beauty'. The dilemma—to promote *and* preserve—is never far from the minds of those who are deliberating on its future.

Things began here in a small way with the formation of the Kilfinane Development Association in 1964. The first big step forward was the selection of the village by RIC for the construction of nine cottages in 1969–71. In 1975–76 Fr Bohan's Rural Housing Organisation built twenty houses, in the process attracting back some who had emigrated from the locality. When Shannon Development was given the responsibility for small industries in the region in 1978 it assisted in the establishment of an electronics assembly business and a workspace centre. In 1982, the chief executive officer of Limerick County Vocational Educational Committee, John Rushe, had the vision to identify an opportunity in the imminent closure of the village's vocational school, transmuting it into an education centre which has proved to be the linchpin of subsequent tourist development. John Quinn, a local man who had been involved in development work both with Macra na Feirme and the IDA and played a part in bringing the electronics enterprise to the village, saw the possibilities both of the centre and of tourism on a wider scale. Macra na Feirme at the time was bringing people into the country to study farming and Quinn succeeded in directing a major proportion of them to Kilfinane. He talked to the key figures in the local tourist industry—a couple of farmers, the owner of a country house, a mán with a few ponies for hire—and the community of interest led, in 1986, to the establishment of Ballyhoura Fáilte Society, a co-operative with both individual and corporate members. In 1988, when the responsibility of Shannon Development was extended to cover the promotion of tourism and industry in the region, it became involved in the setting-up, with the County Limerick VEC, of a sub-committee of Ballyhoura Fáilte tasked with the promulgation of an integrated development plan.

Carmel Fox, with a background as a regional socio-economic specialist involved in agritourism, arrived in Kilfinane from Teagasc in Fermoy in November 1988. A small, tightly-knit community presents its own problems for the outsider—"I don't know who fell out with whom in the past and I probably jump in with my two feet exactly where they shouldn't be"—but it also has its advantages in that she can function with a degree of detachment in her dealings with private individuals, community groups, the State and other representative bodies involved in the development sub-committee. This, and the indoctrination of Polish and other visitors, makes for a full day; particularly as the whole emphasis of the Kilfinane tourist ethos is on individual treatment. Irish Country Holidays (the chosen brand-name for what is provided) aims to bring visitors as close as possible to the life of the people, offering them, for example, a complimentary visit to a farm and tea with the lady of the house as part of the package. Designed with the overseas urban resident in mind, the visit nevertheless delighted two farmer's wives from Carlow, who overstayed their time, if not their welcome, comparing notes with the *bean a' tí*. An information pack for each visitor is another free bonus, and Carmel Fox identifies the co-ordination of information as a very important part of what they are at. How do you go brown trout fishing? You join a club. But each river has its own club. Where can I hire a boat? Who can I get for a ghillie? And maps, always maps. It is a pity that central government, so insistent on the vital role of tourism to the economy, cannot bring itself to recognise this glaring deficiency.

It might appear from the outside that the combined weight of the State and other official bodies on the Ballyhoura sub-committee—the County Council, Teagasc, FÁS, RIC, IFA ... the litany of acronyms seems almost limitless—might have the effect of submerging local initiative rather than encouraging it. But, says Carmel Fox, the reverse has proved the case. The approach over the years before the formation of the sub-committee had been

46. Opening of the Rent-an-Irish-Cottage scheme at Corofin, Co. Clare, July 1970. (Left to right): Naoise Cleary, later to found the Corofin Heritage Centre, Brendan O'Regan and Joe Boland, Clare County Manager (with shovel). George O'Malley, chairman, RIC, is on the extreme right.

47. Paddy Kennedy on home ground, 1 September 1980.

considerable but haphazard, depending very much on who was there at the time. Now there is a five-year plan and a series of one-year achievable targets, enabling all involved to see progress. There is also someone to fall back on. The assistance of Shannon Development in this regard transcends the simply financial (though this is important for small, individual projects). "Motivational support, linking in to other people and systems. It doesn't matter how hare-brained the notion you come to them with, they'll always listen to it … they'll tease you along to tease it out and you'll lose the bits that don't make sense along the way and you'll find the solid core in it. It is quite extraordinary," she adds somewhat enigmatically, "that the organisation can continue to employ people who think with an open mind."

To understand the impact of planned tourist development on places like Kilfinane it is probably necesssary to have experienced it from the beginning. When the RIC scheme was first mooted Pocán, Co. Tipperary, had about fifty inhabitants, "smaller", said Paddy Kennedy in 1990, "than we are now". Of Brendan O'Regan he said "I found him to be a very kind man. The evening he came here he called me aside and said 'I'm telling you here and now we're building cottages here'. He certainly transformed our lives here in the village. From being very parochial and inward-looking, all of a sudden we were meeting people from all walks of life—from the US and all over Europe. It made life much, much more interesting." An American ambassador to Panama, staying in one of the cottages, was obliged to make frequent phone calls at a time when such activity, even on a local scale, demanded reservoirs of time and patience. Curiosity finally got the better of the Limerick exchange: 'Who in the name of Jasus,' asked the operator, 'is phoning the White House from Pocán?'

It was the local priest, who had been involved with Muintir na Tíre, who first proposed the RIC link-up. Paddy Kennedy, who was himself in the road haulage business in a small way and owned the local pub, was sceptical and did not follow up Fr Cooney's suggestion of getting in touch with O'Regan until the priest came back to him again. The application was late, but "they came here one afternoon about three or four o'clock, the first time in our village we ever saw a retinue of maybe three or four Mercedes. We were very impressed. I overheard a high official saying 'Come on, what are we doing here, we're wasting our time'. I wasn't impressing a lot of them, but I played one trump card with Brendan O'Regan. I said to him 'we're so determined to get the Rent-an-Irish-Cottage here I'm willing to give you the site for nothing.'" But Kennedy had to accept something nominal. "According to the rules you had to have a local development association to look for Shannon to come in. We had no parish organisation—nothing."

The parish organisation was formed, *post factum*. Following the opening of the cottages Pocán was selected in 1971 for a pilot scheme for the promotion of handcraft projects in RIC locations by a Mr Lantis of New York in association with Paddy Kennedy and with the assistance of SFADCo. In 1976 it was proposed to buy sites in the village for the erection by the Rural Housing Organisation of five cottages which would then be offered for sale—a Belgian, Mr Van Hemeledonck, had expressed an interest. The plan was that, when not occupied by the owners, the cottages would be available for tourist renting. Such projects (and a similar one to build cottages on farms for which the Department of Transport and Power refused to approve expenditure) were the practical expression of O'Regan's philosophy of 'social tourism', with the RIC scheme acting as the catalyst for subsequent development. In theory the idea appeared perfectly valid and highly laudable: in execution it was to be found wanting.

Pocán's craft industry ran into severe financial difficulties. The Belgian entrepreneur opened a restaurant which proved too ambitious for its location: but the real rot set in at the core of the enterprise, with the RIC itself. The company's board, with up to twenty directors made up of representatives of each village, the County Councils, SFADCo and other state bodies, proved both unwieldy and inefficient. SFADCo terminated its management agreement with RIC on 31 March 1973 but agreed to continue to provide a promotional service whilst remaining a shareholder; in December 1975 the Shannon directors were expressing great concern over its board and management and four years later were seriously exercised by the 'apparent fall, to an alarming extent, in the standards of maintenance and cleaning ... in several villages'[10] having been made aware of a growing volume of complaints and unfavourable reports and believing that there was a real danger that the whole enterprise would collapse. As the single largest shareholder the company anticipated that it might be forced to act in the interest both of the public and private investors.

Paddy Kennedy, himself an RIC board member, and his wife Nancy, an employee of the company and responsible for Pocán's cottages, were in 1990 very bitter about the situation then prevailing. By June of that year brochures required the previous October had still not been forthcoming; the company was employing one maintenance man for the whole RIC scheme throughout the region; Nancy Kennedy, who had eighteen years of hotel experience, complained that she had neither a store nor a laundry—"our washing machines are three miles away from us at the moment and the linen is being stored in the boot of a car"—and had to pay out of her own pocket to get the cottages painted. Those who came after O'Regan, in Paddy Kennedy's view, were bereft of vision. "He would never have sanctioned the kind of bureaucracy we are saddled with."

What went wrong? Even if half the Kennedys' complaints were justified the conclusion is difficult to avoid that mismanagement exacerbated a situation which was perhaps initially attributable to a failure to reconcile a laudable aspiration with its practical possibilities. Sites were developed too quickly in advance of demand. Some of the locations never enjoyed an economic level of occupancy. The logistics of maintenance (traditional cottages, though picturesque, are in this respect very labour-intensive) were never fully worked out. What had begun as an exciting new initiative in Ballyvaghan in 1969 ended, at least in one sense, with the seeking, in March 1991, of offers for the Rent-an-Irish-Cottage company. It was taken over by the Trident Holiday Homes group the following year. 'As long as the local communities treat these cottages as their own, and as a joint effort of the community, they will not fail,' George O'Malley, chairman of RIC, had predicted at the company's first annual general meeting on 19 November 1970. And for a period of years they proved a major attraction both to overseas visitors and the domestic market. But in the view of SFADCo's Jack Bourke in 1990 the follow-through to make the essential linkages with the villages themselves was never done: "They hoped it would happen by osmosis." There were patent failures of integration—the cottages on the hillside outside Corofin, for example, were too far from the village to become part of it—but the decline can be attributed equally, perhaps, to the inability of management to keep abreast of changing tastes in tourist accommodation. There is no doubt, however, but that the RIC scheme benefited—both financially and socially—small communities which would otherwise have remained backwaters and in many cases, though not in all, formed a starting-point for further development.

Pocán owes much of its attraction for visitors to its close proximity to the shores of Lough Derg. 'In wintertime,' wrote W. F. Wakeman in 1852,[11] 'the traveller by steamboat may see upon the surface of some of the larger lakes, as Lough Dearg, fleets of wildfowl, as it were at anchor, undismayed by the approach of the huge vessel, for experience has taught them that the steamer means no harm; approach them when on the lake in a small boat if you can! Here there is beautiful and ever-changing scenery for the lover of the picturesque, finny prey for the angler, game for the shooter, time-hallowed monuments for the antiquary, a field equally rich in matter for the botanist as for the geologist; and for those, as for all, who would seek health by

48. *The original Shannon Development Company's steamer* Countess Cadogan *at the pier in Killaloe, Co. Clare. Built by Bow McLachlan of Paisley, Scotland, she entered the company's service in 1897 when passenger routes on the river were revived. She went to Lough Corrib in 1913.*

49. *Rory O'Hanlon, Minister for the Environment (left) inspects Lough Derg from the Larnchop Pollution boat, Killaloe, January 1992.*

recreation and change of scene, in the noble boats of the Dublin company, a cheap, commodious, and expeditious mode of travelling.'

The noble boats have long been a thing of the past. The vessels of the 'Dublin company'—the Midland Great Western Railway—ceased to operate in the 1860s but were succeeded by those of the prophetically-named Shannon Development Company, whose *Fairy Queen* inaugurated a service between Athlone and Killaloe on 18 June 1897. In the following year six steamers were employed on routes stretching from Killaloe up to Carrick-on-Shannon. The services, assisted by a government subsidy provided under the Railways (Ireland) Act of 1896, did not, unfortunately, realise their potential, and were progressively curtailed from 1904. In the summer of 1914, however, it was still possible to avail of the Special One Day Trip from Dublin. Leaving Kingsbridge (now Heuston) station at 9.15 a.m., it included a rail journey to Banagher, steamer to Killaloe and home again by rail from Killaloe (Lakeside), 'with luncheon and tea on board steamer'. The inclusive ticket was 11s (55p) third class, 14s 6d (72½p) first class. The steamer services ceased on the outbreak of war in 1914, Killaloe lost its passenger trains in 1931 and the irrationalisation of the country's railways in the 1960s removed the last of the branch lines serving the Shannon. And were it possible today to undertake such a pleasant journey, the idle traveller peering over the rail of the steamer with an eye for finny prey might find the waters 'rich in matter' of altogether another category than that lauded by Mr Wakeman.

In July 1988 P. J. Gleeson, a planning consultant and former County engineer with Clare County Council, produced a report on water quality management in Lough Derg which confirmed what local fishermen had been observing since the 1970s—that the lake was threatened by serious pollution caused by excessive amounts of algae growth from nutrients flowing in from rivers and by siltation from Bord na Móna bogs. Two years later a Lough Derg Working Group study document which was examining the creation of a major 'water park' for the area concluded that immediate action was needed to trace the main sources of effluent, to improve agricultural practices, remove algae and control waste from the hire cruisers which are the successors to the lake steamers. Some of these craft are based at Banagher and Killaloe, where the Shannon Region's writ runs, but the biggest concentration south of Athlone is at Portumna—in Co. Galway and therefore 'injun territory' as far as the Mid-West is concerned ... one more regional anomaly which has to be, as it were, taken on board.

Much of the lethargy observable over recent years in the attempt to re-invent Shannon River tourism is attributable to the fact that a wide divergence of interests is involved—many of them, on the face of it, mutually exclusive. Even where local involvement would appear to cohere it is not always easy to stimulate action. There was a great level of apathy in the town generally, a Shannon Development representative said of Killaloe: "not a great sense of entrepreneurship. The way we've done it is probably the most effective: get it to a certain level then get people together, tell them what you're doing". If that formula has the ring of high-handedness, in Killaloe's case it would seem to have worked—up to a point. SFADCo encouraged the formation of a single company, Derg Canal Developments, to focus the concerns of a number of existing bodies concerned with social, sporting, educational and industrial issues as well as tourist development. Some of these were very small indeed: virtually one-person pressure groups as represented by Sara Devane, who teaches at the local school but whose ideas for the future of the lakeside village range well beyond the confines of the classroom.

A walk from the Lakeside hotel, built to cater for the first Shannon tourist boom (the rail extension to the waterside station ran behind it) begins, of course, in Ballina, on the Tipperary shore. "In eastern Europe walls are coming down," said Jack Bourke in 1990, "but Ballina and Killaloe are completely separate places." Across the bridge is the first evidence of the initiative stemming from the new company. Dave Columby's cottage, alias the old lock house on the canal that bypasses the weir, was being renovated as a tourist information office and interpretative centre for the lake (though the manner of its restoration was to provoke a spirited local controversy). Downstream the canal itself, refuge for pleasure craft in various stages of neglect and decay, reflects the fact that hire cruisers are banned from travelling below Killaloe and that few other vessels attempt the intermittently hazardous passage to Limerick and the sea. There are plans at the Limerick end for improving the waterway, but at Killaloe the emphasis is on creating a walking and cycling trail from the existing canal path. A stroll out in this direction and past the school brings you to Clarisford House, the former bishop's palace, which Sara Devane would like to see acquired and refurbished as a business centre, decentralised government offices, a wildlife service . . . anything that would bring new life. And then there is Brian Boroimhe, high-king of Ireland, defeater of the Danes, and a Killaloe man. "If you could re-create an earthwork here on this site . . . you could have a Viking ship coming up the lake . . . . " Lord Killanin, directing the film *Alfred the Great*, sailed two all the way up from the estuary.

Plans for Killaloe itself are perhaps more immediately realisable: in simple terms, to get people off the lake and into the town. "We're hoping to get a critical mass of development between the private and public sector," says Jack Bourke, lapsing into tourism-speak, "that will spawn restaurants and that sort of thing." (In 1991 there was at least one new restaurant of quality—in Ballina.) The dean has put the Late Transitional St Flannan's Cathedral into the project; the ESB, which controls the flow of water on the Shannon in the interests of its power station at Ardnacrusha, is "positive about linking into what we are doing". One problem will be the frail and narrow Ballina–Killaloe bridge, symbol both of what unites and divides. Another will, perhaps, lie in getting enough people onto the lake to get them off—the obstacle on which the first incarnation of the Shannon Development Company foundered. And if they come off in numbers, courtesy of a new lake passenger service, envisaged if not exactly planned, what will happen to the town, on an early spring evening a hushed haven of brooding inwardness. But you can't eat brooding inwardness: is it therefore to be engulfed by plastic pizza parlours, juke-boxed fast food outlets, giant-screen pubs? Perhaps not, if people like Sara Devane retain any say in the matter. "We identified some properties which we really should have acquired—now they're sold. But we have the planning authorities in Co. Clare in on this thing."

Killaloe, tourists apart, is thriving. Sara Devane's school has a roll of 350, which she thinks will soon be 400—"one of the few in Clare that is growing". Her catchment area extends across into Tipperary for twelve or thirteen kilometres, as far on the Clare side as O'Brien's Bridge and Broadford. In commuting terms the range is even wider. Brendan O'Regan lived for some years on the Ballina bank; when he left in 1990 his house was bought by a Guinness Peat Aviation executive. GPA, says Jack Bourke, have a very strong presence in Killaloe: "Some people would say that to get a GPA-type operation to establish here we have to offer a quality of environment, a quality of life ... if only for that it's legitimate to have a dimension that's related to area development; at another level people would say that the era of massive international job-creating investment is over, and that people are going to have to rely on their own indigenous resources to create economic activity and you can only do that by having a very focused approach area by area...." This means that Killaloe must stand both for itself and its wider identity as an element of East Clare if not of the region as a whole—a relationship that must somehow be made to emerge from a complexity of local interests, both public and private, in reaction with Shannon Development in its preferred role as catalyst. It is a situation that will be replicated in other parts of the region as tourism confronts the uneasy dichotomy of 'small is beautiful' and 'big is megabucks'.

"Somebody said to me the other day, 'OK, so what are you going to do with south-west Clare?'" Absolutely nothing, was the response of Shannon

Development's Gerry McKeon: "Just put in quality self-catering accommodation and leave the place alone, because within Europe you will need to be
able to sell space. You can actually have the mix."

Can you? If you walk along the strand from the Siboney Beach Club in
Antigua, West Indies, you come to the Halcyon Cove Hotel. A pier juts out
into the water on which you may enjoy an after-dinner *digestif*, mosquitoes
permitting. On the landward side there are restaurants, sports facilities,
accommodation blocks, shops and boutiques—everything necessary to
convince the North Americans who constitute virtually the entirety of the
clientele that all is for the best in the best of all possible worlds—that is, just
like home. Flown and bussed in, bussed and flown out again, their awareness of the island is limited to, perhaps, the odd air-conditioned sightseeing
trip, their contact with the Antiguans themselves represented by the people
who sweep their verandahs, serve their meals, collect their laundry. They
don't have to know that the island, once a British colony, is now virtually an
American one, dependent upon the US for its tourist revenue and thus for its
livelihood. Virtually everything, even water, is imported since Antigua's
industry, and its staple, sugar, is now virtually non-existent. The capital,
Saint John's, has the turned-in look of a place where nothing ever happens.
Concrete roads are suddenly swallowed up in jungle, and there are no
signposts because the taxi-drivers have taken them all down in an effort to
preserve their livelihood.

"Your daddy ain't your daddy but your daddy don't know," sings the
calypso lady on the beach; but the sense of illegitimacy runs deeper. It is not
unreasonable to attribute it entirely to the development of luxury hotels,
with the native inhabitants living in their rudimentary dwellings outside the
security-fortified enclaves like the Earl of Thomond's peasantry round
Bunratty; but the return to the nineteenth-century concept of tourism as the
preserve of the 'quality' (not many Dublin working-men could have afforded
the 11s 6d for the Special Day Trip on the Shannon) is not something that can
be contemplated with any degree of equanimity.

Current thinking, however, accepts that it is this end of the market that
produces the yield. The spend in Adare Manor, where the daily rate for bed
and no breakfast in summer 1991 was over £100, is ten times greater, it is
suggested, than that of the average coach-tourist. The emphasis has moved
away from doubling tourism numbers to focus on trebling tourism spend.
This entails, inevitably, more 'impactive products' in the jargon: havens for
the rich in the manner of Adare, Mount Juliet, Straffan, Carton, which, while
providing the visitor with every conceivable amenity, effectively insulate
him from the kind of contact with and reaction to the local environment as

represented by Ballyhoura and the broad idea of social tourism. Under this impetus not only the accommodation is hygienically packaged: inverted-commas tourism implies the creation of 'architectural zoos' such as Bunratty Folk Park; the implantation of 'interpretative centres' into sensitive areas such as the Burren, the assumption being that the whistle-stop visitor lacks both the time and the inclination to interpret anything for himself; and, *in extremis*, the remaking of the country in the image of what the tourist is led to expect it to be.

Happily the thinking behind such strategies is not universally accepted. The Burren project aroused such opposition—from a wide range of often inimical interests—that the EC, which was supplying most of the funding, took the unusual step of requesting the Office of Public Works to prepare an Environmental Impact Study. As in the case of the Coto Doñana wetlands in southern Spain, the Burren project served to highlight the real dilemma inherent in tourist development: how to preserve unique and unspoilt areas whilst at the same time improving access for visitors. Doñana, siting its visitor centres on the periphery and rigorously controlling tourist access, has been accused of arrogance and elitism and of ignoring the needs and wishes of the local population. It counters with the view that unless such draconian measures are adopted there would shortly be nothing left for the tourists to come and see. It is a universal problem that admits of no easy solution. SFADCo itself, which announced in 1991 a programme aimed at developing new business ideas in tourism aimed at the overseas market, faces similar dichotomies. Brendan Russell, who devised the six-month course, envisaged new leisure activities, holidays catering for older people and single women, now more inclined to travel on their own. 'They will be products with an Irish flavour and will give Ireland a distinctive edge in product choice,' he said.[12] It remains to be seen whether the resultant flavours will carry an E number.

Antigua ... Malta ... Tahiti (which retreated with the coming of the airport in the early 1960s from being by any standards 'an island paradise' into a mercenary, culturally-exploited and over-priced tourist trap)—it couldn't happen here. Not, certainly, on that scale; but there is no doubt that Irish tourism, of which that promoted by Shannon Development is a significant exemplar, is entering a new phase. Is it socially or politically desirable to create havens for the rich and 'do absolutely nothing with south-west Clare'? Is it even feasible? Is it culturally acceptable to fill the landscape with bungalow-bliss self-catering tourist cottages and preserve the last of the traditional and endangered species of domestic architecture in folk-parks? These, and other questions which address themselves to the tourism 'mix'

[131]

and to the dilemma of advancing the industry whilst preserving the very attractions upon which it is based, have no simple answers—neither in the Shannon Region nor beyond. Meanwhile, a consultative report produced by Shannon Development in 1990,[13] though by early 1992 not adopted as official policy, suggested that 'the region needs a mega-attraction, a major international themed product or park which could establish itself and indeed Ireland at international level'. Leprechaunland, à la Disney? On a more immediate and mundane level the document was concerned with perceived inadequacies in 'public transport, all-weather facilities, night life, campsites, cheap and medium hotels' . . . and 'bed occupancy performance'.

Brian Merriman would have approved.

References

1. Interview on *Mo Cheol Thú*, RTE Radio, 10 February 1991
2. *The Irish Times*, 30 October 1991
3. *Ireland of the Welcomes*, Dublin, May–June 1965, p. 27
4. 'The Bunratty Folk Park', in *North Munster Studies*, Limerick 1967, p. 499
5. *Limerick Leader*, 4 July 1964
6. See p. 188
7. 18 August 1969
8. *The Irish Times*, 9 December 1975
9. 'Community Tourism—the Ballyhoura Case Study', address to the Irish Planning Institute National Planning Conference, 1990
10. Minutes, 15 June 1979
11. *Three days on the Shannon*, Dublin 1852, p. 2
12. *The Irish Times*, 5 July 1991
13. *Planning for Growth: developing tourism in the Shannon Region until 1995*, report by Shannon Development, 1990

CHAPTER 6

On the Way to the Technopolis

In 1991 the city of Limerick celebrated the tercentenary of the treaty which ended the Williamite wars in Ireland. Before the event, which by general consensus was both well-conducted and, given the near-saturation of the festival and commemoration market, well-patronised, there were the usual begrudging voices. The siege was not worth remembrance, local politician and historian Jim Kemmy had claimed at a public debate the previous December. 'If we are to be emotionally aroused and react to the centenary of this national debacle,' said Kevin Hannon, consultant editor of Kemmy's *Old Limerick Journal*, 'let us lower our national flag to halfmast and enfold our treaty stone in a black mantle.'[1]

'It has been dolefully remarked that only Limerick would celebrate a treaty such as that signed in the city 300 years ago,' wrote David Hanly, also a native son, in *The Sunday Tribune.*[2] Was it for this, many wondered with him, the wild geese spread the grey wing on every tide? Nor was scepticism entirely absent from the Sieges and Treaty Symposium held at the University of Limerick on 4 April 1991. In his paper on 'Sarsfield, the man and the myth', Dr Liam Irwin suggested, perhaps only half in jest, that the hero of Ballyneety had sold the Catholic Irish for thirty tuns of French wine. 'And the humorous side of the Limerick personality,' said the *Limerick Leader*,[3] 'sometimes seems calculated to generate just as much heat as the hard edge.'

The symposium, organised and chaired by Professor Noel Mulcahy, dean of the faculty of engineering and chairman of the education and history committee of 'Treaty 300', as the 1991 celebration/commemoration was predictably entitled, produced a scholarly and generally non-controversial overview of the events of 300 years before. It was introduced by the university's president, Dr Edward Walsh, who drew the attention of his listeners to a somewhat later period—the year 1744—when 'the American colonies had three degree-awarding colleges, Harvard, William and Mary, and Yale. These were based on English university colleges, teaching young gentlemen Greek and Latin grammar, rhetoric, mathematics and philosophy. In June 1744, after the commissioners of Maryland and Virginia had negotiated a treaty with the Indians of the Six Nations ... they cordially invited them to send some of their sons to William and Mary College to enjoy the benefits of a classical education.

'The Indians considered the invitation. This was their reply: "We know that you highly esteem the kind of Learning taught in those colleges, and that the Maintenance of our young Men, while with you, would be very expensive to you. We are convinc'd, therefore, that you mean to do us Good by your Proposal.... We have had some experience of it. Several of our young People were formerly brought up at the Colleges of the Northern Provinces; they were instructed in all your Sciences; but, when they came back to us, they were bad Runners, ignorant of every means of living in the Woods, unable to bear either Cold or Hunger, knew neither how to build a Cabin, take a Deer, or kill an Enemy, spoke our language imperfectly, were therefore neither fit for Hunters, Warriors, nor Counsellors; they were totally good for nothing. We are, however, not the less oblig'd by your kind Offer, tho' we decline accepting it; and, to show our grateful Sense of it, if the Gentlemen of Virginia will send us a dozen of their Sons, we will take care of their Education, instruct them in all we know, and make Men of them."'[4] Of marginal relevance, perhaps, to the matter of 1691 but not without significance in the context of the academic institution under the aegis of which the historical examination was being conducted.

In the mid-1950s the College of Technology in the city of Newcastle, New South Wales, housed an embryonic university which, pending the granting of full academic status, was for the time being under the dual tutelage of the New South Wales University of Technology in Sydney and the University of New England in Armidale. The rudimentary arts faculty was entrusted with the provision both of conventional courses leading to arts degrees and 'Humanities' courses—in English, history, philosophy and correlated subjects—for chemical, engineering and other technical students. If it was difficult to convince an incipient steelworker (Newcastle was a major centre of heavy industry) of the relevance to his future of *She stoops to conquer*, it was almost equally so to bring the arts and science faculties themselves together in any form of meaningful dialogue. Someone suggested a forum, subsequently named, with only minimal irony, 'The Ivory Tower', in which each side might learn something of the other's disciplines. The senior lecturer in English led off with a disquisition on one of Milton's sonnets which was not unsympathetically received by the technicians. At the next meeting it was the turn of

[134]

his opposite number in chemistry, who chose as his topic recent developments in the periodic table of elements. The ivory tower toppled shortly thereafter into the apparently unbridgable gap between the School of Humanities and those whom it was its purpose and duty to humanise.

'The School of Humanities—the choice of name is neo-Orwellian—' wrote Patricia Palmer in *The Irish Review*[5] 'is less an arts faculty than its deliberate replacement. Just as the University [of Limerick] was seen earlier to empty arts of their real meaning, so the Humanities School hollows out the recognised forms of an arts programme and fills them instead with unfamiliar shapes and simulacra.' Her criticism of the University of Limerick's 'enterprise culture' underlines the deep academic division that has existed virtually since the government decided to establish in the 1970s a six-man planning board to chart the course of third-level education in the city. Limerick had been campaigning for decades for a fully-independent university on the model of one of the constituent colleges of the National University of Ireland, and the University Project group was represented on a consultative body which also included Paul Quigley, then general manager of Shannon Development. The chairman and chief executive was Edward Walsh.

"One of the best things I ever did," said Quigley, "was to be a member of the board which selected Ed Walsh as first director of the NIHE ... I was never so sure at an interview that this was right." The favourable reaction was mutual: Quigley impressed Walsh as "a very nice person with a sense of mission. I had spent the previous ten years in the kind of university that I think he and others felt Limerick needed". Walsh, who had been teaching nuclear engineering in Virginia, wanted to return to Ireland to work in industry. When the NIHE project was announced following the setting up of the Higher Education Authority by Donough O'Malley, he was urged to apply, was successful, and found himself in Limerick knowing virtually nothing either of the city or the project itself. The empathy with Shannon Development, and with Quigley in particular was, however, quick to make itself manifest—in the first instance in the choice of a site for the new institute. "I had anticipated that we would spend the first x years squabbling about where it should be located. But Shannon Development had brought a group of local authority people together and said 'this guy has been appointed and by the time he arrives in you should have six or eight possible sites'—and this they had."

Before Paul Quigley joined SFADCo as general services manager in February 1960 he had been director and secretary of the Irish Management Institute in Dublin, and this background served to strengthen an already strong awareness as to the vital role of education and training in the programme for industrial development in the region. In July 1968 An Comhairle Oiliúna (AnCO) opened a training centre on the Industrial Estate, the company contributing to the project by leasing the building and assisting in the planning of courses and selection of staff. Quigley himself became chairman of AnCO—a state agency—in February 1971. "We made two decisions of fundamental importance to the subsequent development of the industrial infrastructure in this country," said Tom Callanan: "to go for high-skilled mechanical engineering and high value-added air-freightability.... That led to AnCO. AnCO did not happen as a result of natural growth from the Apprentice Training Board, but because what was happening here was beginning to be seen as something that was applicable nationally."

When SFADCo was given the responsibility for small industry development in 1978 it was clear to Paul Quigley that people would need training at management level. Apart from a few courses in local technical colleges such instruction was only available at the IMI in Dublin. "We decided we needed a training centre here—locally and at a fair price. We came up with a plan for a Regional Management Centre at Plassey." The IMI objected, its then chairman, David Kennedy, attacking the additional cost to the taxpayer. But the project, according to Quigley, involved no such imposition, and it went ahead in the face of such objections and those of the IDA, which "could never see the need for regional management centres". The company called back Lichfield to produce a second report concentrating on the educational needs of the region and effectively influenced a committee that was agitating for a university to press for an institution that it considered more appropriate.

The rancour created by the emergence of the gaudy, high-tech NIHE from an academically conventional chrysalis showed little sign of abating in the course of the first two decades of its existence, academic jealousies deferring only to the sexual in their virulence. Quigley, on his own admission, had a very difficult time as chairman of the governing body from 1975 to 1987; but it was Edward Walsh who sustained—and continued to sustain—the main brunt of the attack. "I took two key words: excellence and relevance. The North Americans believe you can be both. The European universities have not yet accepted this. So that concept was not enormously welcomed." It was also far from being fully understood, and Walsh found he had to "lean over backwards to differentiate myself from the strong presence of the existing university colleges. This annoyed the project committee because we proclaimed what we were not going to do as frequently as what we were going to do".

It also annoyed many within the ambit of academic politics in the country as a whole. The NIHE concept, which Walsh admits was plagiarised unabashedly from North America, involved the integration of practical work with teaching and, as has been seen, a view of the relevance of the traditional arts curriculum seriously at odds with that then prevailing in the established universities. There was no sense of welcome from Trinity, said Walsh. The response from Cork, his own university, was far from helpful, though UCC "suddenly started to realise that Limerick had educational needs". Given his position, as reiterated in an address to new graduates in September 1989[6] that the older universities 'excelled at being irrelevant', he can scarcely have been very surprised; but following his success in securing support from the World Bank, attitudes, he said, changed. "At that point the penny dropped. 'What are they planning in Limerick? Let's stop it!'"

At this juncture national—as distinct from academic—politics also came into play with the fall of the Fianna Fáil government in February 1973 and its replacement by a Fine Gael/Labour coalition. Walsh's recollection of subsequent events lost nothing with the passage of time. "The first lot were about to graduate. The good Richard Burke [Minister for Education] took a proposition into Cabinet which I think was a proposition to make us a separate university. But others in the Cabinet thought otherwise and over a weekend we had to change to the plan to make us a recognised college of the NUI. We were assigned to Cork. Nasty things started to happen. Trinity made an overture to us over lunch. It was heard that we were talking to Trinity. There was a leak suggesting that the mathematics in Limerick were somewhat doubtful—great suspicions that this was Cork. This neutralised us—TCD could not possibly continue to talk." Richard Burke's effigy was subsequently burnt in Limerick; the NIHE's budget was cut by one quarter in 1975 and as negotiations with the NUI over its status continued there were student protests. 'They object to the fact that at the moment diplomas (the three-year course) and degrees (the four-year course) are to be awarded by two different bodies,' wrote *The Irish Times* educational correspondent, Christina Murphy,[7] 'and that students who are at the moment in their final year still do not know who is awarding their degrees.'

Edward Walsh maintained that the whole endeavour came close to complete collapse during this period, but with the return of Fianna Fáil to power in June 1978 the situation recovered and the NIHE Limerick Act of 1980 established the Institute as an autonomous statutory body, paving the way for its emergence as a fully independent university. 'Limerick campaigned for a university,' wrote Christina Murphy, 'but in fact has got something better which has a much greater contribution to make to a developing region such as Shannon than a traditional academic university.' Though this view was steadily to gain ground there remained those, such as Patricia Palmer, with serious reservations concerning the module system which 'encourages

50. *Edward Walsh (left) with Desmond O'Malley at the opening of the Hunt Museum at the National Institute of Higher Education (subsequently the University of Limerick), 14 April 1978.*

51. *The Innovation Centre at Plassey from the air.*

superficial learning and the short-term accumulation of facts. The module system delivers capsules of facts in short bursts and, therefore, is well enough suited to some technical subjects with a defined factual load. What it cannot offer, however, is a framework for exploration in depth, wide reading or sustained thought. To peg "humanities" subjects into such a hostile matrix is, inevitably to do violence to them'.[8] The debate will continue.

☆ ☆ ☆ ☆ ☆ ☆

"The minute I saw it I said that's it." Walsh's acceptance of the proposed Plassey site for the National Institute of Higher Education had been immediate and enthusiastic. The location, some five kilometres from the city centre on the left bank of the Shannon, was clearly the best of the nine possibilities which had been assembled, and with SFADCo's property section acting as intermediary the existing dwelling and seventy acres were acquired for £70,000. The White House—the nickname was to stick for a number of reasons—was to constitute the entire campus from the opening in 1972 with a faculty of twelve until the commissioning of new buildings, the product of an international architectural competition, in 1976. That year Edward Walsh was appointed to the SFADCo board by the minister, Justin Keating, acting on the advice of Paul Quigley, thus formalising an already close relationship. "When I became a director," he said, "I saw that behind it lay a very sophisticated, well-geared organisation. Change created opportunity—even problems created opportunity."

From discussions between Walsh, Quigley and Padraic White, chief executive of the IDA, there emerged the concept of a technological park at the Plassey site as a means not only of preventing available land close to the NIHE from being developed for irrelevant purposes but of confirming the Institute's ideological orientation. 'For anyone who has ever spent any time in that corner of California where microchips are grown,' wrote Douglas Kennedy in 1985,[9] 'the idea of a technological university spawning a technological park is not a new one. . . . In Ireland, however, the development of Plassey Technological Park is a first for the country.' A joint venture involving the NIHE, Shannon Development and the IDA, the necessary land was put together in the 1970s and it was opened in 1980. "What we want to do here is to create an information-rich environment," said Tom Callanan, who became Plassey's chief executive in April 1990, "which means that you have information plus its access to technology woven around an area which has the capability of very high productivity and access to skills. I use the concept sometimes—'A new Florence'—where you're talking about a mixture of culture and craft in a way in which Florence spearheaded the whole change in the Renaissance environment."

A beguiling concept, but one which is quite revolutionary in terms of a national culture which has largely failed to admit the role of science and scientific enquiry. 'The absence of science from the Irish political tradition as a source of ideology,' wrote Dorinda Outram[10] 'points up the isolation of even radical Irish politics from the continental mainstream, where science-as-progress/reason-as-justice has been present ever since the days of Condorcet ....' Plassey's role is seen as a major contribution to redressing this imbalance. In the words of one of its promotional brochures it 'is a unique example of a technopole emerging to meet the needs of the next century'. There is plausible justification for the description 'unique' in the national sense; but the real significance of Plassey lies within the regional context.

As Roy Johnston has put it[11] 'The essence of the "technopole model" of regional development is that a region is defined in terms of a hinterland of a third level college, having a strong research and development component associated with its courses, so that people emerging from its postgraduate schools are in a position to recognise opportunities and become associated with innovative enterprises, catalysing the development of regional economic life. This model was implicit in the decision to found the NIHE in Limerick. The present strong link between the NIHE, now Limerick University, and Shannon Development, our only effective Regional Development Agency, as expressed in the joint management of Plassey Park as an enterprise development area, is an embodiment of the "technopole model"'. Given an added dimension by the presence of the National Microelectronics Applications Centre and the Innovation Centre, opened in July 1980, Plassey would appear to be on course for, in Tom Callanan's words, "creating a centre which will be impervious to the ordinary forces of economic life". By this he does not imply some kind of technocratic Arcadia, but rather the creation of the opportunity for young scientists and engineers to participate in the most advanced technologies without having to go to Munich or Eindhoven to do so ... and with that opportunity, a cultural and social environment that will exert a centripetal pull strong enough keep them at home.

The new University of Limerick Foundation Building, privately financed, will establish a highly specialised research centre with places for some 500 doctoral and post-doctoral students with arts and cultural facilities including live theatre. The irony will not be lost on the traditionalists. "I have seen successful people who have had a strong foundation in science continuing to work in that area and subsequently they have enjoyed the arts," said

52. Heavy industry: the Aughinish Alumina plant on the Shannon estuary.

*53. Small industry: Martina O'Dea,
Coisceim Cheese, Carron, Co. Clare,
14 September 1982.*

Edward Walsh, himself an accomplished musician and art collector. "There may be exceptions to prove the rule but generally Arts people are not in a position to go on and learn the sciences."[12] There is little room, in Dr Walsh's brave new world, for ivory towers.

At a special meeting of the board of SFADCo held in Dublin on 26 October 1977 to consider draft submissions to the Minister for Industry and Commerce on the future role of the company, Dr Walsh voiced his objections to any diminution of its regional industrial functions. Michael Killeen, managing director of the IDA, was then a very powerful figure on the board and was by some accounts most unhappy at the growing importance of the Shannon company in industrial development and wanted it out of it. It was believed that he persuaded Brendan O'Regan that the company could have a future somewhere other than in industrial promotion. The opposition of interests was directly related to the fact that the IDA had never accepted the Buchanan concept of selected major growth areas, preferring to gear the placement of industry to the operation of market forces and the pressures of individual needs. However, for Edward Walsh and others, like Quigley, who thought like him, the creation of a technopolis based on Limerick depended not only on the establishment of industry on the Plassey site itself but on the balancing industrial development of the region as a whole. In respect of Plassey the aim was to be impressively realised with the attraction of Wang and Varian International as 'anchor tenants'; but the change in policy announced by Desmond O'Malley in May 1978 was a major setback to those, Tom Dunne among them, who favoured integrated regional development. At the simplest level, said Dunne, who was to succeed Paul Quigley as SFADCo's chief executive, it came down to "the pragmatical fact of executives based in Limerick looking after industrialists—a matter of geography". The industrialists, he added, did not want to make a fuss about the change, "particularly as they had to start dealing with the IDA".

"SFADCo played a huge part in persuading us to come here," said Cathal O'Shannon of Aughinish Alumina. "It was a joint IDA/SFADCo thing . . . in those days there was no IDA office down here."

From the IDA point of view, of course, it always appeared quite illogical that their national responsibility should be arbitrarily diluted in respect of the Mid-West region, creating, in effect, an embarassingly blank space on the map.[13] This anomaly was not to be ended by the removal from SFADCo of responsibility for large and middle-size development and the announcement of its new role in small industry: in the IDA brochure *Small Industries are Big Business*, dated July 1980, the map exhibits three shades of green: one for Designated Areas, one for Non-Designated, and a third, whether by accident or design the strongest, for Shannon Development. Thus, though the national authority welcomed the opportunity to amend its cartography in respect of major industry it did not react to Shannon's new mandate with any degree of enthusiasm: SFADCo, for its part, welcomed the move as a positive step towards integrated regional development. A draft agreement on the new role was drawn up between the two bodies in advance of the minister's announcement of the operational date of 8 May 1978, but a difference of interpretation arose a year later concerning the criterion of size as it should be applied to a 'small industry'. Did sixty-four jobs being offered by a company called Litex Ltd lift it out of the latter category?

In July 1979 disagreement developed with Michael Killeen over the matter of the Innovation Centre at Plassey, a concept conceived of by Shannon, its sponsors, as making the fullest possible use of the resources of the Limerick NIHE for advancing technology in small industry. Killeen alleged that consultation with the IDA had been inadequate on the matter of the Plassey site as a whole and that the plan itself was, in the view of that organisation, technically unsound and excessively costly. It also failed to make adequate provision for the needs of the IDA, which had at that time two major projects (Wang and Varian) pressing for sites of about eighty acres. In the absence of involvement in the Shannon planning study the IDA had been obliged to prepare its own outline scheme. A compromise was reached which did not entirely satisfy either party—a conclusion not untypical of the continuing relationship between two bodies finding themselves frequently at loggerheads through no inherent fault of their own.

"We have tried to develop and operate a regional policy within a country in which there has been no regional policy and that has brought us fundamentally into conflict situations, because essentially this country is structured with strong national agencies operating out of Dublin," said Tom Dunne. "What you have here is a not very strong but very persistent and tenacious little agency operating down the country and getting into the hair of everybody." And he added, with some measure of defiance, "the day we cease to get into the hair of everybody we cease to be effective."

In 1978 the tenacious little agency found the omens somewhat less than propitious for the new responsibility which had been thrust upon it—a responsibility which it was being called upon to deliver in a disconcertingly short period of time. The company's efforts were to be judged, O'Malley told the Dáil on 1 March 1978, on 'how they go about the job and how relevant

[143]

the plans and strategies that they achieve will be to the development of the indigenous industry in the whole country'. In the wake of the recession of the 1970s he had become concerned at the danger of over-reliance on the multinationals and had observed the success of countries like Korea in licensing-in technology for exploitation by domestic firms. 'The IDA by its very success could create for us a major sociological problem in ten years' time,' he told the Seanad.[14] 'Eighty per cent or even more of our industry will be foreign-owned and foreign controlled. I am worried in a long-term way about that . . . I will not interfere in any way with the IDA's activities. They are regarded by the people of America and elsewhere as the premier industrial development organisation in the world. At the same time we cannot afford to neglect our own people. . . . Another organisation pressing for industrial development in this country, in a way that is not in competition with the IDA, but parallel to it, will achieve useful results without in any sense cutting across the efforts of the IDA or duplicating them. The most successful regional organisation in the country, Shannon Development, should be the one to spearhead an intensive all-out effort to develop entrepreneurship and industrial development among our own people.'

This Seanad speech is particularly interesting in that the minister used it as an opportunity to reassess the role of SFADCo at a crucial juncture in its history. He told the House that he had considered the option of setting up another state board to implement his plan for indigenous industry, but came to the conclusion that this would be a foolish course when he had available a 'highly competent board with a great deal of experience in these matters, with men on the board and in the executive who had shown themselves down through the years to be not just competent but above all else to be innovative'. Though he thought some might prefer to see Shannon Development remaining localised, 'a regionalised second-class IDA', he inclined to the view that it had the ability to respond to the new mandate 'no matter how many begrudgers there may be in the early days when the task is set about'. He foresaw the scheme, should it prove successful in the two-year experimental period, extending under the Shannon aegis to other regions, noting that the company had already expanded to some extent beyond its own borders. 'One of its major castles is in Co. Galway and it was instrumental in helping the establishment of the thatched cottage village development in Renvyle, Co. Galway and in Ballycastle in Co. Mayo. . . . One could see this company developing as a sort of West of Ireland Development Board rather than just a Shannon Development Board.'

Such a prospect can scarcely have provoked much enthusiasm in the SFADCo boardroom, where there was profound concern over the immediate problems of implementing the O'Malley plan closer to home. The minister had made it plain that the company would be judged, not on the criterion of the number of jobs created at the end of the two years, but on the success or otherwise of its strategies in relation to the development of indigenous industry at national level. It was thus not simply a matter of a quick, cosmetic exercise involving the production of employment which might prove to be ultimately unsustainable but would meet a two-year target, but of altering the whole climate of thinking throughout the region in the process of achieving a minor social revolution. The obstacles to such a course were assessed as follows by the company on 16 March 1979: (1) Lack of an industrial base, and consequently of individual skills, in most of the towns and villages outside the sphere of influence of the central area; (2) lack of suitable buildings in practically all locations; (3) lack of specific financial packages geared to the needs of the small-scale, first-time entrepreneur; (4) management deficiencies in varying degrees; (5) lack of drive and willingness to expand on the part of small (often one-man) operations; (6) much of existing small industry classified as 'sensitive'.

Difficulties had already arisen in working on the new plan within the existing County Development system and the company had further identified areas with special problems, including north-west Clare, south-west Limerick, (centering on Abbeyfeale/Athea), south-west Tipperary (North Riding), and Southill housing estate in Limerick city.

Shannon's response to the challenge was to put in place a comprehensive range of support systems. A Field Officer was appointed for each county and for Limerick city to work in co-operation with the County Development teams to source and service projects at local level. A Business Services Division was established to advise small firms on finance, production, product development and marketing, and a 'Matchmaker' service launched to encourage larger industry to seek suppliers among smaller firms. In Limerick city a 'workspace' project inaugurated in April 1981 offered low-cost accommodation and shared facilities and overheads to very small manufacturing businesses. A series of practical handbooks was produced under the title *Mid-West Guidelines* (and subsequently utilised, in translation, by Hommeh, the small business agency in Greece). A periodical, *Enterprise*, was also circulated to over 1,000 outlets.

Youth Enterprise Shannon Ltd (YES) was established 'to promote and encourage the development by young persons of industrial and commercial undertakings at or near Shannon', and a programme undertaken in 1979 among emigrants in Britain and the United States to attract people with job-creating ideas back to the region. A competition was launched in association

54. *The Workspace at Michael Street, Limerick, planned to assist small enterprises through the sharing of basic resources and services.*

55. *Hilary Henry of Lakeshore Foods, Tipperary. Her project was evaluated and assisted by the Limerick Food Centre established by Shannon Development.*

with the Industrial Credit Company to promote craft enterprise. A permanent exhibition of the products of almost 200 small firms was opened in 1979 in Ballycaseymore House, near the airport and a range of new and restored buildings, either on individual sites or in 'clusters' was provided for sale or lease. 'Clusters' was the IDA name, sounding, said Paul Quigley, "like chickens coming in under a hen. So somebody came up with 'Enterprise Centre', and it became a national name". And one of Shannon's more imaginative ventures into nomenclature: though 'clusters' is again back in vogue with a slightly different connotation.[15]

"There was a tremendous feeling in the company," said Quigley, "that now we've got a worthwhile job. One of the first things I did was to go off to America and visit the Small Business Administration in Washington and the Small Business Association of New England. We came back with more possibilities than we actually got done." The company's new chairman, Frank McCabe, who had been appointed managing director of EI at Shannon in 1970 and was subsequently its chief executive, was at the time working in the United States and he felt that a dramatic target, of about 2,000 jobs, must be set and achieved if success was to be measurable. Pat Sheehan, who, like many of his contemporaries, had worked for SFADCo in a variety of capacities, became involved in the setting up of the new Business Services Division which provided the emerging small firms both with advice and practical aid: "We held their hand, went to banks with them."

Paul Sheane, untypical in that he joined the company in 1980 from the private sector, (he was to become its chief executive in 1992), found that "suddenly you were supposed to be an expert on finance and marketing and production . . . a very complex sort of game. A range of situations, a range of companies: between you, you were trying to make a business work. I suppose that's where the real satisfaction came from". He recalled two NIHE graduates who came to him with what they thought was a good idea and believed they could make a business out of it. But "they didn't know anything about business, they didn't know anything about the world, they were still in college. I remember having long discussions with them and saying 'with all due respects you'll never make a business out of this yourselves—you've got to get someone else'". They did: and their company, Ashling Microsystems, was in 1990 employing some seventy people in Plassey.

In the first full year of the programme a total of 2,120 new jobs was approved.[16] Job 'approvals' are, of course, statistically suspect and that form of assessment has been largely abandoned in favour of actual jobs created, but the figure serves to indicate something of the impact of the scheme when taken in conjunction with that for the following year—1,614—which repre-

[147]

sented 140 small industry projects. By August 1980 the minister felt himself able to tell the Dáil, during the course of the debate on the Shannon Free Airport Development Company (Amendment) Bill, that the experiment had been successful. 'The experience gained throughout the pilot role period by the company has, and will continue to be of benefit in identifying and solving the problems of this very resilient sector of Irish industry.' At his direction the company's mandate was extended the same month to include south and west Offaly.

As in the case of Ashling Microsystems, a number of the small firms setting up in business were hoping to link in with the Mid-West's promulgated new role as the 'Silicon Valley of Europe'. Though many of the major industries establishing in the region had a pronounced high-tech orientation, with few exceptions they continued to locate their research and development facilities elsewhere—normally at the overseas parent plant.

'Bye-bye Pie-in-the-Sky, Hello Reality!' was the sobering headline on an article on the future of the Mid-West in *Electronics Report* for December 1984/January 1985. 'The Limerick Region is no longer the "silicon valley of Europe". If it ever looked like becoming so, that day is gone. True, there are thousands of people employed in hi-tech industry and business in the region, but all of the big multi-nationals have, in recent years, concentrated in Dublin, and more especially in Cork. Limerick/Shannon/ Ennis—the golden triangle—is running out of steam.' Although the region had 'a plethora of small Irish-owned support industries', for the most part run by people who had begun their careers as electronics engineers in one of the major companies, the Telesis Report of 1982 had criticised the overall cost of Shannon's 'hand-holding' functions and suggested that the company be more discriminatory in supplying these services.

A judgment such as this must be viewed against the background of a period of severe recession when developmental expenditure was failing to arrest net job losses. An Economic and Social Research Institute report published in November 1986[17] concluded that 'The experience of the Mid-West region constitutes a useful precedent for the successful conduct of the process of decentralisation and for the creation of the conditions needed for promoting innovation and setting up new firms. . . . The cost of the Shannon experience has been high and some of its initiatives could be questioned. However, it is undeniable that a new climate has been created in the region characterised by a remarkable entrepreneurial dynamism. This is manifest, not only in technology and industry in the narrow sense, but also in renovation of towns, adaptation of the services of Shannon Airport and development of cultural activities'.

When the worst of the recession was over the Dublin-based Small Firms Association, in a Mid-West Regional Report issued on 19 November 1990, concluded as a result of a survey of 103 responding firms in the area that 'in addition to the much improved economic condition since 1987, Shannon Development's regional mandate has significantly benefited firms in the Mid-West', though it felt that the company's claim that it had been instrumental in limiting the worst effects of the early and mid-1980s recession and had spearheaded expansion in the post-1986 recovery period needed independent verification. It recommended the formation of a Cabinet sub-committee to promote regional development, review Shannon's effectiveness and achievements and apply the lessons of such a review throughout the country. Describing the company as 'the *only* fully-integrated regional development agency', it suggested that it had made a significant contribution to strengthening the region's small industry and recommended that other agencies operating within the area should come under its overall co-ordinating authority. 'As presently structured,' the report concluded, 'they are an under-utilised source.'

The small industry estate at Smithstown, on the other side of the N19 at Shannon, had been an early example of 'spin-off' development from major industries in the Free Zone. Outside the 'golden triangle', however, removed from direct contact with the high-tech environment, the small industry picture was somewhat different. "If I went to Terryglass or Borrisoleigh," said Tomás O'Domhnaill of Shannon's Nenagh office, "I was more likely to get people who wanted to make hurleys, windows or do general engineering for the farming community ... I couldn't have got, with hindsight, people who would have been happy with the Plassey Technological Park." He recalled a tip-off from a local councillor about the year 1979 that a man was picking up cloth at the local railway station. On investigation it was discovered that his wife was "a stitcher making clothes and he was cutting cloth. They now [1990] have an ultra-modern factory and twenty people working for them". But the scope for such felicitous discoveries was limited. Enquiries had risen from fifty a year in the early days to about 400 in 1990, according to Joe Price in the Birr office, but less projects were resulting proportionately. All the latent possibilities, he believed, had been used up, a view shared by O'Domhnaill. "With the passing of time we had drained out the amount of latent expertise or initiative that was in the county. Not alone were we trying to scrape the bottom of the barrel—we had gone into the ground." Aid to existing enterprises, however, was sometimes fruitful: Banagher Concrete saw the opportunity for a high-tech product and began exporting to the Channel Tunnel project; Tipperary Spring Water was one of the larger suc-

[149]

cesses; an advance factory in Shinrone, a tiny village, was occupied within twelve months. On the other hand attempts to promote initiative in Ferbane were regarded as a failure.

In Co. Clare in 1990 there were 170 small industries in production, employing up to fifty people. "We give aid to anything that replaces imports, has export potential or a niche market," said Martin McKeogh of the Ennis office: the frequently unglamorous business of building on reality.

The two ESB power stations, Tarbert and Moneypoint, are clearly visible from the windows of Glin Castle: "I look at them every day of my life," says Desmond FitzGerald. "The first was a long time ago. When the second one happened I said to myself if there's one there or there's two there it makes absolutely no difference. The estuary's already been spoilt." He was concerned, though philosophical, about the threat to develop a major harbour at Glin: "It's incredibly deep just here—a better site for a port than Foynes. I have always taken the view that probably, sometime, there will be more development here anyway. You have to take stock of the country's scenic areas as a whole and the Shannon estuary, though a scenic area, is not as important as Bantry or Clew Bay or Killary. . . . "

No single aspect of development in the Shannon Region has aroused such deep feeling and been the product of so much utter futility as that relating to the estuary. The first major report—by G. Maunsell and Partners to the Shannon Estuary Company—was published in 1960. *Integrated Development of the Shannon Estuary: A Strategic Study*, by Shannon Development appeared in September 1989. In the interim the estuary had been the subject of some thirty documented investigations including an examination of the potential for tourism and recreation by Nathaniel Lichfield and Associates (1968); a site investigation on a proposed lower channel (Dredging Investigations Ltd), 1970; a report on the investigation of pollution on the Lower Shannon (An Foras Forbartha, 1973); an industrial location study by the same body (1983); a water quality management plan (Limerick, Clare and Kerry County Councils and Limerick Corporation, 1988) . . . and this is only a fragment of the formal paperwork. Newspaper articles, private initiatives, political promises, aborted leglislation, ad hoc committees, County Council resolutions, foreign consultants . . . all have ended in the same stultifying outcome, the result of the inability or unwillingness of any of the interested parties to adopt a common course of action or even to co-operate in any meaningful sense.

"Brendan O'Regan made a bit of an effort following Lichfield," said Desmond O'Malley. "I took it up when I came in here [as Minister for Industry, Commerce and Energy] in 1977. I acknowledged that he had made every effort and he had not succeeded and did not want to go back to it again ... so I picked the then Limerick County Manager, Dick Haslam, who was a very able man and a very committed man and I gave him essentially the same brief.... And the man tried for two or three years and he came back to me and said 'I have tried everything and I can't'. You've no idea of the little parochial suspicions they all have of one another—it's heartbreaking."

'Initially, a Joint Port Committee will be established,' SFADCo stated with totally misplaced confidence in 1970.[18] 'Through the working of this Joint Committee it is anticipated that the various harbour authorities would be given an opportunity of co-operating to the fullest extent in their existing functions, resulting by mid-1972 in the emergence of a single unified authority.' The projected role of the Joint Committee was to promote the estuary and prepare, in consultation with 'various planning authorities', a detailed plan for its full and proper development. These bodies included the harbour authorities at Kilrush/Cappagh, Foynes and Limerick. 'From the viewpoint of the region as a whole', the SFADCo report continued, 'the existence of a unified authority would give undoubted impetus and direction to the promotion and development of the estuary as a location for those industries for which access to sheltered deep water is a critical factor.'

It was not to be. Even the withdrawal of the Limerick Steamship Company's services to Britain and mainland Europe in that same year did nothing to inject a sense of urgency into the situation. "There were awful disputes," said O'Malley, "as to whether there should be two or three members of the Clare County Council on it and why should Kerry have as many as Clare when their shoreline in Clare is three times longer than the Kerry one...." In 1975 the situation, as described somewhat more dispassionately by *The Irish Times*[19] had altered little: 'What has restricted the development of the Shannon Estuary over the years has been the inability of its administrators to speak with a unified voice on matters affecting its development as a centre for maritime industry and major shipping activities. This in turn has deprived the whole region of the benefits that such a development would bring.'

At this point the campaign for a unified authority had been running for some twelve years, and its total failure had prompted Peter Barry, then Minister for Transport and Power, to introduce into the Dáil in July 1975 legislation designed to achieve this end. 'It will effectively combine the interests of the various port authorities that have existed up to now,' explained *The Irish Times*. It did not. The Bill lapsed with the defeat of the coalition government in 1977. In August of the same year the incoming Minister for Industry, Commerce and Energy (Desmond O'Malley) suggested to the SFADCo board that there was a possible role for the company: there was a need, he said, for a body to develop an overall planning framework. The company, of course, had heard that before.

While all this was happening—or not happening—individual plans were being formulated and disparate development taking place. In 1964 Clare County Council was involved in a proposal, backed by D. P. Honan, chairman of Ennis UDC, to build a bridge from the Battery, near Labasheeda, to Tarbert on the Kerry side. The distance was a modest one mile. Lichfield had recommended a causeway across the mouth of the Fergus, and a feasibility study had been produced by SFADCo, together with an outline development framework for the estuary as a whole (anticipating the minister), in 1974. The bridge plan was, perhaps fortunately, rendered largely exiguous by the opening of the Killimer–Tarbert car ferry and the causeway has not, so far, emerged from the planning process. Industrially, however, there were signs of positive movement. Moneypoint, in Co. Clare, was selected as the site of a major ESB coal-burning power station and in 1973 a brochure produced by Alcan Aluminium Ltd of Canada announced that 'an important new industrial complex, based upon an alumina extraction plant, is proposed for County Limerick. . . . It will provide some 800 new industrial jobs, mostly for skilled workers and tradesmen, with a payroll of hundreds of thousands of pounds annually. It will require an average of 1,200 and up to 2,000 construction employees during 1974 until early 1978 when the plant is due to start operations'.

If you approach Aughinish Island from the Askeaton direction and take the back road at Tomileely there is nothing to prepare you for the visual impact of the largest single development in the region since the Shannon hydro-electric scheme of the late 1920s. Little more than a bohreen, it meanders past scattered settlements as yet largely untainted by 'bungalow blight'. Only when you cross the Poulasceala Creek and find yourself on the purpose-built road to the refinery do you realise the extent of the transformation. Security check, visitors' ID, glasses to protect the eyes from the omnipresent red dust: 1,000 acres of processing plant, steam generating plant, marine terminal and, on the western side of the island, a mud-stacking area for the bauxite residue from the refining process.

"We have constant problems watching that it doesn't breach the dykes," says Cathal O'Shannon, who moved from Dublin as Alcan's public affairs director in 1978 when the plans, the subject of delays attributable to various factors including strong opposition on environmental grounds, had just gone through. The plant finally opened in early 1983, following the employment of more than 6,500 people in the biggest construction project in Europe at the time.

From the top of the tower at the marine terminal (the big bauxite carriers from the Republic of Guinea can be turned round in twenty-four hours) you look back over the kind of landscape that breathes fear into those who see the estuary as a priceless natural resource threatened with extinction by the incursion of heavy industry. The fears extend—and extended specifically in Alcan's case—to the possibilites of air and water pollution from the product itself. "When it's windy enough," says O'Shannon, "you get it blowing around"—and from the disposal of the residue. Alcan's response has been to work closely with the County Council and environmental agencies, to plant trees on a large scale and to establish a wildfowl sanctuary that attracts up to 100 varieties of birds. A major local concern was that the Alcan refinery would be followed by the building of an aluminium smelter on the long-standing IDA landbank at Ballylongford in north Kerry: at present the entire product of the refinery is exported to smelters abroad.

The smelter idea, though officially discounted by Alcan on economic grounds, was to prove markedly tenacious. The involvement of Shannon Development with major industry was reinstated in the 1988 extension of the company's mandate.[20] "We were rather glad" said O'Shannon. "I personally was rather glad, because I had known the old SFADCo and I had made the assumption that the new SFADCo would be the same thing. But the animal had changed considerably. The people we are dealing with now [1990] do not necessarily have the same set of abilities. They would seem a little raw to us and perhaps a little unreal in what they say. They talked about an aluminium smelter, but you put an aluminium smelter where there is cheap power and there's no such thing as cheap power here. We spelt this out in considerable detail. Didn't they come back four months later and say we're seriously thinking of suggesting that we ought to have an aluminium smelter. . . !" On the other hand "whenever there seems to be a hint of trouble coming up—for instance there was the threat of a strike by pilots on the river—they were immediately on to us to see what they could do to help . . . they have a good watching brief. We are constantly looking for the possibility of natural gas to replace our imported oil, and SFADCo have always helped us on that particular thing".

Shannon's estuarial role, in essence one of responsibility without effective power, has not proved an easy one to sustain. 'Decisions taken by the government over the past two years have clearly defined Shannon Development as the agency with major responsibility for those functions (including industry and tourism) which most directly impact on the economic development of the estuary,' the 1989 Strategic Study stated.[21] 'No further authority or legislation is needed to enable the company to push ahead, in conjunction with all other interests, with the implementation of the integrated development strategy proposed in this study. However, appropriate financial arrangements will need to be put in place, and most of the new or improved incentives envisaged in the study will require legislation.' The situation was thus, in 1989, only one or two knight's moves from square one. 'In the absence of any other organisation clearly more central to the entire process,' the Study concluded, 'it is proposed that Shannon Development should act in an overall co-ordinating role to ensure that the necessary momentum is generated and sustained.'

If there is about this rather too much of the *déjà-vu*, the company has, on its own initiative, embarked on specific estuarial projects in the tourism area which have at least had the effect of introducing a practical element into what had remained until recently an aridly theoretical debate.

On a wet spring day in April 1990 Kilrush station building, once a busy terminus of the West Clare railway, lies beached in a wilderness of dereliction. 'At the western end of the station,' wrote Edmund Lenihan in the same year, 'we looked across the wasteland we had arrived through and it was hard to imagine the activity that was a daily (and often nightly) feature of the place for almost seventy years, the shunting, the off-loading and the transfer of cargo. Hard also it was to visualise the terror of the railway guard Michael Ryan whose foot became wedged between the rails here during shunting and whose cries went unnoticed as he was run over and killed by wagon no. 27 on 10 March 1933. His tragedy, in a sense, symbolises the tragedy of Kilrush itself, for in spite of the coming of Moneypoint Power Station, it has well-nigh expired almost unnoticed. A town of broad streets, fine houses and great natural endowments had fallen on lean times and a harbour from which great benefits might still be expected now lies choking to death in mud and silt. One can only hope that the proposed multi-million pound marina and its ancillary projects will help to revive a town that deserves far better of native government than it had got over the past half century".[22]

On this wet April day even the minimal fulfilment of such an aspiration seems immeasurably distant. The town itself appears to be sunk deep in terminal atrophy; the broad sweep of Francis Street leading with false promise down to a harbour area where, obviously, nothing has been

56. In the mind's eye: Kilrush Marina site, February 1988.

57. Dream into reality: Kilrush Marina in 1991.

happening with diurnal frequency over the passage of years since the railway terminal closed once and for all. With it (for it had also been, in its day, a through station) there disappeared the extension to Cappagh pier along which, when it was abandoned together with the rest of the West Clare system in 1961, two trains had run in forty-five years. A second look, however, at the instigation of John Hehir of Shannon Maritime Developments, reveals evidence of work in progress at the harbour mouth: giant cranes, caissons, trucks almost up to their wheel-hubs in the coagulating mud. This, explains Hehir, is the first main contract—'the waterworks'—of the Kilrush project, an ambitious plan to provide the town with not only a first-class marina but with a range of ancillary developments that will encompass time-share apartments, permanent housing, a boatyard, maritime-related industries, shops, leisure facilities. . . .

John Hehir, a local man who worked for eleven years for a German company in Kilrush and also at Moneypoint before gaining experience as a project co-ordinator in the Sultanate of Oman, Saudi Arabia and Egypt, was particularly well-placed to put the marina project into perspective. It started, he said, in a strange way. "As part of the planning permission for Moneypoint there was a stipulation that they would allow a certain amount of money for a marina on the site. The ESB were playing with this, but with small boats around where there's boats up to 180,000 tons coming in with coal they decided it wasn't a runner." A number of areas in West Clare realised that there was money available and ideas started coming in. About the same time Shannon Development had been contacted by the then Minister for the Marine, Brendan Daly, who wanted to encourage a major project on the twelve acres of derelict land in Kilrush that included twelve fishermen's cottages and the vestiges of the railway. The two initiatives coalesced.

"A catalyst with teeth," was Brendan Travers' chemically unorthodox definition of Shannon's role in estuarial development. Alley-catalyst or no, the company in this instance took action on its own behalf, setting up a wholly-owned subsidiary, Shannon Maritime Developments, to bring the Kilrush project to fruition. Travers, a maritime enthusiast ("when I'm not working I'm sailing") had been toying with the idea of a marina on the Shannon for some time. Kilrush, for long a depressed area, needed in his estimation something that would combine both tourism and industry. It is a boom town in summertime, said John Hehir . . . once every hour for ten minutes when the traffic comes through off the Tarbert–Killimer ferry. "Over three hundred thousand use the car ferry—we are not getting even three per cent overnighting in this area." Shannon conducted a pre-feasibility study and in 1988 secured £1.8 million in EC Structural Funding, the first time in Ireland that such a payment had been made direct to an individual project.

Up to this point Brendan Travers had been handling the scheme as a sideline to his main executive role with Shannon Development, but the decision was then taken to establish a separate company with himself as managing director. It was in many ways the fulfilment of a dream, though the dream had yet to be given the configuration of reality.

For the yachtsman sailing the Irish coast westabout there is a very long gap between Castletown Berehaven at the tip of Kerry and Galway Bay—a gap which the Kilrush project was designed at least partially to fill. Travers quoted figures—200,000 boats in France, 100,000 in Germany (most located in other countries), 230 marinas in Britain—to suggest where he saw the business coming from: in Ireland, before Kilrush, there were five marinas with about 500 berths. The development was, thus, heavily geared to the overseas market, which he researched in depth, in the process organising the twinning of Kilrush with Plousanne and its marina near Brest. With a boat of his own on Lough Derg, Travers was looking not only at the estuary but at the Shannon as a whole in terms of pleasure cruising with, additionally, the creation of a chain of small satellite leisure harbours on both shores of the estuary itself and the promotion of Inis Cathaigh, or Scattery Island, offshore from Kilrush, as a major tourist destination. The island was bought from its Belgian owners by a consortium consisting of Shannon Development, the Office of Public Works, Clare County Council and Kilrush Community Development Ltd and is the site of a monastery founded in the sixth century by St Senan.

And Moneypoint, Tarbert, Aughinish, Foynes? The sailing man spoke: "Industries, viewed from a boat, are headlands in their own right. To me a certain amount of that makes the whole sailing thing interesting." He stressed, however, the 'certain amount': the challenge facing estuarial development, apart from the still unresolved problem of achieving a unanimity of interests and the organisational structure to implement it, lies in the delicate balance between the attracting of industry and the fostering of tourism. "It is a total contradiction for us to do the marina at Kilrush and put a slurry pit further up the river," said John A. Daly, chairman of SFADCo, in 1991. But the brief of Shannon Maritime was to promote both industry and tourism in a maritime context; that of its parent company to advance the 'integrated development' of the estuary . . . which may not be exactly the same thing. In July 1990 the latter announced that, jointly with the IDA, it was planning to visit twenty selected US corporations in the subsequent year, nearly half of them in the chemical and pharmaceutical sectors.

'Alcan do not rule out the possibility of adding to their smelter capacity in Europe,' insisted the 1989 Strategic Study: '. . . if additional smelting capacity were to be decided upon the estuary would be a suitable location, provided agreement could be reached on electricity costs.' The view from the Clare side, however, was somewhat different. 'In a [Shannon Development] company report recently published, the emphasis is on selling the Kerry side of the estuary to industrialists at Clare's expense,' Councillor P. J. Kelly told Clare County Council in April 1991[23]: 'They are painting a false and misleading picture by inferring that all the resources are on the Kerry side of the estuary. . . . The promotion by Shannon Development is totally biased and the most misleading I've ever seen from a semi-state body.' An extreme view, perhaps, from a vociferous local advocate. On the other hand the company has come under equally strong attack for allegedly squandering public money at Kilrush on a 'white elephant', particularly as the planned ancillary shore developments by the private sector had, early in 1992, as yet failed to materialise. Storm cones may yet be hoisted off Inis Cathaigh.

'Limerick is without exception the pleasantest town in Ireland,' wrote Frank O'Connor in 1947. It is a view that was not always universally accepted. "In the 1960s, rather than overnight in Limerick we would overnight in Ennis or any fucking place," said Cathal O'Shannon of his visits as an *Irish Times* journalist. The recent past had been, to say the least, colourful: the pogrom against the Jews in 1904; the short-lived Limerick Soviet, first outside the USSR, in 1922; the more recent reputation for gratuitous violence—'Stab City'; the stronghold of confraternities and ostentatiously public religious practice; city of derelict old decency and the newly-created instant ghettoes of Moyross and Southill.

"If you look at the outer suburbs of Limerick city," said Desmond O'Malley, "it doesn't make sense the way it's happened. There are three local authority areas, and coming right up to the city boundary there's the Clare County Council. There was permission for 1,000 houses at Corbally on the banks of the Shannon. Somebody pointed out to them that from the planning point of view this was crazy. Their attitude was 'our only function is to maximise the rateable valuation of the county of Clare. They're only Limerick people anyway'." Limerick people, O'Shannon discovered in the 1960s, could be distinctly unfriendly to outsiders. And outsiders included the inhabitants of Co. Clare in general and Shannon in particular.

SFADCo's first direct involvement with the city was in 1966 when it was proposed that a scheme be discussed with the Corporation for the development of King John's castle as a banqueting centre on the lines of Bunratty: the Office of Public Works was to prepare plans. Three years later the OPW indicated that it would not be free to progress such plans for 'about five

58. *Development potential: The Granary, Limerick city, before restoration, December 1988.*

59. *The Granary restored. In 1992 it housed the Limerick office of Shannon Development, together with other tenants.*

60. The restored King John's Castle, Limerick with the 1691 Treaty Stone in the foreground.

61. At the re-opening of the Castle on 3 October 1991 (left to right): Alderman Jim Kemmy, Mayor of Limerick, John A. Daly, then chairman of Shannon Development and An Taoiseach, Charles J. Haughey.

years' and Austin Dunphy, a former OPW architect then with Lardner & Co. of Dublin, was commissioned to work both on the castle and on a site at Arthur's Quay where there were plans to build a hotel. In December 1970 drawings had been prepared and the Corporation had secured the agreement of the Department of Local Government to rehouse the tenants of the local authority dwellings which had been built within the castle walls.

It was proposed to form a public limited liability company with SFADCo as the major shareholder and the Corporation, the Office of Public Works, Shannonside and the general public participating. This project disappeared into limbo, and it was not until twenty years later, in the context of the 'Limerick Treaty 300' commemoration, that the restoration of the castle and its reorientation as a tourist amenity began in earnest with SFADCo playing a leading role. The re-opening on 3 October 1991 by the Taoiseach, Charles J. Haughey, marked the completion of the £4.2 million restoration project in the course of which significant Hiberno-Norse remains were discovered and incorporated into the exhibition area. A new visitor centre by architects Murray O'Laoire, described by Frank McDonald, *The Irish Times* environment correspondent, as 'a brave encounter with the past'[24] was reminiscent of the pyramid building in the Louvre in Paris both in its unrepentant modernity and its ability to provoke strong public controversy.

This leisurely progress of the castle restoration project was reflected in the process of renewal—or lack of it—in the city as a whole. The headlong disintegration of traditional industry (the 124-year-old Limerick Clothing Factory, for example, closed on 29 November 1974 with the loss of 220 jobs) had left in its wake a trail of dereliction which neither private owners nor the local authority appeared to consider as anything out of the ordinary. In 1978, with the announcement of SFADCo's new role in the region, the company believed it was in a good position to work with the city administration towards the adoption of a more dynamic approach and to attract government backing. '. . . the overall prospects of success in city centre development and in integrating industry with this development appeared to the Board to be remote if the city administration were allowed to proceed at its present pace.'[25] A technopolis with a hollow centre, an architectural and cultural vacuum? In the same year SFADCo contributed £5,000 towards a performing arts centre in the city and in 1979 became a formal member of Limerick Civic Week Ltd, but the core of the problem remained untouched. The minister, Desmond O'Malley, was found not to be in favour of a proposal for a Limerick City Development Company involving a range of interested parties. He preferred the sole involvement of SFADCo if it could be achieved without alarming the city administration. In 1980 the two bodies came together to set up the Limerick Urban Renewal Projects Committee.

The Celtic saint Munchin put a curse on Limerick. "We're trying to change that, make our peace with this man 1,500 years later," said Denis Leonard of the Limerick Heritage Trust. Twenty years in the banking business, he experienced 'a late vocation' after meeting, in 1978–79, some civil servants from Dublin who were threatened with decentralisation and felt that in Limerick culturally and in every other way they would be going backwards. Leonard set up a hospitality group through the Junior Chamber, collecting all the literature concerning the city he could lay his hands on. "In the middle of that Quigley introduced the idea of the Civic Trust. It sounded good as a long-term project."

The Civic Trust idea originated in Britain. At Paul Quigley's instigation the first such body in Ireland was set up in Limerick in 1983, closely followed by Belfast. In 1990 there were eight, and an all-Ireland organisation was being established to co-ordinate them. The whole thing, said Denis Leonard, was based on self-help, accepting the fact that the government and state agencies could not do everything. Shannon Development and the revivified Corporation had already undertaken the restoration of The Granary, dating from 1787, by the time the Trust began work. In the first seven years of its existence it completed forty-six projects. "Our development would be in properties that are not municipally owned," said Leonard. "In some cases we get permission to do up a property not tied by statute or unions. We can go into places and do things that other agencies have difficulty in doing. . . . " The eighteenth-century Bishop's palace is a good example. In private owner-ship, it was virtually falling down when the Civic Trust bought it for £1,000. "What I find most pleasing is that I get an awful lot of people in who have an association with the building—who used to live here in its tenement days. They greatly appreciate it." The restoration, costing £160,000 (funded by the National Lottery and the Corporation) has been criticised on the grounds of authenticity by architectural historians, but it is more than a museum: the Trust rents space to deserving and impoverished cultural and social bodies at a nominal cost, a practice that began with the handing over of nearby St Munchin's church, deconsecrated and restored, for the use of the Island Theatre Group.

The re-creation of the city centre is thus as much a matter of people as of place. The Heritage Precinct Plan, produced at the instigation of Michael J. Noonan, minister in the Fianna Fáil government in 1988, aimed not only to restore the mediaeval English town but to create thereby a strong tourist product to persuade visitors to remain in the city rather than just pass through. Castle, cathedral, river . . . with the river, as in cities like Prague, Paris, Frankfurt, setting the scale, establishing the framework. 'At least this much maligned city, which looked so unloved for so long, is moving in the right direction—turning itself to face the River Shannon,' wrote Frank McDonald.[26] And as you stand on a windswept Sarsfield Bridge, the waves beneath breaking white and ragged, the changing perspective emerges through a sudden sweep of Atlantic rain: behind you the long-awaited third bridge; to the right the recreated Arthur's Quay—a restrained shopping centre and an imaginative public park; upriver, the outline of the cathedral shrouded in scaffolding, the solid intrusion of the castle. There are pedestrian routes, new civic offices, a tourist bureau with, as McDonald described it, 'a roofline which recalls the masts and rigging of a sailing ship'. Water-related, the work is reorientating the city in the direction of its noble river and in the process changing its whole face for the better. But only just in time. "Limerick would have disintegrated altogether," in O'Malley's view, "but for the Designated Area tax incentives."

And in human terms? The city is changing, according to Jim Kemmy, on 8 July 1991 unanimously elected its first socialist Mayor, and its continued poor image is now less than fair. 'Every town has good and bad. People continue to think of Limerick as an outpost of backwardness and provincialism, and that is unfair, I think. . . . A lot of the city's poor image in recent years came about because of the usage of catchphrase shorthand journalism to deal with some of the social problems that were happening here.'[27] For former journalist Cathal O'Shannon, however, the city had positively altered for the better, though he admitted that after some fifteen years' residence most of his friends were still 'blow-ins' like himself. It was, moreover, these immigrants, including Corkmen Jack Higgins and Jim Barrett, city manager and city architect respectively, who were to a great measure responsible for Limerick's new image, together, of course, with what has been happening out at Plassey. Limerick may still be on the way to the technopolis as envisaged by Edward Walsh and those who think like him (and many would argue that the siting of the university within the city limits would have exerted a major stimulus towards achieving this end) but the region, for so long directed off-stage, as it were, from Shannon, is now, perhaps, acquiring a more plausible polarity.

"Incidentally," said EC Director Philip Lowe, "I don't think Shannon would ever have developed the cachet it has now had Limerick not also been the focus of a certain degree of development: both in terms of urban renewal and of the academic institution." It is fully in accordance with its perceived role that SFADCo, its enabling function in the physical resurrection of the city now largely accomplished, should be actively encouraging the process to continue under its own dynamic.

References

1. *The Irish Times*, 16 January 1990
2. 13 January 1991
3. 'Limerick Treaty 300: It's dynamite', 15 December 1990
4. Quoted in *Biography and History of the Indians of North America*, ed. Samuel G. Drake, Boston, 2nd ed., 1834
5. Patricia Palmer, in *The Irish Review*, No. 8, Spring 1990
6. Ibid.
7. 'Educational developments at every level', 9 December 1975
8. Palmer, op. cit., p. 17
9. 'Westward Hi', in *Cara*, Dublin, Vol. 18, no. 4, p. 85
10. *The Irish Review*, No. I, 1986
11. 'Science in a post-colonial culture', in *The Irish Review*, No. 8, Spring 1990, p. 72
12. *The Irish Times*, 15 November 1990
13. See p. 175
14. Reply to debate on the second reading of the Shannon Airport Development Bill 1977, 1 March 1978
15. See p. 209
16. Arthur O'Keeffe: *Responding to the Challenges of Small Industry: Strategies initiated by Shannon Development*, (Undated)
17. Robert O'Connor: *The Regional Dimension to Research and Technology Development in Ireland*, p. 47
18. Supplement (1970) to the *Five Year Programme for the Industrial Development of the Limerick, Clare and Tipperary NR region*, p. 19
19. John O'Reilly: 'The Estuary as a Centre for Maritime Industries', 9 December 1975
20. See p. 174
21. *Integrated Development of the Shannon Estuary: A Strategic Study*, Shannon, September 1989, op.cit, p. 83
22. *In the Tracks of the West Clare Railway*, p. 202
23. *Clare Champion*, 5 April 1991
24. 19 November 1991
25. Minutes, 16 June 1978
26. *The Irish Times*, 25 April 1991
27. Quoted in *The Irish Times*, 25 April 1991

CHAPTER 7

A Long Way from Tullyvarraga

Following the O'Malley announcement in March 1978 of its new responsibilities for small industry there was a perception within SFADCo that Brendan O'Regan was probably genuinely unsure as to what was to be the future of the company, that he was tending to orientate it in a direction that his successor, Paul Quigley found difficult to accept. There was a recollection of his saying that he would not object to the company's becoming entirely devoted to the Third World, if it were to turn its back on Ireland completely. "That's a terrible thing to say to people who are bursting their backs trying to do something for this country," was the comment of one of his contemporaries.

This was in the aftermath of O'Regan's resignation from the chairmanship. Frustrated in his immediate local aspirations ("He felt we should be able to intervene in the planning of villages," said Quigley, "that we could help farmers to build holiday homes . . . ") he was reacting against a situation which had become, from his point of view, in many ways untenable by looking for new worlds to conquer. The metaphor, however, is inapposite in two respects: conquering, in the aggressive sense, was never part of the O'Regan philosophy, and the new worlds had been to a significant extent already colonised. As early as 1962 he had been invited to Formosa to discuss the development of industrial estates on the Free Zone model, "where at one stage," said Tom Callanan, "they had 40,000 people employed and we had four-and-a-half." In October 1966 Paul Quigley led a meeting of a UN consultative group on industrial estates in Geneva, and in 1968 Callanan spent three weeks in Yugoslavia as OECD consultant on the proposed Belgrade freeport. An enterprise which had begun as a largely untutored experiment had reached the position in less than a decade where it was possessed of a product with significant export potential, "because", said

Willie Moloney, who was responsible for the SFADCo overseas aid programme from 1981, "we were selling a unique product which was the Free Zone experience ... we were consultants but we were practising consultants".

Ireland's accession to the European Common Market in 1973 served to broaden what was already a strongly outward view. O'Regan saw a role for the country in general, and Shannon in particular, as a median between the developing world and the enlarged European community, and discussed with the SFADCo board the concept of a trade centre based on the industrial estate to act as a shop window for the produce of Third World countries. There was more than a hint of O'Regan social idealism in the concept—in January 1973 the company's objectives were extended by the phrase ' ... and using our experience and facilities to help also the people of less-developed countries'. This caused some unease amongst his colleagues, who wanted the legal and statutory basis for the company's involvement to be verified beyond doubt.[1] As to the proposed trade centre—who would use it? If African countries were seeking a market they would, Quigley suggested, set up shop in London or New York, not "in the middle of the puddle". The proposal was modified to 'the idea of using Shannon for developments which would assist Third World countries'. In October 1972 O'Regan had been asked to undertake a short study of airport development in Monrovia, Liberia. In the same month he wrote to the Taoiseach outlining his ideas on a formal role for the company in the provision of assistance to developing countries.

It is difficult now to travel the underdeveloped world without encountering Irish aid volunteers, whether working within the framework of the government's bilateral aid programme or under the auspices of the multiplicity of NGOs, or non-governmental organisations. It is still slightly unsettling, however, to encounter in the middle of a bog in Burundi a man who would more usually be found drinking in the Hanged Man's Arch pub in Milltown, Co. Kildare and who is doing much the same job as he does at home. In the mid–1980s Bord na Móna were carrying out a contract, in association with USAID and with ONATOUR, the Burundi parastatal peat company, to develop the fuel resources of that country's bogs. If the technology was modified to ensure the employment of a substantial labour force, many of whom walked thirty kilometres to and from the site every day, in essence the procedures, and the resulting product, were entirely similar to those to be encountered on the Bord na Móna workings in Kildare and Offaly: a classic example of what Fr Richard Quinn described as 'an appropriate aid policy for Ireland [given] the similarities between the Irish economy and those of many less developed countries'.[2] In the same context he suggested that 'Similarities in colonial histories and military non-alignment create, as has been suggested, a fund of goodwill towards Ireland and a certain faith in the honesty of Irish intentions as regards aid'. SFADCo found itself, in the early 1970s (and well before such criteria had been officially recognised) in a position to draw upon a corpus of expertise to which it could claim a high degree of exclusivity. In the same way in which Bord na Móna was recognised as one of the leading world authorities on peat technology, exporting both machinery and methodology to much larger economies such as the USSR, so Shannon, as initiators of the airport free zone concept and pioneers in duty-free operations, found itself in possession of a marketable model of the better mouse-trap.

In November 1973 a memorandum prepared by J. Buist MacKenzie at Brendan O'Regan's request advised the company to register its fledgling consultancy service with UNIDO and UNCTAD (respectively the United Nations Industrial Development Organisation and Conference on Trade and Development) and to tender for appropriate projects. The aim, the paper suggested, should be to deal with one country at a time and to restrict activity to the transfer of skills and experience of Free Zone operation. At this point two high-ranking Sri Lankan public servants, Messrs A. Weerartna and P. Murugasu, had already visited Shannon and a tender had been submitted for the proposed development of a Free Zone at Trincomalee. O'Regan was intending to visit Sri Lanka and it was understood that funds were to be made available in the following year's vote for Foreign Affairs. He returned in December from the trip which was extended to include a visit to Cyprus on behalf of UNCTAD, advising his board against tendering for the proposed free ports at Nicosia and Famagusta but confident that the company would be given the job in Sri Lanka. SFADCo was, in fact, to be involved in both projects, receiving a UNIDO contract for advisory assistance to the Greater Colombo Economic Commission and one from UNCTAD for assistance in the drafting of legislation for the free zones in Cyprus.

The company was disappointed in its expectation of funding from Foreign Affairs in 1974, but the government had, nevertheless, moved towards the formalisation of Irish overseas aid. Looking back on a decade of contacts with developing countries, the Department of Foreign Affairs recalled in 1983[3] that 'Before 1974 . . . though by no means insignificant [they] had not been developed within a framework of a comprehensive policy for official development co-operation. There were substantial, long-standing and important private contracts (primarily through the work of missionary organisations); there was contact at political level (primarily through support by Ireland at the United Nations for decolonisation); there was some indirect, official financial support for development (primarily through obligatory or voluntary contributions to the development activities of agencies within the United Nations family which Ireland had joined in pursuit of wider objectives); and there were some directly financed measures in support of developed countries, primarily in response to specific requests such as that from President Kaunda to train administrators for newly independent Zambia.

The latter programme marked the first involvement of state-sponsored bodies with the establishment by the Institute of Public Administration of training courses for the Zambian administrators in the early 1960s. It was not, however, until SFADCo seriously addressed the matter in the early 1970s that the possibilities of the involvement of state bodies on a wider scale began to be explored with government encouragement. The result was the formation, in 1973, of DEVCO (the state agencies' development co-operation organisation) to co-ordinate the work in developing countries of twenty-eight such bodies. Effective from 1975, its first two members were Brendan O'Regan and Tom Dunne: Dunne had been assigned in November 1973 to the new SFADCo role. "There are now very substantial concentrations of industrial development," he said in 1991, "which have come about as a result of people using our help and looking at our model." Following discussions at UNIDO headquarters in Vienna in February 1974 O'Regan expressed himself as satisfied that the organisation was now prepared to deal with the company rather than with individuals as heretofore; in the following months visits were made on behalf of SFADCo to Egypt, Sri Lanka, Guatemala and Cyprus.

In December 1974 O'Regan decided to scale down his activities in the field, having achieved his personal objectives which he categorised[4] as acceptance of SFADCo leadership in industrial free zone development; the change in the UNIDO attitude and the development of joint projects with other state agencies. Advantages accruing to Shannon he saw as its promotion abroad; interest in it as a distribution centre for Third World products (the idea refused to go away) and easier access to markets for Shannon and Irish products generally. Shannon Duty Free shops, he told his board, had received a request to advise on the setting up of similar facilities in Khartoum and Juba in the Sudan and Aer Lingus had been advised of a valuable opportunity in Thailand. There was, however, a note of caution: with the recession at its height at home it would be desirable to maintain a low profile, and the legal and statutory basis for the company's overseas activities should be verified beyond doubt and approval obtained from the

62. *UNIDO international workshop at Shannon, February 1972. Front row: Brendan O'Regan (second from left): on his left Desmond O'Malley. Back row (left to right): Tom Dunne, later SFADCo general manager; Peter Donnelly, company secretary; Tom Callanan and (second from right) Paul Quigley, who was to succeed Brendan O'Regan.*

63. *Peace Conference, Dromoland Castle, Co. Clare, 1988. From left: Ray Joyce, director, Irish Peace Institute, Douglas Gageby, former editor of* The Irish Times *and Brendan O'Regan.*

Ministers for Industry and Commerce and Foreign Affairs. Finance should be kept separate from the company's other activities and no SFADCo funds should be devoted to this work. Finally, 'the company's involvement must be solely in the interest of helping Third World countries and secondary benefits, even though they might ensue, should not be sought'. *O si sic omnia!*

In 1976, the year in which Foreign Affairs finally made funding available for the Shannon development assistance programme, consultancy services were provided for UN agencies in El Salvador, Nicaragua, Cyprus and Egypt. In the following year work was undertaken in Colombia and a course conducted in Cairo for staff of El Nasr City industrial free zone. At the same time, and in common with the growing practice of many state bodies, training courses were provided for overseas students at Shannon. UNIDO held the first international workshop on industrial free zones at the airport in March 1972; the Export Free Zone Study Course, in its 1983 format, was to encompass four weeks of intensive instruction involving visits to Dublin, to AnCO and the Raheen Industrial Estate in Limerick and the participation of the IDA, Bord Fáilte and CTT: it was SFADCo policy to supplement its own consultant teams as appropriate with senior staff from other agencies. The programme concluded, no doubt to the satisfaction of the participating students, with a mediaeval banquet, as did the parallel Tourism Development Study Course. In the period 1975–79 training at Shannon was provided for a total of 227 students from sixty-three countries.

Following the holding of the successful 'Expo 75' exhibition in Shannon Town it was proposed to expand the concept to embrace a full-scale international exhibition involving both Third World countries and 'carefully-selected' multinational firms which, it was hoped (and the hope was clearly Brendan O'Regan's) would lead towards the achievement of a 'One-World Exhibition'.[5] This was to be linked to a permanent centre both for trade and the activities of international aid agencies—a revised proposal which was well received by DEVCO, Foreign Affairs, Córas Tráchtála and others. By July 1976, however, it had been decided not to pursue the concept of a Shannon World Trade Centre as advanced by a private organisation. Were such an idea to prove feasible it should, it was felt, be implemented by the company without the involvement of private enterprise. In the event this ambitious plan remained unfulfilled, at least one of the factors militating against it being the chronic deficiency in eastward air links out of Shannon. The fostering, and subsequent abandonment of this project was a key factor in the development of what Paul Quigley described as "a bit of a push in different directions" as between himself as general manager and his chairman in the period 1976–78.

The established pattern of mobility within the SFADCo organisation was maintained in respect of the new overseas involvement. Willie Moloney, who joined in January 1968 as planning officer, had experience in most areas except finance and administration before taking charge of the aid programme in 1981, frequently working on assignments with Arthur O'Keeffe, another long-serving executive with knowledge of many disciplines. The strategy derived its logic from the fact, as Moloney expressed it, that the company's expertise was vested in a number of individuals. Though the international agencies were employing SFADCo as a body—by virtue of O'Regan's UNIDO agreement—it was the individual input, based on a working lifetime of experience, that produced the results. It was an unusual situation in the context of Third World operations, where the project more usually took precedence over those implementing it, but one which reflects Fr Richard Quinn's analysis of the actuality and potential of Irish aid as being of a personnel-intensive nature rather than relying upon large-scale financial contributions.[6] "We had a major edge against any opposition when we tendered for jobs," said Moloney—not on account of the financial or physical resources at his disposal but because of the acknowledged expertise of a very small group of people in one highly specialised area.

The last overseas assignment Moloney worked on, again with O'Keeffe, before transferring to industrial development in 1984-85 was a contract to provide the government of Indonesia with a national programme for the development of export processing zones and export estates. Tom Callanan, whose experience of overseas assignments between the years 1968-88 embraced El Salvador, Nicaragua, Colombia, Uruguay, Brazil, Argentina, Jamaica and Yugoslavia, wound up his aid experience with a project in the French island of Réunion ("both a Department and a Region of France—unique, almost") and, finally, the company's first representation in the USSR. "My last job," he said, "was in Estonia—to try and convince the Estonians that independence wasn't really the route for them. Political independence means nothing—the old *sinn féin* view—unless you have economic independence. You can't have economic independence unless you have sources of foreign exchange. 'Thank you,' they said politely, 'but of course we are going to have political freedom.' Six months later came the independence statement."

By no means orthodox development consultancy, but at least, for Callanan, a memorable leaving of the field closely coinciding with the withdrawal of Shannon Development itself. At the end of 1988 the board decided that the company's overseas aid activity should be amalgamated with that of International Development Ireland—a body newly-established to combine the consultancy activities of the IDA, CTT and ICC (the state-sponsored Industrial Credit Corporation). 'The purpose of the programme,' a 1983 SFADCo document had put it, 'is to share with developing countries the expertise and experience acquired by Shannon Development in the course of pursuing its own development goals.' It had been, by any standards, a highly interesting exercise in specialised technical transfer.

☆ ☆ ☆ ☆ ☆ ☆

From the outset SFADCo had not been neglectful of its more direct interests overseas. In May 1965 it agreed to participate with Bord Fáilte and others in the establishment of La Maison d'Irlande in Paris: the initial contribution was FF3,000. In 1969 it opened an office in Los Angeles in association with CIE. Even earlier—in 1957—Maeve Fitzgibbon had been sent to New York as a representative of what was then the Sales and Catering Organisation. After a brief return to Shannon in 1961–62 she was back in the United States in 1963, there to remain until 1976 when her retirement as Press and Public Relations Manager, North America, would, noted Vincent Tobin, SFADCo's head of press and PR at the time, 'require considerable re-adjustment within the Division'. She was not replaced.

Working initially out of the Bord Fáilte office in New York, Maeve Fitzgibbon's brief was, "to get people interested in setting up industries as well as developing the tourism aspect. My chief function was to be in touch with people in the communications media, so I ignored all the Irish organisations. . . . I stayed miles away from the United Irish Counties and people like that because they weren't the people we wanted". She had developed good contacts with the American press corps which had passed through in various VIP entourages in the early days at Rineanna, but as a single lady operating in New York in what was then an almost exclusively male environment she was obliged to evolve her own methods. "Bringing them to the Colony or the Four Seasons was just throwing money away— they had too many invites. They liked being asked home." When she did lunch with men in public she found that many were embarrassed at being entertained by a woman and she had to make special arrangements with the restaurant to avoid being seen paying the bill.

Maeve Fitzgibbon's broad function, the promotion of Shannon as 'the gateway to Ireland', did not involve her directly in visits to industrialists, a role performed on SFADCo's behalf by the IDA. However, she was given the special task of encouraging small businesses to consider locating in the Free Zone and became marginally involved in the company's overseas development role, accompanying Tom Callanan in 1976 on a joint IDA/CTT/ SFADCo mission to El Salvador. She was not impressed. "I was horrified at the obvious and callous disparity between the haves and have-nots. I couldn't see any possibility of their developing anything. A sad situation." Not all the candidates pass. But from her base on the sixth floor of 590 5th Avenue, a building which at one time housed Aer Lingus, CTT, CIE, and an array of other Irish public and private bodies (and the disposal of which was at best short-sighted), Maeve Fitzgibbon made a substantial contribution to the creation of an enduring image of Shannon in the USA, to the extent that John A. Daly, who became SFADCo chairman in May 1987, encountered great difficulty at breakfast meetings in telling his hosts where Ireland was but few problems in respect of Shannon.

Other factors, of course, contributed: the historical role of the airport in transatlantic travel; and, at a different level, the enduring popularity of the entertainers from Bunratty, Knappogue and Dunguaire castles on their regular and intensive overseas tours. In the period 1968–69, for example, the Shannon Castle Singers and Farmhouse Entertainers attended the convention of the American Association of Travel Agents (ASTA) in Puerto Rico and were involved in other promotional visits sponsored by SFADCo, Bord Fáilte, CTT, Aer Lingus and CIE. In December 1970 they toured the United States, Canada and the Bahamas and in 1973–74 visited Canada again, Acapulco, Mexico, Britain and the Salon du Cheval in Paris. In 1976, the year which saw the millionth guest at the Shannon mediaeval banquets, they travelled to Holland, Vienna, Zurich, Belgium, Denmark and—to set the seal on the Nieman-Marcus Irish Fortnight—to Dallas, Texas. In 1978, in conjunction with Aer Lingus, they undertook a forty day coast-to-coast tour of the United States.

In 1979 Olaf O'Duill, then director of the Chicago office of the IDA, offered a view of the level of awareness of Ireland in the area for which he was responsible not entirely at variance with John A. Daly's later experience.[7] 'I would suggest,' he said, 'that in the mid-west you probably have a good awareness now among the big companies, primarily because there is such a significant proportion of the major companies of the mid-west already in Ireland—so they know the scene there. They're making money there and they're making products there. But you go to companies that have not got projects in Ireland and it's a different situation. They know nothing of it. They have an image of Ireland probably thirty or forty years behind the United States: rural countryside, thatched cottages ... which is helped, I must admit, by the excellent job the Tourist Board does. We have to overcome that to convince them that we also have a very progressive industrial side to our economy, which is potentially of great advantage to them and to us.'

If it was difficult for the IDA, pursuing its goal with a clear singleness of purpose, the contradictions inherent in the situation were compounded for Shannon Development. Its dual mandate to foster both the image of the Free Zone as a state-of-the-art technological phenomenon and that of the region's tourist amenities drew heavily for the latter upon the image of a romantic Ireland deeply rooted in the past. No organisation, however strongly represented in the market, could hope to reconcile such opposites without falling victim to an acute condition of occupational schizophrenia. SFADCo's solution was to sell the all-embracing 'gateway' concept, building upon an existing awareness of Shannon as a port of entry and developing from there the logic of a sophisticated industrial zone with the resources of a high-amenity hinterland. This, of course, meant more to the potential industrialist than the package tourist; but the latter, once in Shannon and embarking upon the Mediaeval Tour, was not allowed to leave the airport area and its 'jet-age industrial estate' without being informed of something of its genesis and purpose. Though the US view of Ireland was modified to some extent over the ensuing years, the continued fostering of the traditional tourist image, both by Bord Fáilte and by Shannon itself, ensured that the dichotomy remained.

Even where the responsibility of a SFADCo representative was limited to tourism promotion, as in the case of the Paris office in the late 1980s, there were problems of identity, in this instance deriving principally from the ignorance of Shannon, on the part of the target market, as anything other than a transit airport on the North American route. Following the revision of the company's mandate as from 1 January 1988, it became responsible for tourism promotion for the region as a whole, and thus Roisin Kelly, the SFADCo representative in France in 1990, was faced with what was primarily a semantic problem: that of extending the image of Shannon to embrace what was now to be known as the Shannon Region—a locus which, of course, had nothing whatever to do with Carrick-on-Shannon or Portumna and their hire cruisers, perhaps the only aspect of 'Shannon' with which the French might have been expected readily to identify. Her situation was not helped by the fact that most of the brochures available to her for distribution were in English, with which, she said, it was pointless going to consumer fairs.

Since previously the main priority of the Paris office of SFADCo had been to encourage traffic to the airport (with lesser concern as to what happened to it after that) she was continuing to work closely with the airlines: "I try to attract charters into Shannon by making it more attractive than Dublin or Cork." In spite of this strong regional emphasis, she had an excellent working arrangement with Bord Fáilte, frequently occupying the same stand at trade fairs. This helped in the matter of having to explain herself both to the general public and operators not familiar with Ireland: a common phenomenon in Italy, which was also included in her territory. But a policy of selling separate pieces of a small country under confusing labels was one which created many practical difficulties. Should Bord Fáilte's own maps leave the Mid-West, alias the Shannon Region, blank?

This was the IDA's solution, and one which was not to recommend itself to Desmond O'Malley. 'It is important to reiterate the fundamental task that was assigned by the government to Shannon Development on January 1 1988,' John A. Daly wrote in the 1989 annual report: 'it asked the company to become responsible for all aspects of industrial and tourism development in a pioneering, integrated regional development manner. . . . ' The most far-reaching consequence of this new mandate lay in the transfer of respon-sibility for overseas representation in the industrial area from the IDA to Shannon: Willie Moloney became Executive Vice President (a title tailored to American tastes) in New York with a total staff of nine, including himself, to cover the whole country and other personnel were dispatched to Germany and Japan.

There was a feeling in some quarters that the action had been taken not so much to further the fortunes of Shannon as to administer a salutary lesson to the IDA for perceived shortcomings. Whatever the truth of the matter, the reaction of that body was, as might be expected, less than enthusiastic. The new SFADCo overseas representatives entered into their novel role with enthusiasm: in John A. Daly's words, quoting Michael Smith, the then Minister for Science and Technology, 'losing and finding the other people'. After some understandable initial touchiness the two organisations settled down to generally amicable working arrangements in the field, whatever about the situation at a higher level.

Desmond O'Malley, for his part, remained deeply unimpressed. "I could never accept that it [Shannon Development] had a role in promoting that region abroad against the remainder of this country. To take out one tiny region out of a tiny country and ask it to promote itself against the remainder of the country in a world, half of which doesn't even know that the country exists anyway, just made no sense." In 1978, in the wake of his decision to hand over responsibility for small business in the region to SFADCo, the IDA had reacted by shading the lost territory in light brown over the pervading olive green, retaining both the identification Mid-West and the county names.[8] In this new situation their approach was more fundamental. "On a visit abroad I saw the IDA distributing maps of Ireland with two areas blanked out," said O'Malley: "one was Northern Ireland and the other was the Mid-West. I got annoyed about it. On IDA missions abroad in 1989 and 1990 you couldn't even talk about the region. I came out of a meeting with a certain company having talked about Ireland and there sitting at the door waiting to go in was the Shannon representative . . . . " It was a situation rich in ambiguities, not all of them lost on the Shannon people themselves. "I would have a degree of sympathy with the minister's view that Ireland is such a small country that there should be only one body promoting it," said John A. Daly: "but I think that what Shannon Development achieved in a short period certainly merited maybe a longer look at it. Nobody can take from Shannon Development that in that short two years [1988–89] it had produced approximately twenty-five per cent of the new jobs. Brian Lenihan came back from one of his trips as Minister for Foreign Affairs and said 'This change is great! I've noticed a great constructive tension out in the field.'"

There are other views as to whether the tension was entirely constructive. "If you have a number of areas in a country of three and a half million people I wouldn't argue," suggested Philip Lowe of the EC Commission tactfully, "that every one of those regions should have external representation." In the event the experiment was cut short by O'Malley's decision as minister in July 1990 to return to the status quo in the matter of overseas responsibility for industrial development; and, in addition, to restore responsibility for overseas industry already located in the Mid-West to the IDA.

"Before we had a chance to show whether it would work or fail it was taken back off us," said Tom Dunne: "I always felt—and acknowledged it to Dessie O'Malley—that there was a case for what he did in the matter of the overseas promotional work, but I didn't agree with what he did in terms of taking away responsibility for looking after the established foreign industry here. . . . There was no national advantage in taking that away." But the real loser in all this was the concept of integrated regional development and responsibility . . . though it is indeed difficult to envisage eight or nine regional representatives sitting outside the foreign industrialist's door, patiently waiting for the IDA to finish discussing investment in Ireland over an entirely blank map.

'Last year was perhaps the most important in the history of Shannon Development,' its chairman had stated confidently in 1989[9] 'as it was its first year operating under the government's mandate for the integrated development of the region.' Shannon, in this instance as in others, paid the penalty for being the odd man out, the only regional authority capable of speaking with even a muted voice internationally and therefore prone to fall victim to internecine jealousies and what Tom Dunne tactfully described in

1991 as "the current complexion of government thinking". In this sense, if in no other, the 1990 decision was a markedly retrogressive step. "The regional development boat will come in one day," added Dunne philosophically; but on this evidence it would still seem to be a very long way out to sea and setting course in the wrong direction.

☆ ☆ ☆ ☆ ☆ ☆

There is no practicable Great Circle route between Shannon and Belfast. Within the general vicinity of the airport it used to be common enough to come across people who had frequently flown the Atlantic but had never set foot in Dublin; of these, the number who had ever been to Northern Ireland would have been scarcely perceptible. In this sense the distance between Tullyvarraga and Glengormley was far greater than that between Shannon and New York; though it was in the latter city that the Northern civil rights campaign of 1972 and its bloody aftermath first impinged directly on the activities of SFADCo. Maeve Fitzgibbon was recruited by the Department of Foreign Affairs, in company with a number of leading Irish journalists, in an exercise in damage limitation worldwide. She was assigned to Canada with the difficult role both of countering British political propaganda and presenting a positive picture of a Republic untroubled by the events north of its border. At home, Paul Quigley as general manager considered writing letters to friends in the USA 'commenting on events in Ireland in the hope of allaying their fears about conditions here'[10]—an idea subsequently abandoned. Conditions were not good: industrial inquiries and tourism from Britain virtually dried up while Shannon suddenly found itself brought much closer to the North and its problems with the arrival of a substantial contingent of refugees.

Though many of these were to become permanent residents of the new town, for the majority of the Shannon community the six northern counties disappeared once more over the horizon as the tragic sequence of killing and counter-killing dragged on and the representatives of the two traditions appeared to drift further and further apart. Brendan O'Regan, however, was not satisfied that, as far as Shannon was concerned, the matter should end there. In the late 1970s he decided to apply his practical idealism to the state of relations both between the Republic and Northern Ireland and between the two juxataposed communities within the latter entity. The outcome was Co-operation North.

'The first time I saw Co-operation North in action,' recalled the Belfast writer Sam McAughtry,[11] 'I have to admit that it didn't altogether please

[177]

me. There I was, on a gorgeous June morning, ten miles away from my home by the Ards Peninsula in Co. Down, bowling along on my way to the Budweiser Irish Derby at the Curragh ... then, at Mile 10, the bicycles began to appear. Bicycles? I'd never seen so many in my flaming life .... Clearly they weren't professional riders, for there were fat ones and fatter ones, slow ones and easier-going ones, young riders and white-haired riders. Alongside a couple of puffing billies near my own age I called out "What's going on?" "It's the Maracycle," they shouted. "We're going from Belfast to Dublin. Co-operation North, you know".' When McAughtry reached Co. Kildare he learned something of the organisation from a Dublin industrialist whose company had become involved.

'Ever since 1969, when the North was set alight, there have been organisations working to restore some degree of normality in the lives of the people most affected. It took only minutes for me to discover that Co-operation North is not one of those ventures that start off with high hopes and end with an empty clubroom, a table tennis table, and no balls. A carefully planned programme of action has been under way, ever since Brendan O'Regan, the President, thought up the idea in 1979. A one-time chairman of the Shannon Development Company, his philosophy was that North and South should meet in the vital areas of life, and co-operate for their mutual benefit. In the process, the horns and tails of bogey men would fall off, misunderstandings would be removed and, in the economic sector, there was even money to be made by business interests working together, and what's the matter with that?'

There was not much the matter with it. Retiring at the age of sixty from SFADCo, Brendan O'Regan became the first chairman of Co-operation North and succeeded in attracting the support of businessmen, academics, trade unionists, professional bodies and community leaders north and south as well as the variegated cyclists many of whom were more interested, perhaps, in travelling hopefully than in the political significance of their destination. Travelling hopefully, could, however, be applied as a fair description of the manner in which the organisation was to proceed. Its stated aims were 'to promote goodwill and understanding between Northern Ireland and the Republic of Ireland by fostering co-operation in the economic, social and cultural spheres' and 'to engage in investigation and research into common problems and the opportunites for mutually beneficial co-operation'. Two private companies, based in Belfast and Dublin, were formed with a full-time staff and a common board of directors, thus effectively distancing the organisation from its origins in Shannon. For O'Regan, however, the distance was merely physical. 'I'd love to see this region—I mean the County Councils and the people—adopting the policy of Co-operation North and making it a region from which we would go into the North with as many people as possible and invite as many people as possible to come here.'[12] Northerners, he believed, 'see Shannon as a very definite Irish creation whereas Dublin is seen as a creation of the English and those who occupied the country. . . . '

If this postulated view from the Lagan Bridge would strike many as unfamiliar, O'Regan's analysis of the political background could perhaps further be characterised as simplistic. 'We are playing out in Ireland,' he said[13] 'a non-government peace-building operation in the area of Europe that has had the greatest tragedy for so long . . . between two ethnic groups, Irish-Irish Catholic and British-Irish Protestant.' Where this leaves the southern Protestants, the great majority of whom would firmly reject the label 'British-Irish', is not immediately clear. In fairness it must be noted that Co-operation North was involved with the Social Study Conference, Galway, in promoting a discussion on 'Being Protestant in Ireland' at its 32nd Summer School, Kilkenny, 4-8 August 1984, and in the subsequent publication of the proceedings. Other publications, such as *The Co-operation North Guide*—a Directory for North-South Co-operation in Ireland (1985) were more overtly practical, though the foreword to that work restated the organisation's idealistic principles: 'Through its activities it seeks to allay animosities and myths that have inhibited normal interchange and social relationships . . . by bringing out clearly the realistic benefits of economic and social co-operation at every level.' The disillusioned will point to the fact that though such ideals found fertile ground among schoolchildren and cyclists, they failed to penetrate the hard core of mutual aversion or persuade a single paramilitary to hand in his gun.

Such criticisms are recurrent in respect of any initiative in the North-South situation, but O'Regan's application of hard-edged ideals undoubtedly helped to extend the middle ground, if only minimally in the larger context. The experience, and his own evaluation of its impact, prompted him 'to see what the complex at Shannon could do, as it had done in regard to aviation, to put together co-operation to overcome man's greatest enemy, human conflict . . . '. All the world was to become his stage.

From his point of view it was a natural progression, 'a growth from the concept of Co-operation North', as he told the Clare FM interviewer. Believing as he did in Shannon as a centre of 'tremendous human co-operation' (*Ní neart go cur le chéile* was a favourite *seanfhocal*) he saw in its strategic position and neutral connotation the ideal setting for his Centre for International Co-operation. ' The object of it is to build at Shannon a centre

[179]

which will be available for international purposes relative to building peace.' It is an idea, he added, 'whose time has come. I think that Shannon, because it is so productive of new ideas, is ahead of the rest of the world in this manner of thinking at the moment. A lot of people from overseas have said that to me. . . .'[14] In 1986 Ray Joyce was seconded from Shannon Development to direct the new Institute, which opened its offices in No. 1 Tower Block, Shannon Airport. Involving the active participation of Aer Lingus, Aer Rianta, GPA and Stokes Kennedy Crowley/Peat Marwick, it was set up as a consortium with these bodies and the existing Irish Peace Institute, which had been established at Plassey in 1984 with the support and sponsorship of the University of Limerick, the University of Ulster and Co-operation North. An MA course in Peace Studies was instituted in 1987, students attending both Limerick and Ulster universities.

In May 1986 the Irish Peace Institute organised at Shannon an international conference on peace building. 'From this conference,' said Tom O'Donnell, former MEP and then deputy chairman of the Centre for International Co-operation[15] 'a consensus emerged calling for a wide practical programme of international co-operation to complement the academic work of the Irish Peace Institute and which would take advantage of the strategic location of Shannon, almost equidistant from New York and Moscow and with regular flights to and from the USA and USSR.'

The context was Cold War and the principles those which had underpinned the thinking of O'Regan and his colleagues on the pivotal position of Shannon since its inception. Only the thrust—what could be fairly described as a radical dimension in international idealism—was new; but it held echoes of the former plan for Shannon as a Third World focus. The Centre for International Co-operation, which was instituted as a direct outcome of the perceived success of the 1986 conference, adopted a policy of, as O'Regan put it, 'applying the experience of Co-operation North to the international scene'. The letterhead carried a statement of its aspiration 'to exploit Shannon's strategic location, and the track record of its members, to pioneer a path to greater co-operation among nations. It aims to forge international links in a variety of specific areas—in education, youth exchanges, commerce, trade, industry, communications, tourism, science, culture and international conferences'. The long-term goal was global: 'We in Ireland are not working alone in the promotion of international co-operation and understanding through non-governmental agencies,' said Tom O'Donnell.[16] 'There are thousands of such non-governmental international organisations spread over the five continents and we are gradually building up a network of contacts with organisations worldwide similar to ours. We are exchanging

64. *The Japanese connection: Mr Sioda of Sumetoma and Dr Edward Walsh sign an agreement at the University of Limerick, December 1988.*

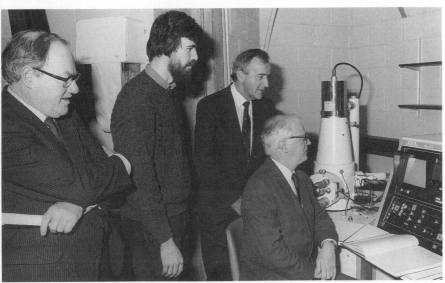

65. *The European dimension: Bruce Millan, EC Commissioner for Regional Affairs (seated) with John A. Daly, chairman, Shannon Development (extreme left) and Albert Reynolds, Minister for Finance, at the University of Limerick, 7 April 1989.*

information, forming friendships and developing joint projects, linking north and south as well as east and west.'

If the bogeymen in the North remained persistently in place those in the East were to shed their horns and tails with almost unbecoming alacrity, radically altering the polarisation of international politics in general and the Centre's main preoccupation in particular. Rightly or wrongly, the pivotal position between Moscow and New York seemed to forfeit something of its pertinence, and it appeared likely, in the wake of these events, that the Centre would move towards a global north-south orientation, turning once more in the direction of the problems and opportunities presented by the Third World. It saw the developments in Eastern Europe, nevertheless, as offering it a new challenge. In May 1987 the Centre had hosted an international conference on the theme 'International Tourism—Passport to Peace'. In April 1990, in the light of events, it convened a second and similar conference to review the position and to restate its own objectives. Ray Joyce, the director, forecast that international tourism would be the single largest world industry by the year 2000 and suggested that it could be a great force for peace 'by fostering respect for inter-cultural differences and traditions and by encouraging friendship and understanding between nations'. In essence, the One Day Tour writ large.

'Flying in an Asahi Chemical helicopter over the 1,700 hectare Tohmi peninsula,' wrote Peter McGill[17] 'where a golf course, "academic park", sports stadium and marinas are all planned, one sees only rugged primeval forest. Driving there in an Asahi Chemical limousine the only signs of human activity are Japanese fisherwomen drying squid on wooden racks on its northern seashore.'

This unlikely location was announced in 1990 as the site for the second University of Limerick campus. In October of the previous year Ed Walsh and Noel Whelan, Dean of Business Studies, learnt that the Asahi Chemical Industry Company, which had had a presence in Ireland since 1973, was interested in investing in European educational facilities in Japan, both to offer its own people easier access to post-1992 Europe and to educate potential European managers in Japanese manners and methods, language and culture with a view to their occupying senior positions in Japanese companies in Ireland and elsewhere in the European Community. The Limerick Business School had at this point been involved in 'distance learning' for about six years, but this proposal lent the term an entirely new connotation. The planned Limerick campus at Nobeoka, on the Tohmi peninsula of Kyushu, Japan's southernmost island, would cater equally for Japanese and European students, with considerable interchange between the two centres. Much of the impetus for the planned development came from the IDA, which held equity in the Asahi acrylic production in Ireland and was anxious to establish closer ties between the two countries. A majority of Nobeoka's population is dependent upon the Asahi factories in that city, and the location of a Limerick University campus there was seen as an imaginative move from both the commercial and the cultural standpoint.

In June 1991 it was announced that Asahi and the University of Limerick were reviewing both the timing and the feasibility of establishing the new university, but that the former was proposing to fund a major chemical study programme under which Limerick students would spend an academic year, funded by Asahi, in Nobeoka, working in the firm's high technology businesses and having the benefit of their research and development facilities. The original invitation to establish a Limerick University campus still stood. Meanwhile planned development at Plassey included a 'Euro-technopole' project 'which illustrates,' said Tom Dunne[18] 'how private interest can be brought into the industrial development process. Working closely with the International Business Incubation Centre (IBIC) in Tokyo, a very broad range of influential and relevant parties in Japan have been brought together to develop the concept of a Japanese Parts Manufacturing Centre to be based at the [Plassey] Park. A complete package appropriate to their needs has been developed based on discussions with potential investors in Japan and Japanese companies already located in Europe. In response to these findings, Shannon Development has allocated forty hectares ... to the development of an industrial parkland for small to medium Japanese companies ... Ongoing promotion is proceeding, with eighteen Irish engineers now placed in six Japanese companies targeted for the Eurotechnopole site'. These initiatives are characteristic of the most recent phase of development in the Mid-West region in its readiness to look far afield and plan for its future in global terms, a readiness most clearly recognisable in developments at the airport itself.

Not all the initiative, however, is confined to the immediate vicinity of the original Rineanna. In an eighteenth-century house at Birdhill, Co. Tipperary, Tony Ryan, chairman and chief executive of Guinness Peat Aviation, officially opened on 1 June 1991 the Tipperary Enterprise Foundation which, through its subsidiary the Tipperary Trading Company, planned to market the county—of which Dr Ryan is a native son—worldwide. The reaction of the IDA to the prospect of discovering a Tipperary representative replacing that of Shannon Development outside the foreign industrialist's door is not recorded, but conceivably the Authority might find some solace in the fact that widespread awareness of the fact that it's a long way to Tipperary could constitute an inhibitingly adverse factor in any programme of individual promotion. Desmond O'Grady, in a footnote to his poem 'Tipperary', points out that *Tiobraid Arann*, (Irish for 'Tipperary') means 'fountain of perception, or enlightenment, or intelligence':

> *It's a long way to Tipperary*
> *it's a long way to go*—and devious.
> It's a torture of twists, about-turns,
> disillusions, disappointments.
> The way to Tipperary appears
> perennially dark with only
> occasional twilights.
> If you decide to go to Tipperary
> set out while you're young, plucky;
> at that age when you're bright-eyed with visions
> of radiant horizons of revelation and achievement
> and you know nothing of twilights or the dark;
> that age when all creation, all life shines clear
> as spring sunlight, bright as light-catching gold.
> When you set out you must go alone.
> There are no maps of the way to Tipperary.
> Your only compass is your own heart. Trust that!

Nobeoka, Moscow, Ballymurphy, New York ... in the outward direction, at least, new light has been dawning on the horizons of revelation and achievement. And in this new light the Shannon enterprise can be seen to have come full circle.

References

1. Minutes, 11 December 1974
2. *The Missionary Factor in Irish Aid Overseas*, Dublin 1980, p. 74
3. *Assistance to Developing Countries: Report for the Year* 1983, p. 4
4. Minutes, 11 December 1974
5. Minutes, 13 February 1976
6. Quinn, op.cit., passim
7. Interview in *Cara*, Vol. 12 no. 3, p. 35

8. IDA Annual Report 1978, p. 8
9. Annual Report 1988, p. 3
10. Minutes, 9 February 1972
11. 'Banishing the Bogey Men', in *Cara*, Vol. 19 no. 6, 1986, p. 33
12. Interview on *Monday People*, Clare FM, 7 May 1990
13. Ibid.
14. Ibid.
15. Speech at Shannon, 13 March 1990
16. Ibid.
17. 'Miyazaki prepares to welcome Irish Campus', in *The Irish Times*, 21 March 1990
18. Address to IMI Business Luncheon (Mid-West branch), 22 January 1992

CHAPTER 8

The Matter of the Route

The impact is more immediate in the case of a large, abandoned railway station from which all tracks have receded. Where an airport is concerned a quiet hour may be the presage either of peak traffic or of terminal decline. For Prestwick, in 1991, it was the latter. Long the rival of Shannon for transatlantic passengers, in April of that year, following the loss of its international traffic to Glasgow, it was handling four flights a day, all US military operations in the aftermath of the Gulf War. The restaurant, the cafeteria, the bar, the skyshop were closed. 'Already,' wrote Lorna Siggins in *The Irish Times*,[1] 'the birds are beginning to take over the empty runway.'

It was rabbits that James Dillon, former leader of Fine Gael, expected to see occupying the deserted concrete of Rineanna: the prophecy was made when the original name was still current. 'I venture to predict,' he had said even earlier—in 1936—'that if in five years' time you suggested that an express airliner from the United States to a point east of Ireland ... would come down on the Shannon to take petrol, the pilot would break his heart laughing.' The ghost of that laughter, the shadowy forms of rook and rodent, were to haunt to a greater or lesser degree those responsible for Shannon airport as long-range jets succeeded thirsty piston aircraft, demands to overfly to Dublin multiplied and traffic, terminal and transit, fluctuated alarmingly in the wake of national and international crises.

Responsibility for the day-to-day functioning of Rineanna/Shannon had been from the beginning vested in the Department of Transport and Power, operating through an airport manager. Colonel P. Maher, the first holder of the office, retired in September 1960, some eighteen months after the formal establishment of SFADCo had injected a new element into the situation. That fledgling body could not but take cognisance of what was happening in the control tower and on the apron and as early as its report to the minister for the period 1 August 1958 to 31 January 1959—whilst it was still constituted as the Development Authority—it stressed the importance of the opening of a route between Shannon and London. 'During the winter season covered by this report,' the document stated, 'there was a very marked decrease in traffic through Shannon both scheduled and unscheduled ... there seems no doubt that the Comet and Boeing 707 and technical improvements in aircraft were mainly responsible.' Routes, and the aircraft operating them, were clearly to be crucial to the viability of the whole Shannon enterprise.

The concept of the Free Zone involved the assumption that firms setting up there would use air freight both to expedite their supplies of raw material and to export their finished products, thus boosting traffic movements and encouraging new services. This, disconcertingly, did not occur: 'The change to air is happening ... more slowly than was expected,' the 1962 SFADCo annual report admitted. The previous September the board had complained that individual firms had not in this respect fulfilled their undertakings to the company: Lana-Knit had switched to surface transport by CIE because of 'inadequate and unsatisfactory freight services to and from Great Britain'. One problem lay in the unfavourable rates and systems imposed by IATA, the International Air Transport Association; but a new tariff introduced in September 1961 removed or reduced these barriers. 'The new rate structure', said the 1962 report confidently, 'makes it worthwhile for the first time to undertake cargo consolidation and "break bulk" at Shannon.' Perhaps; but the SFADCo board had been told the previous November that 'because of the opposition of BOAC [British Overseas Airways Corporation] the potential of cargo consolidation at Shannon (which is closely linked with warehousing) would not be publicised'. In January 1963 the same airline opposed any additional frequencies between Shannon and London. In December 1961 the first large-scale negotiations had taken place in Dublin on the request of the United States that its carriers be permitted to overfly Shannon and terminate in Dublin. The Irish government had in this instance expressed its firm commitment to Shannon . . . but that story had at least another thirty years to run.

Such divergence of objectives as between the company and the carriers was not confined to those of foreign provenance. Aer Lingus, which had opposed rights at Shannon for an Icelandic airline[2] in November 1965, was only prevailed upon to provide additional services between Dublin and Shannon to connect with non-Irish transatlantic flights on the insistence of the minister following pressure from US interests; they were introduced in January 1966 with SFADCo offering to pay fifty per cent of the cost, an offer which was not taken up. In the meantime other carriers had come and gone. International Airlines Inc., of the US, opened an office in Shannon early in 1964 with the expressed intention of transferring its base from California: it went bankrupt in 1967. Shannon Air Ltd commenced charter operations in May 1964, its bankruptcy following in February 1966, a year in which transit traffic at the airport had fallen to 212,226—the lowest since 1953—from a peak of 409,900 in 1958. Constellations and DC7s, the older piston aircraft, were now being phased out. The airport, said Tom Dunne in 1991, "will never ever be fully free from danger. The battle will always be there. I don't think anyone will ever be able to say we've achieved a permanent future for Shannon and now we can turn our minds to something else".

When the new jet runway had opened for traffic on 3 July 1960 Pan Am, the first airline to operate a scheduled passenger flight using jet equipment from Shannon to the United States, was to share international services through the airport with several other major carriers including Sabena, Swissair and Trans-Canada, all fully operational by the time Erskine Childers, Minister for Transport and Power, officially declared the new runway open on 3 November 1960. Training activity, taking advantage of the airport's good meteorological record and low level of daytime traffic, was also on the increase. This latter source of revenue was to continue and prosper, but by 1966 the major carriers had stopped using Shannon as a transit stop and the future looked bleak. In 1968, however, the US supplemental carriers, mostly operating charters, began using an aircraft (the DC 8–60 series) which, on account of its somewhat limited range, found Shannon necessary for refuelling, and traffic, both terminal and transit, began to recover. In the same year Childers announced that the airport would be extended, at a cost of £2½ m, to cater for the growing future of commercial aviation. The plans, designed to respond to the introduction of Boeing 747s on the North Atlantic in 1970, involved the provision of a two-storey terminal building with a pier capable of accommodating as many as ten of the new Jumbos. 'The government's latest move,' concluded the first issue of the *Shannonside Courier* (December 1968) 'is their finest display of faith in Shannon and all those employed there. The development plan heralds the era of the Jumbo jet and will bring a long and prosperous lease of life to the entire Shannonside region.'

Other government moves at the time were greeted with a somewhat more modified enthusiasm. In February 1967, in the course of a review of company policy in the aftermath of the Lichfield Report, SFADCo had entered the caveat that 'any extension on a regional basis of the activity of the company which was primarily concerned with the development of the airport might hamper the carrying out of its main task'.[3] This perceived first responsibility was shortly to be called into question by the announcement that Aer Rianta was to take over the operation of Dublin Airport with the situation as regards Shannon still being discussed. The reaction of the SFADCo board was not favourable. 'The special circumstances existing at

66. *An Taoiseach, Sean Lemass, makes a presentation to Capt. Harold E. Gray on the occasion of the 25th anniversary of commercial flights across the North Atlantic, 1964. Gray piloted the first commercial airmail flight to reach Foynes on 24 June 1939. Brendan O'Regan behind the flowers.*

67. *The GPA Flying-Boat Museum at Foynes, housed in the former terminal building, preserves many relics of a vanished era.*

Shannon,' it suggested in April 1967, 'called for the establishment of a single body, separate from Aer Rianta, to be responsible for all non-technical state services at the airport. It was logical to merge these with the Development Company.'

Aer Rianta, up to this point, had remained—in the public mind at least—a somewhat shadowy organisation, frequently confused both with Aer Lingus, the national airline, and its subsidiary Aer Línte, formed in 1946 to operate the transatlantic service which, following a ten year delay due to a short-sighted political decision, finally commenced operations in 1958. Aer Rianta was, in fact, the parent of both these two state aviation companies, having been established as far back as April 1937 under the legislation setting up Aer Lingus. Sean Lemass had suggested at that time that Aer Rianta might take responsibility for the development and running of Rineanna, but it was not until the introduction of the Air Companies Bill of 1965, described by Minister Childers, as a 'tidying up process', that any move in that direction was made. Under this legislation Aer Rianta was to divest itself of its role as a holding company and to be given the responsibility for the state-owned airports at Dublin, Shannon and Cork. In September 1968 the SFADCo board wrote to the Minister for Transport and Power 'protesting strongly, on the grounds that it was organisationally wrong, against the decision to centralise management of all three airports in one Dublin-based company; proposing that if this decision cannot be reversed Aer Rianta should take over only those functions at present discharged by airport management and that the role of SFADCo should continue unchanged'.

It was too late, however, to turn the tide. On 12 November the board met two Aer Rianta representatives—J. Connor and R. C. O'Connor, the latter an erstwhile SFADCo director—to discuss the arrangements as foreseen by them. In April 1969 Aer Rianta was to take over responsibility for the management of Shannon Airport; in 1970 agreement was to be reached with SFADCo that the Sales and Catering Organisation should hold its commission from the new authority but remain autonomous and that SFADCo should retain its development function. It was also suggested that Aer Rianta would operate through a small headquarters staff at Dublin and include units with a large measure of autonomy at each airport. Brendan O'Regan and Paul Quigley had offered other options: the merger of all management functions in SFADCo—ruled out by the legislation; SFADCo to act as agent for Aer Rianta in day-to-day administrative matters—not acceptable to the latter; SFADCo to be in charge of the airport but with Aer Rianta as their agent for physical planning and construction—not acceptable to Aer Rianta; Sales and Catering to be merged in SFADCo—favoured by Sales & Catering staff and to be further considered. It was also suggested that the latter be reconstituted as a separate state-sponsored body.

The rearguard action was to be fought on two fronts. SFADCo had always been unusual among state-sponsored bodies in that its affairs were the concern of two government departments. Now, with the battle with Transport and Power apparently lost, it turned to Industry and Commerce, which was preparing a Shannon Free Airport Development Company (Amendment) Bill (1970). A letter to the minister sought his agreement for deletion of the phrase ' . . . subject to the overall national responsibility assigned to the IDA' and for provision for retention by the company of the powers it currently exercised at Shannon.[4] In this appeal it was no more successful than in its proposals to Aer Rianta, which had further objected to the merging of Sales and Catering with SFADCo; the proposal now was for the S & C to operate on contract from Aer Rianta instead of directly from the Minister for Transport and Power. All these manoeuvres, labyrinthine in their complexity, must be set against the background of the real fears on the part of SFADCo that control of the airport, and thus effectively of its ancillaries, would pass to Dublin and that the establishing of a working arrangement between the two state companies would prove at least as difficult as in the context of SFADCo's uneasy relationship with the IDA.

This proved to be the case. It had been felt necessary in October 1969 to initiate discussions with a view to achieving a harmonious working arrangement which, a year later, was still exhibiting 'some evidence of strain'. In January 1971, however, the company concluded that 'it was preferable to continue with the modus operandi with Aer Rianta rather than ask the Minister for Transport and Power to define the division of functions. . . .'[5] These were summed up some years later in the report of the Dáil Committee on Public Expenditure (1986) in a manner which suggested that, up to that point, the division had proved somewhat inimical to definition: 'Aer Rianta is responsible for the management of the country's airports including traffic promotion. In the case of Dublin Airport, Aer Lingus and the other airlines undertake some promotion as part of the development of their own traffic and so there is correspondingly less need for promotion by Aer Rianta . . . In the case of Shannon a different arrangement exists. SFADCo has statutory responsibility for terminal traffic and so Aer Rianta is concerned with transit traffic promotion only. But it does have a key role in the servicing of tourist amenities in the area through a management agreement with SFADCo with respect to Shannon Castle Tours . . . Apart from duplication this has also led to conflict and confusion. This contrasts with the degree of co-operation between SFADCo and the IDA.'[6]

The latter observation no doubt provoked a wry smile in certain quarters; but lest SFADCo be accused of sulking in its tent in the matter of relationships with other state bodies it is only reasonable to point out that Aer Rianta was to encounter similiar difficulties at Dublin in its working arrangements with its former subsidiary Aer Lingus.[7] For the moment SFADCo could only regard this incursion into its established field of operations as an inhibiting factor. Brendan O'Regan, in his introduction to the 1972–73 annual report took it upon himself, however, both to explain and reassure. 'The fact that our work is similar, or complementary, to the work of national agencies like the IDA, Bord Fáilte and Aer Rianta, can be confusing to those not familiar with it. They may suspect duplication of effort and unproductive competition as between state agencies. In practice, we have made agreements with other agencies, spelling out working procedures, so that any wasteful duplication is avoided.' A brave try—but the characteristic Shannon sting was in the tail: 'Looking westwards from Dublin, the picture may be confusing. Looking outwards from Shannon, it is a clear—if necessarily complex—picture.'

"It has been most of its life under threat of overfly at one time or another," O'Regan recalled in 1990 "and the threat has really stimulated new activities and new ideas." The campaign by US interests to gain access to Dublin at Shannon's expense grew in intensity through the late 1960s and early 1970s,[8] culminating in an announcement by the US authorities on 18 August 1971 that they were terminating the right of Aer Línte to serve New York as from 18 August 1972. The year's grace was patently an exercise in brinkmanship, but the situation was sufficiently serious to embarrass the Irish government, which did not relish the prospect of a major rift with Washington. A hearing of the case by the US Civil Aeronautics Board was fixed for early 1972 and Brendan O'Regan was asked to submit written evidence on behalf of the Shannon interests. His lengthy document—nineteen foolscap pages—traced the history of the Shannon enterprise to date. 'There is a common idea that the Irish purpose in confining transatlantic landings to Shannon is to support Aerlínte,' it began. 'I will show that this is a mistaken view. The Irish purpose is to:

"develop Shannon in the interest of the Irish economy as a whole

" to maintain a pattern of tourist movement which is in the best interests of the whole Irish economy

" to foster Shannon as a major port and focus of commercial and industrial activity in the west of Ireland

" thus to revitalise the West and counteract the drift of all activity and population to the east of Ireland or further east to England

" and to bring about a healthy demographic and cultural balance in the life of the nation."

The final paragraph of the document completed the full statement of what might be termed the philosophical basis of the whole endeavour: 'The positive input by Irish interests in new tourism products and in air freight has had much wider effects than are measurable in terms of that input. A rise in business at an airport has a cumulative effect. The more business there is, the more frequent and diverse are the air services to cater for it. The more frequent and diverse the services, the more traffic is attracted to use them. The Development Company, which had used that snowball effect for growth, is fully conscious that a similar effect would occur in decline.'

This similar effect was foreseen, presumably, as a melting snowball; but the prospect of such deliquescence did not wring the hearts of the Americans. The obligation to land at Shannon, the president of TWA had observed in 1966, 'is somewhat akin to suggesting that, because parts of northern New England are economically underdeveloped, non-US flag carriers should deposit their passengers at Skowehegan, Maine'[9]—the kind of comparison that was again to be made when the campaign against the Shannon stopover was renewed from another direction in the late 1980s. In the event, and after protracted political, commercial and diplomatic manoeu-vrings, the first cause was lost. In June 1973, some twenty-eight years after the issue had initially been raised, a revision of the bilateral treaty between the two countries permitted one US airline to serve Dublin ... via Shannon. Pan American was awarded the route but decided it did not, after all, want it. The role fell to TWA, whose brief tenure ended in 1979, the airline pleading the inability to operate profitably. Subsequent undertakers were, for similar stated reasons, to come and go. *Parturiunt montes, nascetur ridiculus mus*: though perhaps the timorous nature of the mouse born following the protracted birth pangs of the Shannon mountains was attributable in some degree to the fact that the airport had, for the moment, preserved its status as the country's first and obligatory port of entry on the transatlantic route.

It was, however, more than a little shaken by the experience. 'Now that Dublin rights had been granted to a US carrier it was even more necessary that there should be an agency giving special attention to the promotion of Shannon,' the SFADCo directors concluded in August 1973: 'otherwise it was probable that the size and commercial power of Dublin city would force expansion of all facilities there, including the airport, at the expense of the Shannon region.' There was equal concern as to the attitude of their political masters: 'In the Department of Transport and Power it was recognised that originally the company was the only body to which the function of Shannon traffic promotion was appropriate; but there was now some doubt that, in changed circumstances, it was still appropriate ... if the regional activities were to expand still further it might be that the company should withdraw more and more from traffic promotion'—though the Department, it was believed, recognised that there was no other body to undertake the task. The board further expressed its concern at the decline of traffic at the airport at a time when total transatlantic movements were on the increase.

A major element in the problem was the continuing failure to secure the establishment of routes to the east. "If you looked back to 1959," said Gerry McKeon, who joined SFADCo in 1969, "you can really say that we didn't create many new services ... our only real achievement was to get scheduled flights to London."

'Potential for growth of European traffic ... is severely restricted by the absence (other than the London service) of direct services from European countries,' the 1974 SFADCo Annual Report complained. Ireland's accession to the EEC in 1972 had, in this respect, made little difference. In April 1974 a joint Aer Rianta/SFADCo aviation committee decided to engage a consultant, and though the desired scheduled connections with mainland Europe largely failed to develop the picture was somewhat better in respect of charter operations catering for the tourist trade. On 9 December 1975 *The Irish Times* reported that 'in the first nine months of this year, European terminal traffic [at Shannon] jumped by a respectable 6% to 127,000, and with charter series due to come in next summer from Dusseldorf, Frankfurt, Amsterdam, Berlin and Brussels, the growth in Europe may again be better than on the Atlantic'.

Economic recession on both sides of the Atlantic combined with the effects of the violence in Northern Ireland had seriously affected the volume of flights from the United States, but Jack Ryan, Aer Rianta's manager at Shannon and a colleague of Brendan O'Regan's since Rineanna days, achieved something of a breakthrough in persuading a number of major carriers operating between the US and destinations in eastern Europe, central Europe and Africa to stop-over at Shannon. Between January and September 1975 transit traffic increased by thirteen per cent over the same period in the previous year, with consequent benefit to the duty-free shop and the expanding mail order business. The provision of inflight meals and revenue from landing charges and the supply of fuel contributed substantially to Aer Rianta's earnings. Shannon offered not only economic incentives to transiting aircraft but also the advantages of a relatively uncrowded airspace. A major new user was Aeroflot, one of whose captains

68. *Tony Ryan, founder of Guinness Peat Aviation, in his office in Shannon Airport House, 20 June 1978. In the previous February he had written to the author: 'It is appropriate at the moment for us to become a little more well known in the community, particularly in the financial sector, as we are in the process of launching a scheme of aircraft investment.' In early 1992 GPA was the largest company leasing modern-generation aircraft in the world.*

69. *The purpose-built GPA headquarters at Shannon.*

'raised a few horse laughs when he radioed Shannon to enquire how many aircraft were ahead of him waiting to land'.[10] For the year 1975 the airport's total passenger throughput, terminal and transit, totalled 1,031,900, compared with the 571,300 of its Scottish rival Prestwick. 'We have got to be careful not to become fat and happy with the increase in transit traffic,' a spokesman for Shannon Development told *The Irish Times* air correspondent Jack Fagan: 'This is the white underbelly, it provides finance for the airport but not for the region as a whole. Therefore the most important thing now is to increase terminal traffic.' Or, in Brendan O'Regan's more expressive phrasing: 'We must reach into the sky and pull the business down.'

'EEC membership will greatly enhance the attractiveness of the Region to industrial development,' he had predicted in 1972, a year in which employment at Shannon fell by 382 compared with the previous twelve months. 'Now that Ireland has joined the European Economic Community, Shannon's strategic crossroads location offers even greater scope for business enterprises established within the Airport Zone,' claimed a SFADCo publication of April 1973, maintaining the upbeat note. This, however, was not simply a repackaging of existing incentives: *Shannon Airport House—Ireland. A Strategic European Location for Office Operations* made up in innovation for what it lacked in titular concision. In offering office space in a purpose-built block it was in effect taking the first significant step towards the encouragement of service industries to locate at the airport. The concept was a novel one to many people who still saw employment in terms of the repetitive processes of the production line; and financial services in particular were not looked upon with any great favour by the Department of Finance: 'people just playing around with money,' as Paul Sheane, who joined SFADCo in 1980, categorised the official attitude. Within two years, however, Shannon Airport House had secured a tenant who was to demonstrate his ability to engage in that activity in an unequivocally effective manner.

'When GPA was established here in Shannon in 1975 with a team of six people, including a secretary,' said its founder, Tony Ryan,[11] 'our role was primarily that of an agent. For instance, we identified leasing or purchase requirements in the Southern Hemisphere and then matched them with surplus aircraft from the Northern Hemisphere. This was a fairly easy exercise in 1975 and '76 when we were still affected by a world recession—a lot of aircraft were around and a lot of airlines needed help in finding homes for them. When the recession ended in 1977 the market changed and we had to go from an intermediary to a principal role where we acquired our own aircraft and leased and controlled them ourselves. This led to the formation of Air Tara, a fully-fledged airline with its own management structure, pilots and engineers—but without routes of its own.'

Tony Ryan's aspirations, in the event, verged on the side of modesty: in September 1991 GPA was the largest undertaking of its kind in the world, with ninety-seven airline customers in forty-six countries and a fleet of 313 aircraft. "Initially," said Niall Greene, who joined GPA from Aer Lingus in 1976, "we had to give the government an undertaking as to how much traffic we could generate for the airport. We used to stick our tongues firmly in our cheeks and make the most outrageous promises that we could with some degree of honesty get away with. We have out-performed these undertakings to an extent no one could possibly have envisaged."

GPA had developed out of Tony Ryan's involvement in aircraft leasing while still an employee of Aer Lingus: ' ... we established that there was a leasing requirement beyond what Aer Lingus had to offer,' he said. 'We were also clear that there were two definite ingredients required to develop that market: technical and operational expertise (and Aer Lingus certainly had that) and financial expertise. Just prior to that time, in 1973, Aer Lingus had bought ten per cent of the Guinness Peat Group, an amalgam of Guinness and Mahon, the old-established Irish merchant bankers, and Lewis and Peat, a very diversified company trading mainly in South East Asia and South America. Capitalising on the relationship between Aer Lingus and the Guinness Peat Group it was natural that the two main shareholders should come together in what became Guinness Peat Aviation.'[12]

By 1991 the GPA shareholding, spread across a range of investors, bankers, other leasing companies and manufacturers, had broadened to become roughly one-third North American, one-third Japanese and one-third European. Whilst the executives, several of them distinguished ex-diplomats, remained largely Irish the list of co-opted directors read like an abridged international *Who's Who*: former Taoiseach (and ex-Aer Lingus employee) Garret FitzGerald; former EC Commissioner and Irish Attorney General Peter Sutherland; former British Chancellor of the Exchequer Nigel Lawson; former chairman of ICI, Sir John Harvey-Jones; Shinroku Morohashi, president of the Mitsubishi Corporation —to name only some of the more prominent. Describing the GPA boardroom as 'one of the most exclusive in Europe', *The Independent on Sunday* (London) added: 'More astonishing is that this exclusive group has been brought together by a train-driver's son from Tipperary who founded his company only fifteen years ago with capital of $50,000. ... '[13] The group profit in 1991 was $1.2 million per employee—"unheard of," according to Niall Greene, "in almost any industry."

What *The Independent on Sunday* described in the same article as 'a nondescript building beside Shannon Airport' was subsequently abandoned for a purpose-built headquarters in keeping with GPA's growing status—

sited not in Monaco, or the Isle of Man, or the Cayman Islands, or in any other secure tax-haven but within easy walking distance of where it all began. GPA, according to regularly recirculated rumours, had been about to forsake Shannon on several occasions, but, claimed Greene, there never had been any truth in any of them. "A lot of people tried to attract us out of Shannon," he admitted, "but we never considered it ourselves." The location conferred a number of very obvious advantages in the taxation field and with them other attractions. "One of the great advantages for those of us in Shannon is that we work very hard, do a lot of travelling and it's been a very good place to come back to . . . your job, your family, the big outdoors." GPA had, on this basis, no trouble in attracting Americans, Danes and Icelanders of the requisite quality. But, said Greene, "sometimes we have had problems with [Irish] people who see great advantages to living in Dublin and great disadvantages to living anywhere else." As regards relationships with SFADCo: "They are our landlords: of necessity we work very closely. We've had our ups and downs. GPA is a very good totem pole for Shannon Development. If you can build a financial services global company in Shannon with all the problems we used to have then you have to be able to do a lot of other things here as well to a high standard." SFADCo, for its part, fully acknowledged Tony Ryan's contribution. "What GPA has done for Shannon," as Arthur O'Keeffe put it, "can never be repaid."

It is not untypical of GPA that a visit, in April 1991, to the site of the new aerospace industry at the far side of the airport from their head office—a ten minute car drive—should have involved the use of a helicopter. But from the aerial vantage point it was possible to see how the new development related to Shannon as a whole and to its historical genesis: the vestiges of the never-completed flying-boat base; the town, expanding from its nucleus on Drumgeely Hill; Smithstown, offshoot of the Free Zone; and in the distance Bunratty, its old stone bridge relegated to a backwater by the construction of the new dual carriageway. The future, however, lay immediately below. Site work for the new project was well under way, but the area still offered the appearance of a small rural community served by a fragmentary network of bohreens drifting off in the general direction of Ennis. All this, of course, would be changed: and within a few short months the last evidences of a rural environment would have finally receded from the close vicinity of the airport. The six aircraft bays, each big enough to take a Boeing 767, would dwarf the SRS hangar on the terminal building side—itself a structure which, in Shannon terms, could be classed as an historic building.

On 19 March 1960 the *Clare Champion* carried a photograph of a 'giant aircraft hangar . . . being built for Seaboard & Western'—an operator which had been using Shannon for scheduled cargo services since 1955 and which had also leased Constellations to Aer Línte before that airline acquired its own fleet for the transatlantic service. Seaboard & Western cargo services ended in 1962, but the hangar, which they had leased, was reoccupied some little time later by the American-owned Shannon Repair Services, a new company with a licence from the Federal Aviation Agency (FAA) permitting it to work on US-registered aircraft. It traded successfully, but, following a downturn in business in 1966 which threatened it with closure, was acquired by Aer Lingus, which had itself been involved in maintenance at the airport and had originally been very unhappy about the government's decision to licence a rival to perform work which it was already doing. Under its new management SRS expanded its operations and developed into a compre-hensive maintenance, overhaul and handling agency, with a particular expertise in the executive jets which were beginning to figure significantly in Shannon traffic patterns. To reflect its new status its name was changed to SRS Aviation (Ireland) Ltd.[14]

Though Aer Lingus continued to concentrate its principal maintenance activities in Dublin the existence of SRS at Shannon supplied the inter-national credentials necessary for the airport's further expansion into aviation-related activities and probably made it easier—though in this case, perhaps, not by much—for Dara Hall and Harry Ryan, two young local men whose entrepreneurial vision extended from Drumgeely Hill to the Urals, to secure a contract for repainting Aeroflot aircraft. "They went out and learnt how to do high-quality aircraft painting," said Niall Greene, "and for a long time worked in other people's facilities." Once established in Shannon the operation expanded to a degree that a new company involving both GPA and Aer Rianta, GPA Expressair, was set up to handle it. The travel-stained Ilyushins and Tupolevs sank out of the skies onto the Shannon runways with gratifying regularity in the late 1980s: pending completion of custom-built facilities the repainting was carried on in the old Lockheed hangar dating from the early Rineanna days. But even before the break-up of the USSR, GPA recognised that political changes and the cyclical nature of the airline industry could cause the business to evaporate as dramatically as it had appeared. It was already well advanced in the planning for a major new project.

Robin Wilson, born in Dublin, educated in England, had spent most of his working life in Britain and the US and had never anticipated coming back to Ireland—certainly not in the course of employment. As president of Western Airlines in the mid-1980s he had been involved in the sale of six aircraft to GPA and "could not help but be impressed with the dynamism of the organisation". At the suggestion of Tony Ryan he joined the company in 1988 but found himself visiting six countries on GPA's behalf before he succeeded in setting foot once more in Ireland. One of these countries was Switzerland, where a meeting had been arranged to discuss the projected Shannon Aerospace facility. At this stage the concept of a major maintenance plant had not been finalised. Would GPA do it on their own? Would they even do it in Shannon? At least two other locations had been strongly urged upon them. "A fairly major selling job had to be done on GPA and their partners," said Arthur O'Keeffe of SFADCo, "that this was the best of a number of possible locations.... Where we were involved was convincing the partners that the kind of skills were available and that the incentive package, a fairly substantial one, was as good as or better than they might obtain elsewhere. Would it have happened without us? Perhaps, perhaps not. I don't think it would."

Wilson, whose appointment was as managing director of the newly-formed GPA Technologies, had run maintenance operations for two large US airlines and was fully aware that GPA, small in numbers and with no relevant experience, faced a marketplace problem: starting with the support of an established reputation was crucial. GPA had enjoyed good relations with Swissair, and Wilson's discussions with them made it clear that they could not continue as they were: they were running out of maintenance capacity in Switzerland and finding it impossible to recruit the right people at an acceptable price. Swissair had already undertaken an independent evaluation of possible outside locations for their own planned maintenance facility and narrowed them down to three, one of which was Ireland. "So then," said Robin Wilson, "we took it a step further. It was clear to them that having GPA as a partner would probably swing it." Swissair would continue to be responsible for wide-bodied aircraft and component maintenance; and with the GPA fleet consisting largely of narrow-bodied types—MD80s and 737s—it seemed an ideal arrangement. But Swissair, for their part, did not want to become involved in 737s, which were not represented in their own fleet. "They suggested we looked at a 737 operator as a partner," said Wilson. "They mentioned Lufthansa." The German airline, as it happened, had been also been conducting a far-reaching analysis of its maintenance requirements and had reached similiar conclusions. Just before the collapse of the Berlin Wall it agreed to participate as the third Shannon Aerospace partner; a little later and its eyes would have turned decisively eastward.

John Horgan, former chairman of the Labour Court, undertook the task of explaining the niceties of Irish industrial relations to the Germans and Swiss ('because I've seen a thousand ways not to run a business') and it was agreed

70. *Early stages of the Shannon Aerospace project at Shannon Airport, a joint venture between GPA, Swissair and Lufthansa.*

71. *Work proceeding at the new Shannon Aviation Park early in 1992.*

that a single union, SIPTU,[15] would act for those of the planned workforce of 1,000 who sought union representation. Advertisements appeared in January 1990 to recruit the first 100 trainee aircraft maintenance technicians for a two-year programme to commence the following April and to include periods of study and tuition with Lufthansa in Germany and Swissair in Switzerland. 'The successful applicants,' the announcement concluded, 'will be required to demonstrate a strong commitment to live and work in the Mid-West.' Amongst those selected from the 1,900 who responded were five girls, two from Co. Limerick and two from Co. Clare. A year later the Germans and Swiss were expressing themselves as extremely impressed with the quality of the intake, and senior management from their two airlines were taking up residence in the Shannon region on five-year contracts. The day and the hour of the arrival of the first aircraft for maintenance—14.00 on 19 September 1992—had been decided down to its precise identity: a Swissair DC9, registration HB INA.

☆ ☆ ☆ ☆ ☆ ☆

'May I suggest an achievable set of objectives for the Irish aviation industry?' Tony Ryan requested of a meeting of the Irish Airline Pilots' Association on 8 March 1990. Assuming assent he went on to outline these objectives as follows:

'We should determine to *double* its size at the end of each of the next five-year periods;

'We should secure for Ireland the establishment and operation of a central registry for all European civil aircraft in the same fashion as all 295,000 US aircraft are registered in Oklahoma—this to replace the present unco-ordinated and costly national patchwork approach;

'We should dramatically increase the amount of aviation-related manufacturing in Ireland, taking advantage of the many opportunities now emerging as a result of our development of the Shannon Aerospace park;

'While there is obviously a limit to the amount of travel that can be directly generated by a population of only 3.5 million people, there is huge scope to exploit Ireland's unique geographic position as a crossroads between East and West.'

'Civil aviation is fundamental to social and economic growth and to the support of civilised living,' he continued. 'Ireland has achieved the criticial mass of activity necessary to make our country a leading world centre for civil aviation; we should see ourselves as being to civil aviation what Silicon Valley is to electronics or Zurich is to banking.'

Though the discourse would have been different in detail this might have been Brendan O'Regan talking. If the two men offer a marked contrast in almost every personal respect they share the same vision (though Ryan, for his part, might be nervous of the word) of a role for Shannon and by implication for the country as a whole on the world stage. Before that particular piece of jargon had gained currency O'Regan was committed to establishing a 'critical mass' in terms of the industrial development of the Free Zone; and, of course, his devotion to the 'crossroads' concept has already been extensively documented. Ryan, imbued with something of the same creative restlessness and a similar impatience with no-hopers, begrudgers and little-Irelanders, shares—though he expresses it somewhat differently —O'Regan's strong loyalty to his roots and, stemming from that, to the region as a whole. Of his rescue and restoration of the Bolton Library in Cashel (though across the 'border' in South Tipperary and therefore beyond the Shannon Region limits), Ciaran MacGonigal wrote, in a comment not unexpressive of the metropolitan viewpoint: 'It is an amazing collection to have outside Dublin. . . .'[16] The comparison between the two men can be pushed too far, but Shannon has, to say the least, been fortunate in the succession.

By early 1992 the 'critical mass' in aviation terms was well on the way to meaningful agglomeration. GPA itself, through GPA Technologies, was, in addition to Shannon Aerospace, operating three companies involving the provision of spares and aircraft repainting and had announced a joint venture, Shannon Turbine Technologies, with Sulzer Brothers to be located in the 110-acre World Aviation Park, formally opened on 23 September 1991 by the Minister for Industry and Commerce, Desmond O'Malley. This, he said, was a key initiative being taken by Shannon Development to create a primary centre for aerospace operations in Ireland. The company, he said, 'has played a key role in bringing together all the diverse elements that exist in Shannon's aviation infrastructure. With a track record of over thirty years in successful Industrial Free Zone development and promotion at Shannon, I believe that the company is ideally placed to accomplish this task and to spearhead a new era for Shannon in aviation terms. . . .' On the same day he made the official announcement of the establishment of Acromil, the US aerospace components manufacturer, in the Free Zone.

This momentum had been given an initial impetus with the sponsoring by GPA in 1990 of a Chair of Aircraft Engineering in the University of Limerick, an initiative followed by the decision of Robin Wilson, who had been involved in the selection of the appointee and who had "got to know and greatly respect the University and its contribution to the area", to

[203]

72. *The first tanker arrives at Shannon with Russian oil, 1 June 1980.*

73. *Victor Bowman, president of Acromil, with Desmond O'Malley, Minister for Industry and Commerce and John A. Daly, chairman of Shannon Development at the launch of the project at Shannon, 23 September 1991.*

embark upon a new academic career as an adjunct professor whilst retaining his links with GPA as chairman of Air Tara and board member of Shannon Aerospace.

In the meantime Aer Rianta, the airport authority, had been strengthening its links with its second most important airline customer, Aeroflot. Aer Lingus remained in first place, though in the early 1990s it was in the process of being overtaken by the Soviet airline's expansion of its routes to North America consequent upon its winning rights to carry passengers between Shannon and Washington. In April 1991 Aeroflot's general manager in Ireland, Boris Krivchenko, announced that Shannon would become the hub for its transatlantic operations, new services originating in the Soviet Union to connect with onward flights to fourteen destinations on the American continent. At the same time he made public the formation of a new company, Aeroshannon, which was to be a joint venture involving Aeroflot, Aer Rianta and its subsidiary Aer Rianta International to develop these services. Events in the Soviet Union were, however, to cast their shadow. While Aeroflot retained its identity immediately following the establishment of the Commonweath of Independent States and proceeded with its plan to construct accommodation at Shannon for its overnighting crews, airlines bearing the colours and insignia of the new republics began to make their appearance. On 5 January 1992 Aeroflot Moscow Airlines inaugurated its services out of Shannon with a flight to Miami carrying 120 Tipperary hurling team members and supporters.

Aer Rianta had itself built upon the strong Soviet connection, which had developed both from the Aeroflot services and from the establishment of a USSR oil terminal at the airport in 1981, to secure a contract to install and operate the first duty-free facility at Moscow's Shermetyvo 2 airport. A joint Aer Rianta-Aeroflot company, Aerofirst, was established for the purpose and the new shop, constructed in its entirety by the Dublin firm Modern Display Artists (MDA) was formally and jointly opened by Soviet Minister for Civil Aviation, Alexander Volkov and his Irish counterpart, John Wilson, on 12 May 1988. Aeroflot personnel, according to Liam Skelly, Aer Rianta's deputy chief executive, were proud of the achievement 'and to be proven correct in their choice of partner. This is one of the most exciting projects', he said, 'that Shannon and Aer Rianta has [sic] embarked on for a long number of years.'[17] Aer Rianta personnel became permanent Moscow residents.

'The refurbishing of their living quarters in a nearby Hotel,' wrote the Moscow correspondent of *Runway/Airports*[18] '. . . is nearly complete and the hotel has taken on a distinctively Irish flavour with snooker, darts and regular videos from home. The smell of bacon, sausages and black pudding mingle easily with the odours of more traditional Russian dishes as do the discussions on the relative merits of Irish brown bread and Russian Blakk.' In the following years Aerofirst opened two other duty-free and two hotel shops in Leningrad and a duty-free facility on the Soviet-Finnish border, with others in prospect. In 1990 the floor area of the Moscow duty-free shop was extended from 332 to 499 square metres; and in September 1991 the Minister for Foreign Affairs, Gerard Collins, opened 'The Irish House on the Arbat', a shopping complex operated by SITCO, the Soviet Irish Trading Company, a joint venture involving Russian interests, Aer Rianta and Computer Support Services, Shannon.

If these new ventures in aviation, both in the industrial and entre-preneurial sectors, marked another turning-point in the history of Shannon the re-orientation was, in the light of other events, not untimely. The admission of North American airlines to Dublin whilst obliging them to maintain the compulsory Shannon stop did no more than put the lid on a pot which would clearly continue to simmer. To change the metaphor, the anti-Shannon lobby was simply being washed down in preparation for its occupation by a new body of objectors, this time from the east rather than the west. Towards the end of the 1980s the objections manifested themselves in an organised manner in the form of the Fly Dublin Direct Committee, a body with close links with the Dublin Chamber of Commerce. In March 1990 a report[19] produced at the committee's instigation by Colm McCarthy of Davy Kelleher McCarthy, a Dublin firm of economic consultants, concluded that 'the compulsory stop at Shannon is inhibiting the expansion of North American tourist capacity into Ireland, is preventing the development of Irish long-haul aviation and is diverting traffic to British and other foreign airlines. The benefits of the policy, such as they are, are exclusively local. . . .'

The day after the document was published Shannon Development and Aer Rianta announced the formation of Shannon Airport Marketing, to ensure, according to Aer Rianta's chief executive, Derek Keogh, that 'with a synergy between the two companies no opportunity for bringing traffic to Shannon and thus to Ireland was lost'. Though marketed under a new FLY SHANNON label the idea was simply the old 'gateway' strategy refurbished in response to the new threat. As Gerry McKeon of SFADCo explained: "Aer Rianta handle the three Fs—fuel, fees and food—and we handle the logistics, analytical stuff and promotion . . . Now you've a team up there that can meet any airline and talk about the three Fs and the promotional support. It's a bit of a departure—some people here felt that we gave away bits of our birth-right. But I worked on the basis that the man in the street doesn't really care who put the Shannon–Bristol service on the ground. . . ." The object of the exercise was to attempt, once again, to attract scheduled carriers from Britain and mainland Europe and also to find a replacement or replacements on the North Atlantic for Pan American which withdrew (for the second time) from the route on 17 February 1990. "I see some sense," added McKeon, "in eventually pulling the western airports together, creating a critical mass."

Response in the region itself, particularly when in April 1990 the Minister for Tourism and Transport gave permission for transatlantic charters to overfly Shannon and land at Knock, was somewhat less measured. Donal Carey, a Fine Gael TD, said that Clare County Council should call for Minister Seamus Brennan's resignation. 'He doesn't know the business and has spent his time genuflecting to the likes of O'Reilly and Smurfit up in Dublin. To hell with Connacht and Cork. Shannon should be made into a hub airport.'[20] There was much more in this vein, and little evidence of popular solidarity with the sister western airport. "I was ashamed of Shannon when they attacked Knock," said John A. Daly, then SFADCo chairman and a former Aer Rianta director: "I recognised [in Monsignor Horan, its prime mover] a kindred spirit to Brendan O'Regan .... The attack was so anti the spirit of Shannon. I am very worried about the attitude towards Shannon Airport per se, and the very emotive and defensive manner in which everybody talks about the overflying issue."

The Shannon Status Committee, formed in response to the pressure from Dublin, sponsored its own economic research[21] which reached conclusions broadly supportive of the status quo; but many Shannon Region people privately, and some publicly, admitted that some modification of the policy was inevitable. Amongst the latter was numbered, somewhat controversially, Edward Walsh of the University of Limerick, who in a wide-ranging interview with the *Limerick Chronicle* (20 November 1990) said that ' This idea of clinging to the sacred air rights for Shannon is clinging to a model that was very good in the past but will not survive within the European Community regulations. We can hang on to it, maybe delaying the day. Inevitably, Shannon will be overflown. And if our efforts have been directed to preventing it being overflown, and not making good reasons why aircraft want to come here, then we're not only going to be overflown but we'll be left without the kind of things that will safeguard the future'. Emphasising that he was speaking from an academic standpoint rather than in his role as a director of Shannon Development he continued: 'I believe strongly that the best strategy for this region is to support a deal which involves overfly and investment,' stressing the importance of the establishment of eastward connections. 'The Atlantic,' he added, 'doesn't matter too much.'

In fact, to the cumulative ironies, over the years, of the transatlantic debate had been added, as the controversy continued, the serious falling-off in traffic consequent upon the US recession and the Gulf War and its replacement by a remarkable increase in tourism from mainland Europe. Shamrocks and the kissing of the Blarney stone were out: *Does your mother come from Ireland?* gave way to more authentically ethnic music of greater appeal to those of Parisian or Milanese parentage, souvenir shops had to pension off the plastic leprechauns, ditch the kitsch and restock with goods of altogether another orientation. In the light of this development, which appeared to be as permanent as anything in the airline/leisure business, some of the edge was inevitably taken off the confrontation. However, the Dublin lobby continued to insist that business traffic to the US was going in volume over London Heathrow (in spite of the hazards there of interlining baggage, inconvenient changes of terminal and the lack of normal transit facilities for Irish-originating passengers). It also insisted that the Shannon stop was inhibiting US and Canadian airlines, particularly the latter, from serving Ireland and that tourist traffic really wanted to go to Dublin, although some fifty to seventy-five per cent of it still seemed happy to deplane at Shannon. As the events of previous decades had shown, however, foreign airlines could not be relied upon to maintain a service even when their immediate demands had been met; and Ireland, in US terms, remained a largely insignificant destination in the context of Europe as a whole. Early in 1992 it seemed likely that the controversy would eventually result in some form of compromise, with Shannon retaining part of its existing terminal traffic and Aer Lingus, for example, being permitted to operate a planned Los Angeles service direct from Dublin. Repeated promises of an early decision by the responsible minister, Máire Geoghegan-Quinn, remained, however, unfulfilled, with supporters of the Dublin and Shannon lobbies becoming increasingly more vocal.

With local interests continuing to predict nothing but economic ruin as the result of any change, Brendan O'Regan adopted a characteristically optimistic outlook. 'Anybody who flies from Shannon to any of the international airports on the other side of the Atlantic will realise that air transport is expanding all the time and there will be plenty of business for all Irish airports.'[22] Ed Walsh, equally positively, favoured a five-year government subsidy similar in function to that formerly given to Aer Lingus to stop at Shannon: 'Redirect that. The quid pro quo in this region is to say, okay, we accept that it is in the national interest—and it is—to overfly Shannon. But in return for that, because we have built our way of life and our enterprise around it, it would be disruptive to some enterprise that is located here and

[208]

certainly some enterprise would have to relocate. . . . There is a real cost. Now let's sit down, let's be pragmatic. Let's have a scenario for the future.'

☆ ☆ ☆ ☆ ☆ ☆

This study must halt on the prudent side of prediction. The measure of what might in the future be achieved can, however, to some extent be calculated upon the record of what has gone before. The airport, where the story began, is likely to remain as the cohesive focus of the region in that it continues to provide much of the rationale for developments in the area of tourism and seems likely to succeed in its new aviation-related role. Its position as an east-west crossroads, so consistently supported by Brendan O'Regan, was considerably strengthened by its acquiring pre-clearance facilities operated by the US Immigration Service; though that Service's refusal to allow pre-clearance to passengers on the inaugural Aeroflot flight to Miami in April 1990 suggested that the Cold War thaw was then not yet complete. The airport's status received somewhat similarly anomalous confirmation in its use, in controversial circumstances, by the US forces in the course of the Gulf War and it continued to be the somewhat unwilling and, in spite of decades of experience, ill-prepared recipient of refugees from inimical political systems seeking asylum together with others with more mixed motives.

As a centre, however, the airport will key, but not control, the development of what seems likely, against all the odds, to coalesce ultimately into some kind of formal entity wearing the emblem of the Shannon Region— with a rejuvenated Limerick city asserting a more central role. Whether this entity will continue to include north Kerry or south-west Offaly, whether it will ever acquire a coat of arms or sport a football team are matters for marginal speculation. The only thing that can safely be said is that the regionalisation process has gone too far in the area to be put into reverse, and whatever the reluctance of central government to devolve power and the funding necessary to give that power a reality, the movement towards greater regional independence in Europe as a whole will inevitably register its effect even on the Community's outer margins.

Not, perhaps, too quickly. 'One must question real commitment to regional development in Ireland until adequate resources, political direction, and, most importantly, real decision-making authority is given to the regional bodies,' said John A. Daly, launching the 1989 Shannon Development Annual Report. On the evidence of the 1991 local government legislation that commitment would seem at best lukewarm; though the publication in January 1992 of the report of the Industrial Policy Review

Group[23] seemed to endorse the Shannon initiative by calling for greater emphasis on regional structures for industrial development. 'I am encouraged by the fact that some of the key recommendations ... amount effectively to a recognition of the ability of individuals and organisations in this Region to work together in order to maximise development potential,' said Tom Dunne in one of his last public utterances before retiring as SFADCo's managing director. What form such recognition may take remains a matter for speculation.

In the meantime this curious entity, whether operating under its unwieldy acronym or as the more acceptable—if still confusingly-named— Shannon Development, would seem likely in the immediate future to continue to act in loco parentis, a role which, for all its changes of direction, forced and unforced, it has evolved and sustained virtually unsupported in the wider regional context and which still constitutes the only model upon which further development in this area could feasibly be based. J. Buist MacKenzie, the Scottish consultant who had advised Brendan O'Regan on its formation, told a SFADCo meeting held in his honour in 1973: 'Shannon's great success has been based on creativeness, enterprise and innovation. And this was not innovation in a protected market in a small country. It was innovation in the competitive global market which is the world today. . . .' Or as the 1986 *Report of the Committee on Public Expenditure* more cautiously assessed it: 'Within the Irish government system SFADCo is a unique organisation in that it combines a number of somewhat different functions and has even at times reported to different Departments. This singularly confers upon the Company a special status which is sometimes regarded as being a source of strength. . . .'

Pending the statutory establishment of the autonomous Shannon Region and consequent consultation with the office of the Chief Herald, SFADCo should perhaps consider the interim replacement of its current somewhat involuted shamrock symbol with a representation—possibly along the lines of the 'active enzymes' of the old washing-powder commercials—of a catalyst with teeth.

References

1. 13 April 1991
2. See p. 60
3. Minutes, 9 February 1967
4. Minutes, 8 January 1969
5. Minutes, 27 January 1971

6. Report by the Dáil Committee on Public Expenditure (1986), op. cit., p. 21ff
7. Bernard Share, *The Flight of the Iolar*, pp. 236–237
8. Share, op.cit., pp. 137-154
9. Share, op. cit., p. 142
10. *The Irish Times*, 9 December 1975
11. 'Mr Ryan's Airline', in *Cara*, Vol. 13 no. 1, 1980, p. 27
12. Ibid.
13. 11 February 1990
14. See *Irish Air Letter* Nos 180, 181, December 1989–January 1990
15. Services, Industrial, Professional and Technical Trade Union
16. 'The Opulent Eye', in *The Irish Times*, 29 June 1991
17. *Runway/Airports*, June-July 1988, p. 23
18. Ibid.
19. *The Shannon Stopover Policy: Impact on Tourism Growth and on the Aviation Industry*, Davy Kelleher McCarthy, Dublin 1990
20. *The Clare Champion*, 20 April 1990
21. *Shannon's Transatlantic Gateway Status: an Analysis*, Envision Marketing Consultants and University College Galway 1990
22. *The Irish Times*, 21 April 1990
23. 'A time for change: industrial policy for the 1990s', Dublin 1992

Select Bibliography

MANUSCRIPT SOURCES

State papers, Department of the Taoiseach; SFADCo board minutes; reports and other documents as referenced.

PRINTED SOURCES

AVIATION

Anon: 'Aviation on the Shannon', in *Irish Air Letter*, Dublin 1985

Cuddy, Michael and others: *Shannon's Transatlantic Gateway Status: an Analysis*, Envision Marketing Consultants and University College Galway, 1990

Dunne, Tom and others: *Shannon Airport: 50 years of engineering*, Shannon 1987

Irish Air Letter, Dublin

Mc Gahern, Ray: ' The potential of aviation for wealth and employment creation in the Irish economy', in *Administration*, Vol. 39 no. 2, pp. 167–193, Dublin 1991

O'Sullivan, R. W.: 'An Irishman's Aviation Sketchbook', in *Irish Aviator*, Dublin 1988

Share, Bernard: *The Flight of the Iolar, The Aer Lingus experience, 1936–1986*, Dublin 1986

GENERAL

Bohan, Harry: *Ireland green. Social planning and rural development*, Dublin 1979

Bohan, Harry (Ed.): *Roots in a changing society, Social justice for rural Ireland*, Shannon 1982

Breen, Richard and others: *Understanding contemporary Ireland*, Dublin 1990.

Delany, Ruth: *By Shannon Shores*, Dublin 1987

Flanagan, Patrick: *Transport in Ireland 1880–1910*, Dublin 1969

Gilmore, Hilary: *Irish art heritage from 2000 BC, Design legacy from the Mid-West*, Dublin/Shannon 1983

Girvin, Brian: *Between Two Worlds*, Dublin 1989

Kearney, Richard (Ed.): *Across the frontiers: Ireland in the 1990s*, Dublin 1988

Lee, Joseph (Ed.): *Ireland–Towards a Sense of Place*, Cork 1985

Lenihan, Edmund: *In the Tracks of the West Clare Railway*, Cork 1990

McCarthy, John F. (Ed.): *Planning Ireland's future: the legacy of T. K. Whitaker*, Dublin 1990

Palmer, Patricia: 'Apples, arts, amnesiacs and emigrants: the university connection', in *The Irish Review*, No. 8, Spring 1990

Share, Bernard: 'Throw up your hat on a windy day', in *Ireland of the Welcomes*, Vol. 18 no. 6, pp. 24–29, Dublin 1970

REGIONALISM

Boylan, T. A. and M. P. Cuddy: 'Regional industrial policy: performance and challenge', in *Administration*, Vol. 32, Dublin 1984

Buchanan, Colin and partners: *Regional studies in Ireland*, Dublin 1968

Callanan, Tom and Brian: *Local Government in Ireland–the Regional Dimension*, (unpublished)

CII Small Firms Association: *Small business trends*. Regional Report no. 3—the Mid-West Region, Dublin 1990

Clout, J. O. (Ed.): *Regional Development in Western Europe*, 2nd ed., Chichester 1981

Hutterman, A.: 'Shannon 1976: the industrial estate and its regional implications', in *Irish Geography*, 11, pp. 179–183

Kupper, V. I.: 'Socio-geographical aspects of industrial growth at Shannon', in *Irish Geography*, 6, pp. 14–29

Lichfield, Nathaniel and associates: *Report and advisory outline plan for the Limerick region*, 2 vols, 1967

Newman, J. J.: *New dimensions in regional planning. A case study of Ireland*, Dublin 1967

O'Connor, Robert: *The Regional Dimension to Research and Technology Development in Ireland*, Economic and Social Research Institute report, Dublin 1986

O'Farrell, Patrick N.: 'Regional development in Ireland: the economic case for a regional policy', in *Administration*, Vol. 18, Dublin 1970

Shannon Free Airport Development Co.: *Five Year Programme for the Industrial Development of the Limerick, Clare and Tipperary NR region*, Shannon, 1969 and 1970 (Revised)

Shannon Free Airport Development Co.: *Shannon facts and figures 1974*

Various: 'Regionalism', five essays in *Administration*, Vol. 18, Dublin 1970

Viney, M. (Ed.): *An appraisal of regional planning in Ireland: seven seminars*, Dublin 1969

Walsh, F.: 'The growth-centre concept in Irish regional policy', in *Maynooth Review*, 2, pp. 22–41

SHANNON TOWN

Downes and Meehan in association with Frederick Rogerson: *Shannon Free Airport—preliminary proposals for industrial and community development*, Dublin 1962

O'Carroll, Cian: *Shannon: Ireland's New Town*. Town and Country Planning, London, February 1978

Ryan, Fr Liam: *Shannon: Ireland's New Town*: A Social Survey, Shannon 1969

Shannon Free Airport Development Co.: *Estates Manager's report*: 'Housing at Shannon, the case for a new approach', Shannon 1969

Shannon Free Airport Development Co.: *Social Trends in Shannon Town, Report of a Special Census*, Shannon 1975

Shannon Free Airport Development Co.: *Viability study: Shannon Town Centre 6,000 population stage*, Shannon 1967

Sheppard Fidler, A. G., and associates: *Shannon New Town—a reappraisal and medium-term structure plan*, Epsom 1972

Index

Acromil, 203, 204(p)
Adare Manor, 130
Aer Lingus, 29, 47, 53, 168, 173, 180, 190, 197, 205
  and Aer Rianta, 192
  freight services, 187
  Los Angeles service, 208
  and SFADCo, 60–61
  SRS, 199
Aer Línte, 190, 192, 199
Aer Rianta, 116, 180, 194
  and Aeroflot, 205–6
  and Shannon Airport, 188–92
Aer Rianta International, 205
Aerlínte, 60–61
Aerofirst, 205–6
Aeroflot, 93, 103, 194, 196, 199, 205, 209
Aeroshannon, 205
Agriculture, Department of, 60
Air Companies Bill, 1965, 190
Air Corps, 36, 40
Air France, 41
Air Tara, 196, 205
aircraft. see aviation
Alcan Aluminium Ltd, 152–3, 157–8. see also Aughinish Alumina
American Association of Travel Agents (AATA), 173
American Export Airlines, 41
American Export Lines, 42
AnCO, 62, 136, 170
Andrews, Mark Edwin, 114(p), 115
Annacotty, Limerick, 73
Antigua, 130, 131
Archaeological Society, Shannon, 95
Ardnacrusha, 129
Argentina, 171
Arthur's Quay, Limerick, 161, 163
Asahi Chemical Industry Company, 182–3
Ashling Microsystems, 147, 148

Askeaton, Co. Limerick, 66
Athlone, Co. Westmeath, 5
Aughinish Alumina, 72, 141(p), 142. see also Alcan
Australia, 9
aviation
  early transatlantic services, 29–31, 39–40, 41
  flying–boats, 26–31
  jet aircraft, 53–4
Avro Anson, 40

Bain, D., 38(p)
Ballina, Co. Tipperary, 14, 128
Ballycaseymore House, 147
Ballycastle, Co. Mayo, 144
Ballyhoura Fáilte Society Ltd, 119–21, 131
Ballylanders, 66
Ballylongford, Co. Kerry, 12, 153
Ballyorgan, Co. Limerick, 119
Ballyvaghan, Co. Clare, 6, 117, 125
Banagher, Co. Offaly, 127
Banagher Concrete, 149
Barcs, Mr, 67(p)
Barrett, Jim, 163
Barrett, Maureen, 16
Barrington, T. J., 8, 11–12
Barry, Patrick, 12
Barry, Peter, 151
Battery, Labasheeda, 152
Bavaria, 24
Baxter, Rev., 95
Beary, Jim, 119, 120
Beddy, Dr, 52, 68
Belfast Civic Trust, 162
Belgium, 23
Birdhill, Co. Tipperary, 183–4
Birr, Co. Offaly, 5, 12, 81, 149
Blaney, Neil, 10, 82–3
Blum, Jorgen, 67(p)
BOAC, 33, 35, 40–41, 187

Bohan, Fr Harry, 74, 118–19, 120
Boland, Joe, 122(p)
Bolton Library, Cashel, 203
Bord Fáilte, 19, 21, 109, 170, 172, 192
    O'Regan chairman, 56
    regional divisions, 8, 18, 175–6
    and RIC, 117
    and SFADCo, 71, 116
    traditional image, 173–4
Bord na Móna, 5, 127, 166–7
    locomotive, 13(p)
Bourke, Jack, 125, 129
Bow McLachlan, Paisley, 126
Bowman, Victor, 204(p)
Boynton, Jesse, 38(p), 44(p)
Brazil, 171
Brennan, Seamus, 207
Britain, 52, 60, 102, 186–7
    advertising in, 70
    New Towns, 82
    transatlantic services, 29
    wartime aviation, 33, 35, 37, 40–41
Broadford, Co. Clare, 129
Brophy, T., 10–12
Brougham, Finbar, 17
Brown, E. T. S., 63(p), 64
Brunt, Barry, 7
Buchanan Report, 10, 70, 142
Bunratty Castle, 104(p), 105–8, 111, 158,
    198
    folk park, 108–9, 112–15, 131
Bunratty Entertainers, 106(p), 107, 173
Burke, Richard, 137
Burlington, 74
Burls, John, 65
Burren, Co. Clare, 131
Burundi, 166
Bus Éireann, 66
Byrne, Paddy, 5

Cage, Ted, 82
Callanan, Tom, 9, 62, 68, 165, 169(p)
    chief executive, Plassey, 8, 139–40
    developments officer, 59–61
    and ODA, 171, 172–3
    on O'Regan, 51
    and Shannon town, 83
Campbell, Captain D., 38(p)

Canada, 29, 173, 177, 208
Candy, J. P., 26, 29
Cappamore, 66
Carey, Donal, 207
Carton House, 130
Casey, Edward F., 58
Cashel, Co. Tipperary, 15
Castle Tours, 116
Castleisland, Co. Kerry, 18
Castletroy, Limerick, 72
Catholic Church, 94–5
Central Fisheries Board, 16
Centre for International Co-operation,
    179–80, 181
Channel Tunnel, 149
Childers, Erskine, 57(p), 59, 67(p),
    114(p), 117, 190
    Air Companies Bill, 188
    and Bunratty Castle, 107, 108, 112
Chile, 97
Chinchilla Breeders' Association, 61
Chinchilla (Ireland) Ltd, 60
Chubb, Basil, 56
Church of Ireland, 94–5
Civic Trusts, 162
Civil Aviation, Report on, 1948, 47–8, 51
Clancy, Bart and Jim, 88
Clann na Poblachta, 52
Clare, Co., 15, 17, 21–2
    small industries, 150
Clare Chemicals, 67(p)
Clare Council of Trade Unions, 66
Clare County Council, 12, 82, 101, 102,
    117, 150, 158, 207
    Inis Cathaigh, 157
    SACTAS, 48
    and SFADCo, 10–11
    and Shannon Estuary, 152
Clare Development Team, 22
Clarisford House, 128
Cleary, Naoise, 122(p)
Clipper III, 39
Clonmacnoise, Co. Offaly, 5
Clonmacnoise and West Offaly
    Railway, 5, 13(p)
Club na Sionna, 93
Co-Am-Co, 60
Co-operation North, 65, 177–9, 180

Co-operation North Guide, The, 179
Coalition Government, 1973, 74, 137
Cobh, Co. Cork, 47
Coisceim Cheese, 141(p)
Collins, Gerard, 206
Colombia, 170, 171
Colón Free Zone, 59–60
Columby, Dave, 128
Comhairle Oiliúna, An (AnCO), 62, 136, 170
Comhlucht Siúcre Éireann, 53
Commonwealth of Independent States (CIS), 205
compulsory stop-over, 46, 52, 192–6, 206–9
    deletion recommended, 54
Computer Support Services, Shannon, 206
Condell, Frances, 100
Conference of Peripheral Maritime Regions, European Committee of, 12
Congested Districts, 22
Connaughton, Gus, 38(p)
Connolly, Jim, 21
Connolly, Neil, 101
Connor, J., 190
Conradh na Gaeilge, 93
Cooney, Fr, 123
Córas Iompair Éireann (CIE), 116, 172, 173, 187
Córas Tráchtála (CTT), 56, 170, 172–3
Corcanree, Limerick, 72
Cork Airport, 190
Corofin, Co. Clare, 122(p), 125
Corofin Heritage Centre, 122
Costello, M. J., 53
Coto Doñana, Spain, 131
Countess Cadogan (steamer), 126(p)
County Development teams, 22, 69, 145
Coward, Noel, 109, 110
Crag Cave, 18
Craggaunowen Castle, Co. Clare, 108, 117
Cratloe Rovers Football Club, 100
Crawley New Town, 82
Critchley, General, 42
Cronan estate, Shannon, 97
Crosby, Bing, 50(p)
Crossroads pub, 87

Custom House, Limerick, 108
Customs Free Airport (Amendment) Act, 1958, 58
Cyprus, 167, 168, 170

Daly, Brendan, 156
Daly, John A., 6, 113(p), 160(p), 173, 181(p), 204(p), 209
    on compulsory stop–over, 207
    and Kilrush marina, 157
    and role of SFADCo, 175, 176
Danaher, Kevin, 109, 112
Davy Kelleher McCarthy, 206
De Beers, 55, 63(p), 64–5, 85, 100
de Graff, Mr, 112
de la Tocnaye, Le Chevalier, 16
de Paor, Liam, 74
de Valera, Éamon, 22, 31, 32(p), 46, 51, 53, 83
Defence, Department of, 35, 37, 40
Delap, R. H., 38(p)
Dempsey, J. F., 53, 60
Derg Canal Developments, 128
Devane, Sara, 128, 129
DEVCO, 168, 170
Di Lucia, Manuel, 20–21
Dilger, John, 59, 61, 110
Dillon, James, 186
Dillon, Michael, 74
Dixon, Bill, 47
Donnelly, Peter, 58, 169(p)
Dooley, Pat, 5
Dowley, Bob, 38(p), 44(p)
Downes and Meehan, Messrs, 83, 88
Dredging Investigations Ltd, 150
Dromoland Castle, Co. Clare, 45, 169(p)
Drumgeely Community Centre, 94
Drumgeely Hall, 100
Drumgeely Hill, Shannon, 198
Drumgeely shopping centre, 87
Drumgeely Town. *see* Shannon town
Dublin Airport, 45, 46, 188
Dublin Chamber of Commerce, 206
Dublin region, 9–10, 96
    reverse emigration, 21
Dugdale, Dr Rose, 73
Dunguaire Castle, Co. Galway, 107, 114(p), 115, 173

Dunne, Tom, 59, 78, 169(p), 188, 210
  and industrial estate, 66, 168
  and regional development, 142, 143, 176–7
  on Shannon town, 83
Dunphy, Austin, 161

Economic and Social Research Institute (ESRI), 148
Egypt, 168, 170
EI, 65, 66, 68, 147
El Nasr City free zone, 170
El Salvador, 170, 171, 173
Electricity Supply Board (ESB), 16, 129, 150, 156
Electronics Report, 148
Emergency Powers (no 315) Order, 1944, 46
Ennis, Co. Clare, 22, 45, 70, 71, 81, 85, 96, 150
Ennis Urban District Council, 152
Enterprise, 145
Enterprise Development Unit, 77
Environmental Impact Studies, 131
Estates Arbitration Committee, 99
Estonia, 171
European Community (EC), 131, 182
  definition of regions, 23–4
  Ireland joins, 74, 194, 196
  Structural Funding, 156
European Parliament, 7
European Social Fund, 20, 21
Expo 75, Shannon, 170
Export Free Zone Study Course, 170
External Affairs, Department of, 29, 31, 37

Fagan, Jack, 196
Fairy Queen (steamer), 127
Falls Hotel, Ennistymon, 31
Farranfore airport, 6
FÁS, 121
Feakle, Co. Clare, 77–8
Federal Aviation Agency (FAA), 199
Feldman, Jacob, 58
Ferbane, Co. Offaly, 150
Ferenka, 72–3
Fergus river, 62, 152
Fianna Fáil, 51, 52, 56, 77, 102, 137, 162

Finance, Department of, 37, 53–4, 87, 100, 170, 196
Finance (Miscellaneous Provisions) Act, 1958, 22, 58
Fine Gael, 51, 76, 137
Firgrove House, 45
FitzGerald, Desmond, 45
FitzGerald, Desmond, Knight of Glin, 16–17, 150
FitzGerald, Garret, 197
Fitzgibbon, Maeve, 109–10, 111, 172, 177
Fitzgibbon, Marjorie, 75
Fly Dublin Direct Committee, 206
flying-boats, 26–31, 34(p), 37, 39, 40
  decision on, 41–2
Flynn, Dr Bill, 97
Foley, Donal, 74
Folklore Commission, 109
Foras Forbartha, An, 150
Foras Tionscal, An, 52, 68
Foreign Affairs, Department of, 167, 170, 177
Fox, Carmel, 119, 120, 121, 123
Foynes, Co. Limerick, 17, 109
  airport established, 26, 29–31
  airport restaurant, 31–3, 35–6, 42
  harbour authorities, 151
  wartime development, 33, 35, 42
France, 10, 174
Free Day promotion, 110–11
Free Zone. see Shannon Free Zone
freight services, 57(p), 60–61, 187
Freud, Clement, 106(p)

Gaelic Athletic Association (GAA), 7
Gaeltarra Éireann, 10
Gageby, Douglas, 169(p)
Galbally, Co. Limerick, 6, 66, 112
Gallico, Paul, 110
Galvone, Limerick, 72
Galway, Co., 62
Garland, T. & Company, 60
Garrett, George A., 52
Gaynor, Fr, 95
Geaney, Dr and Mrs, 18
Geoghegan-Quinn, Máire, 208
Geological Survey, 1859, 18
Germany, 24

Gibney, Frank, 60, 81, 82, 83
Gleeson, P. J., 127
Glen of Aherlow, 6
Glenanaar, Co. Limerick, 119
Glin, Co. Limerick, 16–17
Glin, Knight of, 16–17, 150
Glin Castle, 150
Glynn, Josephine, 95
Gorbachev, Raisa, 113(p), 115
Gort, Lord, 104(p), 107–8
GPA Expressair, 199
GPA Flying-Boat Museum, Foynes, 33, 189(p)
GPA Technologies, 200, 203
Granary, Limerick, 159(p), 162
grants
    role of SFADCo, 68–71, 78
    Underdeveloped Areas, 22
Gray, Captain Harold E., 38(p), 39, 189(p)
Greater Colombo Economic
        Commission, 167
Greece, 24, 145
Greene, Niall, 197, 198, 199
Grogan, Mr, 34(p)
Guatemala, 168
Guinness, Arthur, Son and Company, 87
Guinness Peat Aviation (GPA), 108, 129, 180, 183, 195(p), 199–200, 203
    established, 196–8
Guinness Peat Group, 197
Gulf War, 186, 208, 209

Haight, Bob, 44(p)
Hall, Dara, 199
Hallowell, H. Thomas, 49, 61–2
Hamburg Free Zone, 58
Hamilton, Fr M., 46
Hanafin, John, 19–20
Hancock, F. G., 36
Hanly, David, 133
Hannon, Kevin, 133
Harris, John D., 98
Harty, Dr, bishop of Killaloe, 95
Harvey, W. T. D., 33
Harvey-Jones, Sir John, 197
Haslam, Richard, 9, 151
Haughey, Charles J., 160(p)
Haughey, Maureen, 113(p)

Headfort, Lord, 38(p), 42
Hedges, Captain, 38(p)
Hehir, John, 156
Heidseick, Jean-Marc, 67(p)
Henry, Hilary, 146(p)
Heritage Precinct Plan, Limerick, 162–3
Herrema, Tiede, 73, 74
Higgins, Jack, 163
Higher Education Authority (HEA), 135
Hiller Helicopters, 58
Hogan, Dick, 7–8
Holford, Lord, 82
Holycross Abbey, 6
Hommeh, Greece, 145
Honan, D. P., 152
Horan, Monsignor, 207
Horgan, John, 200
Hunt, John, 108
Hunt Museum, UL, 108, 138(p)

Iceland, 61, 187
Imperial Airways, 29, 31, 37, 40
Inchiquin, Lord, 22, 38(p), 45, 115
Indonesia, 171
Industrial Credit Company (ICC), 147
Industrial Credit Corporation (ICC), 172
industrial development, 21
    closures, 73–4
    local rivalries, 14
    overseas investment, 77, 144
    and SFADCo, 68–71, 77–8, 142–50
    Shannon Airport House, 196
    small industries, 72, 143–50, 165
    Whitaker plan, 56
Industrial Development Act, 1969, 68
Industrial Development Authority (IDA), 5, 17, 19, 120, 139, 147, 183, 191, 192
    and Asahi Company, 183
    established, 52, 56
    land bank, Ballylongford, 12, 153
    and ODA, 170, 172
    and overseas investment, 77
    overseas promotion, 172–6
    regional divisions, 175–6
    regional management centres, 136
    and SFADCo, 59, 68–71, 78, 111, 142–4
    small industry development, 72
    takes on regional planning, 74

Industrial Policy Review Group, 209–10
industrial relations, 200, 202
  Limerick, 72–3
Industry and Commerce, Department
  of, 26, 37, 52–4, 170, 191
  and Foynes, 33, 35
  and Industrial Estate, 56
  SFADCo to report to, 68
  Shannon Airport development, 45–6,
  47
  and Shannon town, 83
Inis Cathaigh (Scattery Island), 157
Innovation Centre, Plassey, 138(p), 140,
  143
Institute of Public Administration
  (IPA), 168
*Integrated Development of the Shannon
  Estuary: A Strategic Study*, 150
Integrated Rural Development (IRD), 23
Inter-Party Government, 1949, 51–2
International Air Transport Association
  (IATA), 187
International Airlines Inc., 187
International Business Incubation
  Centre (IBIC), 183
International Development Ireland, 171–2
International Dynamics Industries, 57(p)
interpretative centres, 131
Irish Airline Pilots' Association
  (IALPA), 202
Irish Coffee, 35
Irish Country Holidays, 121
Irish Farmers' Association (IFA), 121
Irish Independent, 101
Irish language, 93
Irish Management Institute (IMI), 76,
  83, 135, 136
Irish Peace Institute, 180
Irish Transport and General Workers'
  Union (ITGWU), 51
Irish Wildlife Conservancy, 16
Irwin, Dr Liam, 133
Island Theatre Group, 162
Italy, 175

Jamaica, 171
Japan, 182–3
Johnston, Roy, 140

Jones, Bill, 61, 83, 85
  and Shannon town, 85–6, 94, 96, 97
Jones, Eileen, 85
Joyce, Ray, 111, 169(p), 180, 182

Kaunda, President, 168
Keating, Justin, 74, 75(p), 76, 77, 79, 139
Keating, Michael, 98(p)
Kelly, Henry, 74
Kelly, P. J., 158
Kelly, Paddy, 39
Kelly, Roisin, 174
Kelly-Rogers, Captain J. C., 75(p)
Kemmy, Jim, 133, 160(p), 163
Kennedy, David, 136
Kennedy, Douglas, 139
Kennedy, Nancy, 124–5
Kennedy, Paddy, 15, 122(p), 123–5
Keogh, Derek, 206
Kerry, Co., 17–19
  North Kerry, 6
Kerry County Council, 18, 150
Kerryman, The, 18–19
Kilconry, Co. Clare. *see* Foynes
Kilfinane, Co. Limerick, 66, 119–21, 123
Kilfinane Development Association, 120
Kilfinane Education Centre, 119
Kilkee, Co. Clare, 20–21
Kilkenny, Co., 7–8
Kilkishen, Co. Clare, 118
Killaloe, Co. Clare, 14, 126(p), 127–9
Killanin, Lord, 128
Killeen, Michael J., 68, 78, 142, 143
Killimer-Tarbert car ferry, 18, 152, 156
Kilmihil, Co. Clare, 66
Kilrush, Co. Clare, 151, 154–8
  Marina, 155(p), 156–8
Kilrush Community Development Ltd,
  157
King John's Castle, Limerick, 107, 158,
  160(p), 161
King's County. *see* Offaly, Co.
Kinlay, Howard, 12
Kirwan, Helen, 43(p)
Kirwan, Lal, 43(p), 45
KLM, 41, 48, 109
Knappogue Castle, 107, 114(p), 115, 173
Knight's Inn, Shannon, 103

Knock Airport, 207
Korea, 144
Krivchenko, Boris, 205

Labasheeda, Co. Clare, 66
Labour, Department of, 20
Labour Court, 51
Labour Party, 51, 76, 137
Lakeshore Foods, Tipperary, 146
Lakeside Hotel, Killaloe, 128
Lana-Knit, 65, 73, 187
Lantis, Mr, 124
Lardner & Co., 161
Larnchop Pollution boat, 126(p)
Le Brocquy, Louis, 110
Lee, J. J., 9–10
Lemass, Sean, 22, 28, 31, 42, 52–4, 67(p),
        189(p), 190
    and Foynes, 35
    opens Foynes, 29
    and Shannon Airport, 37, 40, 46
    and Shannon Industrial Estate, 58
    and Shannon town, 83
    Whitaker plan, 56
Lenihan, Brian, 101, 176
Lenihan, Edmund, 154
Leonard, Denis, 162
Lep Transport, 61, 83, 85
Leydon, John, 30(p), 31, 53
Liberia, 166
Lichfield, Nathaniel, and Associates,
        150, 151
Lichfield Report, 10–11, 152, 188
    second, 136
Limerick, Co., 17–18, 22
Limerick Business School, 182–3
Limerick Chamber of Commerce, 46
Limerick city, 45, 69, 71, 209
    redevelopment of, 19–20, 158–63
    SFADCo investment in, 72
    and Shannon town, 85, 86, 93, 96
    Treaty 300, 133–4, 161
    Workspace, 145, 146(p)
Limerick Civic Week Ltd, 161
Limerick Clothing Company, 45
Limerick Clothing Factory, 161
Limerick Corporation, 10–11, 150, 162
Limerick County Council, 10–11, 150

Limerick County VEC, 120, 121
Limerick Food Centre, 146
Limerick Heritage Trust, 162
Limerick Soviet, 158
Limerick Steamship Company, 151
Limerick University, 163
Limerick Urban Renewal Projects
        Committee, 161–3
Limerick Wine and Food Society, 45, 107
Lindbergh, Charles, 29, 37, 39–40, 46
Local Government, Department of, 83,
        101–2
Local Government Bill, 1991, 9
Local Government (Planning and
        Development) Act, 1963, 8
Loch Cutra castle, Gort, 108
Loftleidir, 61
Lough Derg, 15, 16, 125, 127–9, 157
Lough Derg Working Group, 127
Lowe, Philip, 23, 24, 163, 176
Lufthansa, 41, 200, 202
Lynch, Christopher, 112, 115
Lynch, J. C., 58
Lynch, Jack, 63
Lynch, Joe, 38(p)

McAughtry, Sam, 177–8
MacBride, Sean, 52
McCabe, Frank, 147
McCarthy, Colm, 206
MacCochlans, 7
McCoy, Gerard T., 38(p), 39
McDonald, Frank, 161, 163
McElgunn, J., 58
MacEntee, Sean, 40
McGill, Peter, 182
MacGonigal, Ciarán, 203
McGrath, Fergal, SJ, 85, 90
McHugh, Joe, 11
McInerney Builders, 91
MacKenzie, J. Buist, 56, 58, 83, 167, 210
McKeogh, Martin, 150
McKeon, Gerry, 130, 194, 206–7
MacMathuna, Ciarán, 74
McNamara, Michael, 81, 89, 93, 94
MacNeice, Louis, 31
Macra na Feirme, 120–21
MacSharry, Ray, 23, 24

Maher, Colonel P., 58, 186
Maison d'Irlande, La, 172
Malta, 119–20, 131
Maracycle, 178
marinas, 156–8
Maunsell, G., and Partners, 150
Mayo Composite, 30(p)
Mediaeval Tours, 118
Merriman, Brian, 74, 77, 132
Mid-West Guidelines, 145
Mid-West Region, 6, 12, 76, 183
    and Bord Fáilte, 175–6
    industrial development, 69–70, 147–8
    Irish Times report, 74
    responsibility for, 142–3
    tourism, 110–12
Mid-West Regional Report, 1990, 149
Mid-Western Regional Tourism
        Organisation Ltd. *see*
        Shannonside
Midland Great Western Railway, 127
Mill, Dr, 87
Millan, Bruce, 23, 181(p)
Miltown Malbay, Co. Clare, 117
Modern Display Artists (MDA), 205
Moloney, Willie, 166, 171, 175
Monahan, Patrick, 87
Moneypoint, Co. Clare, 152
Moneypoint Power Station, 20, 150, 154
Monteagle Hotel, 30(p), 33
Morohashi, Shinroku, 197
Moscow Airport, 205–6
Mother and Child Scheme, 52
Mount Juliet, Co. Kilkenny, 130
Moyross, Limerick, 158
Muintir na Tire, 93, 118, 123
Mulcahy, Noel, 56, 133
Mullingar, Co. Westmeath, 5
Munchin, St, 162
Murphy, Christina, 137
Murphy, Noel, 113(p)
Murray O'Laoire, 161
Murugasu, P., 167
Musical Society, Shannon, 95

National Association of Tenants'
        Organisations (NATO), 99
National Building Agency, 82–3

National Economic and Social Council
        (NESC), 8
National Institute of Higher Education
        (NIHE), Limerick. *see* University
        of Limerick
National Lottery, 162
National Microelectronics Applications
        Centre, 140
National University of Ireland (NUI),
        79, 135, 137
Nenagh, Co. Tipperary, 14, 149
Nenagh Anglers' Association, 16
Nenagh river, 15–16
New Towns Commission, 82
New Zealand, 26
Newcastle College of Technology, 134–5
Newcastle West, Co. Limerick, 17
Newfoundland, 29
Newmarket–on–Fergus, Co. Clare, 46
Nicaragua, 170, 171
NIHE Limerick Act, 1980, 137
Noonan, Michael J., 162
North Kerry, 6, 12
North Tipperary, 15–16
Northern Ireland, 97, 175, 177–80

O'Brien, N. A., 71
O'Brien's Bridge, Co. Clare, 129
O'Carroll, Cian, 82, 83, 90, 91, 93, 112,
        113(p)
    Croí na Sionna, 100–101
O'Connor, Frank, 77, 158
O'Connor, R. C., 58, 59, 190
O'Connors, 7
O'Dea, Martina, 141(p)
O'Domhnaill, Tomás, 14, 15–16, 149
O Donnabháin, Diarmuid, 96
O'Donnell, Tom, 180, 182
O'Driscoll, T. J., 30(p), 31, 41, 116
O'Duill, Olaf, 173
O'Dwyer, Tom, 24
OECD, 165
Offaly, Co., 7, 148
    South Offaly, 5–6
Office of Public Works (OPW), 16, 26
    and Bunratty, 107
    Burren interpretative centre, 131
    Inis Cathaigh, 157

King John's Castle, 158, 161
Shannon Airport, 37, 45
O'Grady, Desmond, 184
O'Hanlon, Rory, 126(p)
O'Keeffe, Arthur, 76, 171, 198, 200
O'Kelly, Sean T., 35
Old Ground Hotel, Ennis, 31, 42, 46–7, 49(p)
O'Malley, B. G., 116
O'Malley, Desmond, 5–6, 45, 138(p), 169(p), 176, 203, 204(p)
   industrial development plan, 143–5
   and Limerick, 19, 158, 161, 163
   and regional development, 7, 12, 18, 142
   and regional tourism, 175
   on role of SFADCo, 76–8, 165
   and Shannon Estuary, 151–2
O'Malley, Donough, 12, 68–9, 135
O'Malley, George, 107, 116, 122(p), 125
O'Melaghlins, 7
ONATOUR, 166
One Day Tour, 111, 115
O Nuanáin, Seán, 88, 93
Oppenheimer, H. F., 63(p), 65
Orde, Campbell, 41
Ordnance Survey, 81
O'Regan, Brendan, 10, 22, 44(p), 67(p), 68, 96, 129, 142, 189(p), 203, 207
   and Aer Rianta, 190–92
   changing role of SFADCo, 77–9
   Co–operation North, 177–9
   on compulsory stop–over, 46, 192–3, 208
   and Industrial Estate, 56, 58
   on Lemass, 53
   opens Foynes restaurant, 31–3
   and regional development, 71
   resignation of, 79, 165
   SFADCo's consultancy role, 165–72
   SFADCo's early days, 58–61
   Shannon Airport restaurant, 35–6, 42, 45, 48, 51
   and Shannon Estuary, 151
   and Shannon town, 81, 83
   and social development, 76
   and tourism development, 107, 109–12, 117, 122(p), 123, 125

O'Shannon, Cathal, 72, 109–10, 142, 152–3, 158, 163
O'Sullivan, R. W., 36
Outram, Dorinda, 140
overseas development aid (ODA), 166–72

Palmer, Patricia, 135, 137
Pan American Airways, 33, 35, 37, 41, 45, 109, 188, 193, 207
   Clipper III, 27(p)
   concentrates on land-planes, 42
   DC4, 44(p)
Panama, 58
Peace Conference, Dromoland Castle, 169(p)
Peat Marwick, 180
peat technology, 166–7
Pink, W. B., 61
Plassey Technological Park, 8, 13(p), 138(p), 139–40, 142, 143, 149, 163, 183
Pocán, Co. Tipperary, 14–15, 123–5
Portumna, Co. Galway, 127
Posts and Telegraphs, Department of, 37
Pozzy, Colonel, 48
Prestwick Airport, 186, 196
Price, Joe, 5, 12, 149
Public Expenditure, Committee on, 71–2, 102, 191
   report, 1986, 210
Puerto Rico, 58, 173
Pyle, Fergus, 21–2

Quigley, Paul, 14, 73, 75(p), 82, 169(p)
   on Lichfield Report, 10, 11
   and Limerick Civic Trust, 162
   and NI, 177
   and O'Regan, 78
   and regional development, 70
   role of SFADCo, 76, 165, 170, 190
   and Shannon town, 83
   and small industries, 147
   and Walsh, 135–6, 139, 142
Quin, Co. Clare, 117
Quinlivan, John, 39
Quinn, John, 120–21

Quinn, Pat, 101
Quinn, Fr Richard, 166, 171

Radburn system, 89
Raheen, Limerick, 72
Raheen Industrial Estate, Limerick, 170
Railways (Ireland) Act, 1896, 127
refugees, 97, 209
regional development, 7–9, 175–7,
    209–10
  definition of region, 23–4
  excessive centralisation, 9–10
  Lichfield Report, 10
  local rivalries, 14–16
  RDOs, 11–12
  role of SFADCo, 68–71, 142–50
Regional Development Organisations
    (RDOs), 11–12, 25, 70
regional tourism organisations, 116
Rent-an-Irish-Cottage scheme, 14,
    116–17, 122(p)
  Kilfinane, 120
  Pocán, 123–5
Renvyle, Co. Galway, 144
Republic of Ireland
  established, 52
Réunion, 171
Revenue Commissioners, 81
Reynolds, Albert, 181(p)
Rineanna. see Shannon Airport
Rinuccini, Cardinal, 112
Rippen (piano manufacturers), 61
Romac, 58
Roscrea, Co. Tipperary, 15
Rossiter, Stuart, 119
Rural Housing Organisation (RHO), 74,
    118–19, 120, 124
Rushe, John, 120
Russell, Brendan, 131
Russell, George (AE), 10
Ryan, Harry, 199
Ryan, J. G., 58
Ryan, Jack, 110, 194
Ryan, Fr Liam, 81, 91
Ryan, Michael, 154
Ryan, Tony, 108, 183, 195(p), 196–7, 198,
    200, 202
Ryan survey, 1964, 89

Sabena, 188
St John's school, Shannon, 88
St Munchin's church, Limerick, 162
St Senan's school, Shannon, 88
Sales and Catering Organisation, 51, 58,
    87, 108, 111, 172, 190–91
Sarsfield, Patrick, 133
Scarriff, Co. Clare, 66
Scattery Island (Inis Cathaigh), 157
Schildhauer, Commander C. H., 41
Schipol Airport, Amsterdam, 48
Scotland, 24
Seaboard & Western, 198–9
Senan, St, 157
SFADCo, 17, 19–20, 21, 22, 81, 99, 119,
    194. see also Shannon Industrial
    Estate; Shannon town
  and Aer Rianta, 188–92
  area covered by, 6–9
  Business Services Division, 145, 147
  consultancy role, 165–72
  consultative report, 1990, 132
  established, 58–9
  future development of, 77–9, 142,
    209–10
  and IDA, 59, 68–71, 78, 111, 142–4
  and industrial development, 153
  Kilrush marina, 156–8
  as model, 14
  overseas promotions, 110, 111, 172–6
  and railways, 6
  and RDO, 11–12
  and regional development, 10–11,
    68–71, 74, 76, 142–50
  role of, 15, 17, 18–19, 21–2
  staff recruitment, 83
  Strategic Study, 1989, 154, 157–8
  and UL, 135–9
  women in, 109
Shannon Aerospace, 200, 201(p), 203, 205
Shannon Air Ltd, 187
Shannon Airport, 194. see also
    compulsory stop-over; Sales and
    Catering Service; Shannon
    Airport Restaurant
  and Aer Rianta, 188–92
  building of, 37, 39–40
  choice of site, 36–7, 38(p)

development of, 17, 53–4
duty-free shop, 47–8, 50(p), 168, 194
established, 35–6
first landings, 38(p), 40
future role of, 202–3
immigration clearance, 209
international routes, 112, 186–8
mail-order business, 51, 194
need for extension, 45–7
strikes, 39, 51
tourism information bureau, 109–10
working conditions, 45
Shannon Airport Catering Service Staff
    Training and Advancement
    Scheme (SACTAS), 48
Shannon Airport Development
    Authority, 8
Shannon Airport Development
    Company, 54
Shannon Airport House, 195(p)
Shannon Airport House - Ireland, 196
Shannon Airport Marketing, 206–7
Shannon Airport Restaurant, 35–6, 42,
    45, 48, 51
    menus, 43(p), 49(p)
Shannon Aviation Park, 201(p)
Shannon Castle Singers and Farmhouse
    Entertainers, 173
Shannon Castle Tours, 191
Shannon Community Association, 87,
    94, 97, 100
Shannon Development. see SFADCo
Shannon Diamond and Carbide, 63,
    64–5, 100
Shannon Diamond Group, 100
Shannon Enterprise Centre, 147
Shannon Estuary, 18, 60, 80–81
    development plans, 150–54
    Kilrush marina, 156–8
Shannon Estuary Company, 150
Shannon Free Airport Development
    Company. see SFADCo
Shannon Free Airport Development
    Company (Amendment) Bill,
    1970, 191
Shannon Free Airport Development
    Company (Amendment) Bill,
    1980, 148

Shannon Free Zone, 22, 55, 68, 149, 172,
    174, 196, 203. see also Shannon
    Industrial Estate
    early industries, 61–5
    established, 58–60
    freight traffic, 60–61, 187
    further acquisitions, 200, 202, 203
    job creation estimates, 88
    as model, 165–6, 167, 170
    and Shannon town, 81
Shannon Golf Club, 97, 98(p)
Shannon Heritage, 112
Shannon Hotel Management School, 48,
    67(p)
Shannon Industrial Estate, 21, 49, 55–68,
    83, 87
    AnCO, 136
    closures, 73–4
    Factory No. 1, 57(p)
    female workforce, 65–6
    genesis of, 56, 58–9
    industrial relations, 66, 68
    problems of, 65–8
Shannon Industrial Zone, 14
Shannon International Hotel, 48
Shannon Maritime Development, 156,
    157
Shannon Region, 5–6, 7–9, 174
    RDO, 11–12
Shannon Repair Services (SRS), 198–9
Shannon River tourism, 127–9
Shannon Status Committee, 207
Shannon Tenants' Association, 99
Shannon town, 45, 70, 80–103
    churches, 88, 93, 101
    community activities, 93, 95–6, 100
    Croí na Sionna, 92(p), 93, 99–101
    early citizens, 83, 85–7
    electoral representation, 99, 101–2
    established, 80–87
    Expo 75, 170
    house–building, 87–8, 94
    isolation of, 93
    landscaping, 90
    name of, 81
    Outline Development Plan, 83, 88–91
    place-names, 91, 93
    population estimates, 88

refugees, 97
religion, 94–5
rent strikes, 93, 99
schools, 88, 93, 94–5, 96–7
shops, 87, 88
social development, 95–7
sports facilities, 96, 97
Shannon Town Alliance, 97, 98
Shannon Travel, 116
Shannon Turbine Technologies, 203
Shannonbridge, Co. Offaly, 5, 6
Shannonside, 21, 116, 117–18
Shannonside Courier, 116, 188
Sheahan, T., 117
Sheane, Paul, 147, 196
Sheedy, Tom, 66
Sheehan, Canon, 119
Sheehan, Pat, 147
Sheppard Fidler report, 80, 88, 89, 91
Sheridan, Joseph, 35
Shinrone, Co. Offaly, 150
Shorts C Class flying-boat, 34(p)
Sicily, 24
Sieges and Treaty Symposium,
    Limerick, 133
Siggins, Lorna, 186
Sioda, Mr, 181(p)
SIPTU, 202
Sisk, John, and Co. (Dublin) Ltd, 101, 103
SITCO, 206
Sixmilebridge, Co. Clare, 62, 81, 118–19
Skelly, Liam, 205
Small Business Administration,
    Washington, 147
Small Business Association, New
    England, 147
Small Firms Association, 149
small industries, 72, 143–50, 165
Smith, Michael, 175
Smithstown, Shannon, 149, 198
Smyth, W. T., 117
Social Study Conference, Galway, 179
South Africa, 65
South Offaly, 5–6, 12
Southill Development Co-Op Society
    Ltd, 19, 20
Southill estate, Limerick, 19–20, 145, 158
Southill House, 20

Soviet Irish Trading Company (SITCO),
    206
Spain, 131
SPS, 49, 61–4, 85, 87
    established, 55–6
    training personnel, 86
Sri Lanka, 167, 168
SRS Aviation (Ireland) Ltd, 199
Standard Pressed Steel. *see* SPS
state-sponsored bodies, 53, 76, 191
    and overseas aid, 168–72
Stephen's Green Club, 31
Stokes Kennedy Crowley, 180
Straffan House, 130
Strong, Rupert, 41
Sudan, the, 168
Sulzer Brothers, 203
Sutherland, Peter, 197
Sweden, 82
Sweeney, Maxwell, 33
Swift, Carolyn, 115
Swissair, 188, 200, 202
Switzerland, 200
Syntex, 74

Tahiti, 131
Tait, Sir Peter, 20
Tarbert, Co. Kerry, 18–19, 152
Tarbert-Killimer ferry, 18, 152, 156
Tarbert Power Station, 150
Tasman Empire Airways Ltd (TEAL), 26
Taylor, Chris, 64–5, 85–6
    and Shannon town, 88
Teach Ceoil, Murroe, 113(p)
Teagasc, 121
Telesis Report, 1982, 148
Thackeray, W. M., 17
Thailand, 168
Thomond, Earl of, 115
Thompstone, Kevin, 97
Thurles, Co. Tipperary, 6, 15
Tipperary, Co., 6, 14, 66
    North Riding, 10
    North Tipperary, 15–16
Tipperary Enterprise Foundation, 183
Tipperary Spring Water, 149–50
Tipperary Trading Company, 183
Tobin, Vincent, 172

Tourism and Transport, Department of, 207
  tourism development, 105–32
  community projects, 17
  Limerick, 158–62
  need for maps, 120, 121
  negative side of, 130–32
  One Day Tour, 111, 115
  regional divisions, 175–6
  RIC, 116–17
  river tourism, 125–9
  traditional image, 173–4
Tourism Development Study Course, 170
Town Commissioners, 102
Town Improvements Act, 1854, 102
Toynbee, Arnold, 105
Tradaree, Shannon, 90
trade unions, 66, 68, 202
Tralee, Co. Kerry, 5, 6, 18–19
Tralee and Dingle Light Railway, 6
Tralee Borough Council, 18
Trans-Canada, 188
Transcontinental and Western Air (TWA), 46
Transport and Power, Department of, 68, 83, 124, 186, 190, 193–4
Travers, Brendan, 156–7
Treaty Stone, Limerick, 160(p)
Trident Holiday Homes, 125
Trinity College Dublin, 137
Trippe, Juan T., 29, 37, 39–40
Tullyglass, Shannon, 85, 94
Tullyvarraga Hall, 100
Tunney, Michael, 14, 18
TWA, 47, 48, 193
  DC4, 44(p)

Údarás na Gaeltachta, 18
Ultra High Pressure Units (Ireland), 63
UNCTAD, 167
Underdeveloped Areas, 22
Underdeveloped Areas Act, 1952, 10
UNIDO, 167, 168, 171
  workshop, 169(p), 170
United Nations, 165, 167–8, 170
United States, 64
  and compulsory stop-over, 52, 54, 192–6
  industrial investment, 61–2, 66, 68, 86, 144
  recession, 208
  SFADCo marketing in, 110, 111, 116, 172–6
  Shannon Entertainers tour, 173
University College Cork (UCC), 137
University of Limerick (UL), 13(p), 23, 25, 55–6, 75(p), 180
  Aircraft Engineering chair, 203
  Asahi campus, 182–3
  development of, 134–9
  Foundation Building, 140
  Hunt Museum, 108, 138(p)
University of Ulster, 180
urban development, 82
  New Towns, 96
Uruguay, 171
Urwick, Orr and Partners (Ireland), 56
US Civil Aeronautics Board, 192
US Immigration Service, 209
US Naval Air Transport Services, 41
USAID, 166
USSR, 171, 199, 205
  duty-free shop, 205–6

Van Hemeledonck, Mr, 124
Varian International, 142, 143
Vaughan, Kevin, 22, 33, 62, 107, 111, 117
Vereker family, 107–8
Victoria and Albert Museum, 108
Volkov, Alexander, 205

Wakeman, W. F., 125
Walsh, Dr Edward, 25, 133–9, 163, 181(p)
  and Asahi campus, 182–3
  Plassey Technological Park, 139–40, 142
  on Shannon stop-over, 207, 208–9
Walsh, J. J., 68
Walsh, Joe, 55–6, 62, 64
  and Shannon town, 85–6, 96
Walsh, Patrick, 15
Wang, 142, 143
water pollution, 127
Waterford, Co., 7–8
Weerartna, A., 167
West Clare Railway, 5, 156

Western Airlines, 199
Westport, Co. Mayo, 81
Whelan, Noel, 182
Whitaker, T. K., 53, 56
White, Padraic, 139
Wickenhagen, Professor, 48
Williamson, Paul, 108
Wilson, John, 205
Wilson, Robin, 199–200, 203, 205
Workspace, Limerick, 145, 146(p)
World Aviation Park, 203

World Bank, 137
World War II, 33, 40
    airport expansion, 45–6

Yankee Clipper, 30(p)
Young, John, 19, 20
Youth Advisory Council, Shannon, 96
Youth Enterprise Shannon Ltd (YES), 145
Yugoslavia, 165, 171

Zambia, 168